Teaching Classroom Guitar

Teaching Classroom Guitar

Steve Eckels

Published in partnership with
MENC: The National Association for Music Education

ROWMAN & LITTLEFIELD EDUCATION
A division of
ROWMAN & LITTLEFIELD PUBLISHERS, INC.
Lanham • New York • Toronto • Plymouth, UK

Published in partnership with MENC: The National Association for Music Education

Published by Rowman & Littlefield Education
A division of Rowman & Littlefield Publishers, Inc.
A wholly owned subsidiary of The Rowman & Littlefield Publishing Group, Inc.
4501 Forbes Boulevard, Suite 200, Lanham, Maryland 20706
http://www.rowmaneducation.com

Estover Road, Plymouth PL6 7PY, United Kingdom

British Library Cataloguing in Publication Information Available

Library of Congress Cataloging-in-Publication Data

Eckels, Steven Zdenek.
  Teaching classroom guitar / Steve Eckels.
    p. cm.
  "Published in partnership with MENC: The National Association for Music Education."
  ISBN 978-1-60709-388-6 (cloth : alk. paper) — ISBN 978-1-60709-389-3 (pbk. : alk. paper) — ISBN 978-1-60709-390-9 (ebook)
   1. Guitar—Instruction and study. I. Title.
    MT580.E35 2009
    787.87'193071—dc22   2009032417

Printed in the United States of America

Contents

PART V: INTERMEDIATE SKILLS

PART VI: REMEDIAL TECHNIQUES

PART VII: THE GUITAR ROOM, GUITARS, AND INDEPENDENT STUDY

Preface

In reality, guitar class is a general music class that happens to use guitar.

Because you are a busy person, I have written this book in a very direct style. You may read it chronologically, or you can skip around to chapters that are of immediate interest to you. If you are interested in solo classical guitar, look ahead to chapter 29. It is my hope that you can scan the chapters and section headings to quickly find the information you are looking for. The strategies included here are ones that I developed in working with seventh through twelfth grades. Because scheduling and students vary greatly, feel free to modify the strategies to meet your individual needs.

There are many guitar methods available, and a good method book is one of the pillars of your classroom resources. This books not method book. The purpose of this book is to give you the techniques and strategies to utilize, elaborate on, and reinforce the information presented in the method book of your choice. In chapter 37 I list some recommended publishers.

Student engagement in any class is improved when the content presented is relevant to them, be it popular or classical music. Student engagement and enthusiasm is improved when students feel they have a choice in what they work on. Therefore most methods must be supplemented with popular songs and/or classical literature. The repertoire of popular music provides songs, on all skill levels, that make guitar class an attractive offering for young people. I encourage you to get excited about the possibilities by carefully studying the popular songs, keys, and artists in the figure following and marking your favorites. They are arranged by skill level. Each year the list grows. Throughout the book I will make suggestions for songs that I have found to work especially well. For those teachers interested

in a more performance-based or classical approach, I have included chapters on finger-picking, solo guitar, and ensembles. I also highly recommend my book *A Modern Method for Fingerstyle Guitar*, which guides students in a classical or solo guitar direction.

POPULAR GUITAR SONGS, KEYS, SKILL LEVEL, AND ARTISTS

Skill Level One – Preliminaries

Riffs on One String

Flaming Ice Cube
Distorus Maximus
Skydiving Fish
Power in G

Melodies on One String

Amazing Grace, hymn
Twinkle, Twinkle, Little Star
Love Me Tender – Elvis
House of the Rising Sun, blues
On Top of Old Smokey, Western
The First Noel, Christmas
Scarborough Fair, English folk song
Star Wars, movie theme
Ghost Riders in the Sky, – Johnny Cash
Bouree – Bach
Fur Elise – Beethoven
Play By Ear: Happy Birthday, Jingle Bells, Row, Row, Row Your Boat

Skill Level Two – Getting Started

Lion Sleeps Tonight –C– movie theme
Blue Eyes Cryin' In the Rain –C– Willie Nelson
I Walk the Line –C– Johnny Cash

Worried Man Blues –G– Carter Family
Folsom Prison Blues –G– Johnny Cash
Good Night, Irene – G– Lead Belly
Tom Dooley –G– folk

Ain't Nobody Here But Us Chickens – C– blues

Jambalaya –D– Hank Williams
Achy-Breaky Heart –D– Billy Ray Cyrus
Surfin' USA – D– The Beach Boys

Let the Good Times Roll –A– blues

Man of Constant Sorrow – E – movie theme

Eleanor Rigby – Amin– The Beatles
El Condor Paso –Emin– Simon and Garfunkel

Skill Level Three

Big Rock Candy Mountain –C– movie theme
The Bismarck –C– Historical
Blowin' in the Wind –C– Bob Dylan
Brown-Eyed Girl –C– Van Morrison
Don't Think Twice It's All Right –C– Bob Dylan
Feelin' Groovy –C– Simon and Garfunkel
Farther Along –C–Dolly Parton
Friends in Low Places –C– Garth Brooks
I Still Miss Someone –C– June Carter Cash
Jamaica Farewell –C– Reggae

The John B Sails –C– Reggae
Margaritaville –C– Jimmy Buffett
My Home's In Montana –C– Western
Obladi Oblada –C– Beatles
Streets of Laredo –C– Western
Under the Boardwalk –C–
Wildwood Flower –C–Maybell Carter

All God's Critters Got a Place . . . –G– Bill Stains
Amazing Grace –G– Hymn
Country Road –G– John Denver
Down to the River to Pray –G– Oh Brother . . .
King of the Road –G– Roger Miller
Marine's Hymn –G– Armed Forces
Mr. Tambourine Man –G– Bob Dylan
Stand By Me –G– Ben E. King
Take Me Out to the Ball Game –G–
Times They are a Changin' –G– Bob Dylan
Where Have All the Flowers . . . –G– Pete Seeger
Yellow Submarine –G– The Beatles

Battle of New Orleans –D– Nitty Gritty Dirt Band
Can the Circle Be Unbr . . . –D– The Carter Family
Home on the Range –D– Western

I'm a Believer –D– Neil Diamond
In the Pines –D– Lead Belly
Leaving on a Jet Plane –D– John Denver
Red River Valley –D–
This Land is Your Land –D– Woody Guthrie
The Unicorn Song –D–

Get Together –A– The Young Bloods
Git Along Little Doggies –A– Western
Oh What a Beautiful Morning –A– *Oklahoma*
Kumbaya –A– folk song
Silver Bells –A– Christmas song

Blue Suede Shoes –E– Elvis Presley
Higher Ground –E– gospel
Malaguena –E– Spanish traditional
What I Say –E– Ray Charles

Ghost Riders in the Sky –Amin– Johnny Cash
Gilligan's Island –Amin– TV theme
Hotel California –Amin– Eagles
Jamin' –Amin– Bob Marley

Secret Agent Man –Emin–

Skill Level Four – Power Chords

Fortunate Son –G– Creedence Clearwater Revival
Jet Airliner –G– Steve Miller, Riff Study
Johnny Be Good –G– Chuck Berry, scale study
Joy to the World –G– Three Dog Night
Rockin Around the Christmas Tree –G– Christmas Tune
Smoke on the Water –G– Deep Purple
Twist and Shout –G– The Beatles
Wild Thing –G– Jimi Hendrix
You Really Got Me – G– The Kinks/Van Halen

Sunshine of Your Love –D– Cream

Jumping Jack Flash –A– Rolling Stones
Hound Dog –A– Elvis
Old Time Rock and Roll –A– Bob Seeger

Day Tripper –E– The Beatles
I Saw Her Standing There –E– The Beatles
Pride and Joy –E– Stevie Ray Vaughn
Steppin' Stone – E– The Monkees

Born to Be Wild –Steppinwolf– Emin

Skill Level Five – Finger Picking

Bonney Banks of Loch Lommond –C– Irish
Colors of the Wind –C– Pocahantas
Desperado –C– The Eagles

I Can't Help Falling in Love –C– Elvis Presley
Let It Be –G– The Beatles
Love Can Build A Bridge –C–
Love Me Tender –C– Elvis
Morning Has Broken – C– Cat Stevens
The Rose –C– Amanda McBroom
Simple Man – C– Lynard Skynard
Titanic Theme –C– movie theme
Today –C– Irish Rovers
What a Wonderful World –C– Louis Armstrong
Wind Beneath My Wings –C– Bette Midler

Danny Boy –G– Irish
December –G– Collective Soul
Every Breath You Take – G– Sting/The Police
Freebird –G– Lynard Skynard
Hallelujah –G– Leonard Cohen
Imagine –G– John Lennon
Let it Be –G– The Beatles
Time of Your Life –G– Green Day

Banks of the Ohio –D– bluegrass
Blue Moon of Kentucky –D– Bill Monroe, bluegrass
The Garden Songs –D– John Denver
Give Yourself to Love –D– Kate Wolf
One Last Breath –D– Creed, easy
One Last Breath –D– Creed
Vincent –D– Don McClean
What It's Like –D– Everlast
Wonderful Tonight –D– Eric Clapton

Here Without You –Amin– 3 Doors Down, riff
House of the Rising Sun –Amin– The Animals
Scarborough Fair –Amin– Simon and Garfunkel

Behind Blue Eyes –Emin– The Who
Cemetery Gates –Emin– Pantera
Nights in White Satin –Emin– The Moody Blues
Scarborough . . . –Emin– English folk song duet
Stairway to Heaven –Emin– Led Zeppelin
Wish You Were Here – Emin– Pink Floyd

Skill Level Six

All You Need is Love –C– The Beatles
American Pie –C– Don McClean
Desperado –C– The Eagles Duet
Free Falling –C– Tom Petty
I Will –C– The Beatles
We Shall Overcome –C– civil rights song
White Christmas –C– Christmas song
Yesterday –C– The Beatles

Bridge Over Troubled Water – G– Simon and Garfunkel
Frosty the Snowman –G– Christmas Song

Heart of Gold, Neil Young –G– Neil Young
La Bamba –G– Richie Valens
Lean on Me – G– Al Green
My Girl –G– Smokey Robinson
My Girl – bass
Sunshine on My Shoulders –G– John Denver
Wild Word –G– Cat Stevens

Here Comes the Sun –D– The Beatles
Keep On the Sunny Side –D– Oh Brother . . .
Moon Shadow –D– Cat Stevens
Sweet Home Alabama –D– Lynard Skynard

The Wind –D– Cat Stevens
With A Little Help From My Friends –D– The Beatles

Jingle Bell Rock –A– Christmas song
Travelin' Band – A– Creedence Clearwater Revival
For What It's Worth –E– Buffalo Springfield

Sounds of Silence –Amin–Simon and Garfunkel
Walk Don't Run –Emin– surf guitar

California Dreamin' –Amin– Mamas and the Papas

Skill Level Seven – Barre Chords

All My Lovin' –C– The Beatles
Blue Christmas –C– Christmas Song
Rocky Mountain High –C– John Denver
San Francisco –C– John Phililips
Sittin' on the Dock of the Bay –C– Otis Redding

Leroy Brown –G– Jim Croce
Proud Mary –G– Credence Clearwater Revival
Tequila Sunrise –G– The Eagles

I Can See Clearly –D– Jimmy Cliff, Reggae
I Wanna Hold Your Hand – D– The Beatles
In My Life –D– The Beatles
Take it Easy –D– Eagles
Wedding Song – D– Paul Stookey

Pretty Woman –A– Roy Orbison

Under the Bridge –E– Red Hot Chili Peppers

Happy Together –Dmin– The Turtles
In A Gadda Da Vida –Dmin– Iron Butterfly
Layla –Dmin– Eric Clapton
People Are Strange –Dmin– The Doors

Skill Level Eight – Passing Chords

Annie's Song –C– John Denver

Bojangles –C– Jerry Jeff Walker
City of New Orleans –C– Steve Goodman
Don't Know Much – Sam Cooke/James Taylor
Dust in the Wind –C– Kansas
Dust in the Wind – Duet
Have Your Ever Seen the Rain? –C– Creedence Clearwater Revival
Landslide –C–Fleetwood Mac
Landslide – Picking Study
Lonestar –C– Nora Jones
Tenessee Waltz –C– country standard
The Weight –C– The Band
When A Man Loves a Woman –C–
Yesterday –C–The Beatles
Your Song –C– Elton John

The Best of My Love –G–The Eagles
Blackbird –G– The Beatles
Dancing in the Moonlight –G– movie music
Puff the Magic Dragon –G– Peter, Paul, and Mary
You've Got a Friend –G– Carole King
Redemption Song –G– Bob Marley/Reggae
Tears in Heaven –G– Eric Clapton

Fire and Rain –D– James Taylor
How Sweet It Is . . . –D– James Taylor
You Are the Woman –D– Firefall
Michelle –A– The Beatles

Gypsy Anthem –Amin– Gypsy Jazz
Riders on the Storm –Emin– The Doors

And I Love Her –Dmin– The Beatles
Time in a Bottle –Dmin– Jim Croce
While My Guitar Gent . . . –Dmin– The Beatles
While My Guitar Gently Weeps – The Beatles

Bluegrass Tunes

Charlie and the MTA –C–
I'll Fly Away –D– Oh Brother Where Art Thou?
Rocky Top –G–
Rolling in My Sweet Baby's . . . –G– Bill Monroe
Shady Grove –Emin–
Sourwood Mountain –C–
Wreck of the Old 97 –G–

Skill Level Nine

Cattle Call Waltz –C– Western
Down on the Corner – C – Creedence Clearwater Revival
Heartbreak Hotel – C– Elvis Presley
Limbo Rock –C– Caribbean
Peace Train –C– Cat Stevens
White Christmas –C– Bing Crosby

Your Cheatin' Heart –C– Hank Williams

Blue Hawaii –G– Elvis Presley
Crazy –G– Patsy Cline
Don't Know Why –G– Norah Jones
Hey Good Lookin' –G– Hank WIlliams
I Hope You Dance –G– Inspirational
In the Still of the Night –G– 1950s, The Platters
Jazz blues in G major and minor
Jazz blues in B Flat major
Ring of Fire –G– Johnny Cash

Blue Christmas –D– Christmas Tune
Cold Cold Heart –D– Hank Williams
I Can't Help it if I'm . . . . –D– Hank Williams
I'll Be Your Baby Tonight –D– Bob Dylan
Let it Snow –D– Christmas Song
Only You –D– 1950s/Platters

I'm So Lonesome I . . . –E– Hank Williams
Susie Q –E– Credence Clearwater Revival

Black Magic Woman –Amin– Santana
Black Magic Woman – riff
Hava Nagila –Amin– Israeli Folk Dance
Minor Swing –Amin– Gypsy jazz
Summertime –Amin– George Gershwin

I Shot the Sheriff –Emin– Bob Marley
Moondance –Emin– Van Morrison
Moondance –Duet
Evil Ways –Gmin– Santana

Skill Level Ten

The Christmas Song –C– Mel Torme
Georgia On My Mind –C–Ray Charles
Have Yourself a Merry Little Christmas –C–
Oh Susannah –C– James Taylor, reharmonization
Somewhere Over the Rainbow –C– duet
I'll Be Home For Christmas –G–
Satin Doll –G– Duke Ellington
Sleepwalk –G– Richie Valens

Carolina On My Mind –D– James Taylor
Twilight Time –D– The Platters

Color My World –F– Chicago

Sweet Georgia Brown – B flat
Winter Wonderland –B flat

Polka Dots and Moonbeams – Duet
Polka Dots and Moonbeams – E flat Frank Sinatra

Europa –Amin– Santana Duet
Light My Fire – Amin– The Doors

Section Eleven – Guitar Solos

For a more complete list of classical solos check with you local music retailer.

Classical Solos

Star Spangled Banner
Andante in Amin, Ferdinando Carulli
Romanza, Spanish traditional
Leyenda, Isaac Albeniz
Bouree in Emin, Bach
Lagrima, Francisco Tarrega
Greensleeves, English
Carol of the Bells, Russian
Pachelbel Canon, Pachelbel
Jesu, Joy of Man's Desiring
Malaguena, Spanish traditional
Concerto De Aranjuez, Josquin Rodrigo
Für Elise, Beethoven
Moonlight Sonata

Popular Solos

Is Anybody Out There, Pink Floyd
Nothing Else Matters, Metallica
Sanitarium, Metallica
To Live is to Die, Metallica
Stairway to Heaven, Led Zeppelin
Stairway to Heaven
Over the Hills and Far Away, Led Zeppelin
Thunderstruck, AC/DC
Dream On, Arrowsmith
Always With Me, Always With You, Joe Satriani
Boogie Shuffle, Steve Eckels
Yesterday, The Beatles
Blackbird, The Beatles
Classical Gas, Mason Williams
Diary of a Madman, Ozzie Osbourne
When You Wish Upon A Star, Disney theme
Georgia, Ray Charles
Sign, Eric Clapton
Somewhere Over the Rainbow
Miserlou – surf guitar
Pipeline – surf guitar
Tequila – surf guitar
Wipe Out – surf guitar

Section Twelve – Famous Riffs

Emin – Smoke on the Water, Deep Purple
Emin – I Shot the Sheriff, Eric Clapton/Bob Marley

Emin – Gold Finger
Emin – James Bond Theme
Emin – Enter Sandman, Metallica
Emin – Iron Man, Black Sabbath
Amin – In a Gadda Da Vida, Iron Butterfly
Amin – Sunshine of Your Love, Cream
G – La Bamba, Richie Valens; My Girl, Smokey Robinson

Here are more songs I added to the list each year:

2007

Amarillo by Morning, George Straight (D)
Daughters, John Mayers (D)
Do Re Mi, The Sound of Music (C)
Don't Fence Me In, Texas Swing (D)
Kansas City, blues (A)
Me and Bobby Mcgee (C)
Purple People Eater, Novelty (E)
Route 66, Nat King Cole (E)
San Antonio Rose, Texas Swing (G)
Wayfarin' Stranger, Spiritual (Amin)
Wish You Were Here, Pink Floyd (G)
Why Georgia , John Mayers (G)

2008

Autumn Leaves, Jazz Standard (Amin)
Colorado Train, Western (C)
Don't Know Why, Nora Jones (Bb)
Fields of Gold, Sting (C)
Gone Forever, 3 Days Grace (Bmin)
Good Hearted Woman, Waylon Jennings (D)
Hey Jude, The Beatles (C)
I Can't Get Started, Bix Biderbeck (A)
I'm Yours, Jason Mraz (G)
Iris, The Goo Goo Dolls (D)
It Starts in My Toes, (G)
Knockin On Heaven's Door, Dylan (G)
Lemon Tree, Peter, Paul & Mary (D)
Luchenbach Texas, Willie Nelson (D)
Morning Has Broken, Cat Stevens (G)
My Own Two Hands, Jack Johnson (Emin), (G)
Okie From Muskogee, Merle Haggard (C)
Oh Darlin', The Beatles (A)
On the Road Again, Willie Nelson (C)
Rivers of Babylon, Reggae (G)
Run For the Roses, Dan Fogelburg (C)
Scarborough Fair, Simon and Garfunkel (Amin)
Seven Spanish Angels, Willie Nelson (D)
Stardust, Nat King Cole (G)
Sway, Micheal Buble (Amin)
Tennessee Flat-top Box, Johnny Cash (G)
The Very Thought of Your, Tony Bennet (Eb)
Touch of Gray, Greatful Dead (E)
Wayfarin Stranger (Emin)

2009

Beauty and the Beast – A – Disney tune
Cat's in the Cradle –E– Harry Chapin
Daydream Believer –G– The Monkees
Eye of the Tiger –Amin– Survivor
Four Strong Winds –G– Neil Young
I'd Rather Be With You –C– Joshua Radin
In the Moon of Wintertime –Emin– French Carol
It's Now or Never –G– Elvis Presley
Jumper –C– Third Eye Blind
Needle and the Damage Done –D– Neil Young
Norwegian Wood – D– The Beatles
Ohio – Dmin– Neil Young
Sitting, Waiting, Wishing –Jack Johnson
Somewhere Over the Rainbow, Ukulele Style –C–
Tree Little Birds –A– Bob Marley
Under the Sea – G– Disney Tune
Up Around the Bend –Creedence Clearwater Revival
Venus –Emin– Shocking Blue

FRACTION NOTATION

You will notice that this book contains no standard notation. I occasionally communicate strings and frets by using fractions. If you see a fraction such as 1/6, it means "the first fret of the sixth string." A zero indicates an open string. For example, 0/6 means the open sixth string. Two other helpful symbols follow:

RH   right hand
LH   left hand

VERBAL INSTRUCTIONS

The classroom guitar instructor is in some ways like an exercise coach who leads the class using verbal instructions. You can avoid confusion by not using the terms *up* and *down*. It is better to refer to the left hand as moving to the left (descending in pitch) or right (ascending in pitch). If you prefer, you can say "toward the nut" or "toward the sound hole." The same holds true for the right hand. Say "toward the sound hole" or "toward the bridge," or "toward the treble" or "toward the bass." If you use the terms *up* and *down*, half the class will move one way, and the other half will move the opposite way, which is quite humorous.

THE REST POSITION

The most important position for guitar class is the rest position. When you give the instruction to rest, it means students should rest their right forearm over the strings, and their left hand should wrap around the neck, effectively muting the strings. The guitar is an "irresistible manipulative," and the rest position should be modeled, practiced, and reviewed as a way to create a more comfortable learning environment.

UNPITCHED PRACTICE

Whenever you can, perform exercises while the strings are muted with the left hand. This enables students to hear the rhythmic precision better and keeps the noise level to a minimum. It also allows students to concentrate on one skill at a time.

EAR PLUGS AND MICROPHONE

If you don't own them already, make an appointment at your local audiologist to be fitted for musician's earplugs. I recommend the maximum filter. Earplugs will protect your ears and help you avoid noise fatigue. Inexpensive earplugs can be obtained at your local pharmacy. There is no cure for tinnitus (ringing ears), which is caused by prolonged exposure to loud noise, so prevention is invaluable. Using a microphone is an effective way to protect your voice and for the students to hear you more clearly. With the use of an audio mixer you can connect one to your class stereo system.

ADVANCED STUDENTS

Never underestimate a student's potential. On the one hand, a student's success may consist of playing simple melodies or riffs. On the other hand, some students may be able to perform classical concert material. Show respect for your advanced students by having them work as mentors. Monitor mentors to be sure they don't intimidate or distract other students. Provide a "custom agenda" for them by having challenging materials and assignments prepared in advance. I provide ideas throughout the book. Many basic songs can be adapted by having them play (1) without looking at their hands, (2) in higher positions on the neck, (3) using all barre, triad, or jazz forms, or (4) using fills or improvisations. Another useful strategy is to present classical guitar solos that include chord symbols. The advanced students can play the solo while the rest of the class plays the chords. Students who are planning to become or considering becoming music majors should be directed to study *this* book. Classroom pedagogy and instructional strategies will be an important tool for earning a living later in life.

REMEDIAL STUDENTS

Be prepared to offer remedial students a song pack of melodies that can be played *by fret number on a single string*. Remedial students may also participate by singing or playing percussion. Another option is to encourage them to play bass, which requires fewer notes than guitar. In Montessori education, students observe for the first year, participate for the second, and are mentors for the third. Students blossom in their own time if they are encouraged and inspired to be good observers and listeners. Everyone can, and must, participate on some level. Chapters 33, 34, and 35 address special techniques for remedial learners. Being prepared and meeting the needs of diverse learners is one of the most satisfying aspects of classroom teaching.

RELATIONSHIPS

Strive to develop positive relationships. Inspiration, which is one of your greatest gifts to your students, is the result of your relationship. Some students will follow every instruction you give exactly, and others will find it difficult to learn in a group situation. Ironically, some of the best students are rebels who march to the beat of their own drummer. In this case, it may be more appropriate to assist such students in more limited ways and to work with them as a guide in helping them reach their highest learning and creative potential. Teenagers especially need a certain amount of freedom. Regardless of their learning styles, developing a positive relationship can have a positive influence in students' lives even beyond the classroom.

On the first day of class pass out index cards and collect the names and daytime phone numbers of parents. Explain that parents can provide insights into each student's learning style and that music can be a fun family activity. Try to talk with all parents at least twice a semester.

Don't be shy about asking colleagues for ideas and advice. Solicit and listen to feedback and constructive suggestions. Some of the best lessons I have learned have been from general music teachers and band, choir, and orchestra directors. Always reflect on and learn from your own experience.

THE FUTURE OF GUITAR EDUCATION

It is one of my professional goals that classroom guitar be offered to all music-education students since such course of study offers so many benefits. Guitar is inexpensive, portable, and part of the popular and classical music cultures. Students are drawn to this instrument because of its simplicity and potential for rhythmic expression. It can be enjoyed with friends, in social situations, with families, and in church. It is an ideal instrument for teaching music theory and general music. It introduces a whole new group of students to the benefits of music education.

THE SPIRITUAL DIMENSION OF TEACHING

I believe that both student and teacher are enriched and engaged by acknowledging the spiritual dimension of the classroom. Teaching philosophies and styles can certainly vary, but I would rather light a spark than pound a nail. Some maxims that have guided me follow.

- Teaching is the greatest vocation.
- Every student is a miracle.
- If the eyes are the windows to the soul, my classroom has many windows.

I hope that you are excited and inspired to read what follows.

Steve Eckels, 2009

Acknowledgments

I acknowledge the work of three educators who have made a monumental impact on the foundation of guitar education: I extend my special thanks to William Bay of Mel Bay Publications for encouraging my professional development as an author; and to Will Schmid and Nancy Marsters for advancing guitar in public education and for serving as my mentors and role models at different times. Special thanks to the department chair at Flathead High School, Allen Slater, for his encouragement and consultation throughout this learning adventure. Thanks to the administrators at Kalispell School District #5 for their interest in guitar as a means of serving their students. Thanks also to my wife, Barbara, for providing the environment in which this book could be written and for managing my catalog of recordings and books, which are available through our website, guitarmusicman.com.

I

INTRODUCTION

1

Effective Planning

Use the Six S's to remember the elements of guitar-lesson planning: salutation, strength, scales, sight reading, songs, and skills.

INITIAL THOUGHTS

- Become as familiar with your method book as you can.
- Go chapter 22 in this book and mark the songs that you are interested in teaching.
- Your lesson plan will vary depending on the characteristics of the class, the time of year, the time of day, the length of the class period, and your personal philosophy.
- You must constantly evaluate each student's understanding and skill and be flexible enough to make adjustments during the lesson as needed.
- Let the students help you with tomorrow's lesson plan by listening to their questions and requests and by observing their progress. Then . . .
- Write down your ideas for tomorrow's lesson plan during pauses in the class period.
- Do not overload students in one day. If you feel they have received enough instruction for one day, allow them time to practice, process, and fully absorb the material.
- It is usually better to have short, frequent practice pauses than longer ones.
- Make a list of songs and skills for the week and for the two-week proficiency cycle. Observe the students carefully, and work through only the amount of material that matches your students' needs. For example:
  - o Week one: Introduce and practice "The Lion Sleeps Tonight" in the key of C; read the melody to "Ode to Joy" using the first two strings.

  - o Week two: Prepare for the proficiency examination to be administered on Thursday. A good assessment for the first two weeks could be to ask each students to perform the C, F, and G chords as used in "The Lion Sleeps Tonight" and to read the notes C, D, E, F, and G as written in "Ode to Joy."

EFFECTIVE UNIT PLANNING: THE TWO-WEEK PROFICIENCY CYCLE

A unit of approximately ten class periods provides a good opportunity to introduce, ingrain, assess, and perform new skills and songs. Mastery of skills will take longer. The following unit cycle is designed for instructors who meet with their classes daily. If you meet on a different basis, you should modify the general framework to meet your needs.

USE ROUTINE TO YOUR ADVANTAGE

Students appreciate the predictability, safety, and comfort provided by using a routine or pattern during the two-week proficiency cycle. For example, introduce and practice a new skill on Monday, ease off and provide more practice opportunities during the week, review the following Monday, provide assessment on Thursday, and play songs on Friday. Let's examine the cycle in more detail.

WEEK ONE: INTRODUCING AND INGRAINING NEW MATERIAL

Monday and Tuesday: Presentation and Workout

Introduce and rehearse the new materials. Short practice points should be interspersed with direct instruction to ensure that the students are tracking and to assign mentors if possible.

Midweek: Practice and Instructor Feedback

As students become aware of what and how to practice, the class will appreciate, and benefit from, time devoted to fully absorbing the new material. Be sure they have their own copy of each piece or book to take home and practice. After the group warm-up and review, have the students practice individually, or in pairs, while you circulate and work with individuals or small groups. After students receive your coaching, have them "pass it on" by helping a friend. Wednesday is a good day for a written worksheet that reinforces the skills you are working on. Worksheets should be checked and their material performed, where appropriate, during class. At the end of the class each student should place his or her worksheet in an individual hanging file. Place an open cardboard file box near the exit. On a regular basis, remind the students of the assessment date approaching on Thursday.

Fridays

Friday is a special day with a mood of its own—a good day to release energy through the rhythm and movement of playing and rehearsing songs. Playing songs provides the opportunity to apply skills in a fun way. I like to give students a proficiency slip so that they know what to practice on the weekend. The slip is a reminder of the required proficiency skill, the date of the assessment, and how they will be graded. The more specific you are about your expectations, the better the students will meet them.

WEEK TWO: LEADING UP TO THE PROFICIENCY ASSESSMENT

Monday Review

On the second Monday, students will need a review of the material learned the previous week. It should be much like the first Monday, with the entire class period devoted to direct instruction interspersed with practice points. Remind students that Thursday is the formal assessment day.

Midweek

Tuesdays or Wednesdays are good days for written worksheets that reinforce the proficiency requirements. During practice points circulate, work with,

observe, and assess individuals. Figures 1.1, 1.2, and 1.3 provide pages for converting notes to grids and/or tablature. (Delay beginning work on tablature with students who are learning the staff because there will be confusion between the five-line staff and the six-line tablature staff.) You can customize the worksheets by adding the notes that you are currently working on. Place the notes either on the grid or on the staff, and have the students add the missing note name, note head, or finger location on the grid. Students could also write the melody for the "Ode to Joy" on staff paper and add the fingerings and note names. You will find many more worksheets and ideas for assessment in the next chapter.

Second Thursday: Formal Assessment

Take a look at the assessment possibilities in the next chapter, and use whichever assessment matches your style and you feel best serves your students. Always review the skill and allow a few moments for students to practice before giving the test. Congratulate students on the rewards of accomplishing something new.

DAILY PLANNING

The Role of Guitar Class in the School Day

It is useful to reflect on the context of guitar class within the school day. Guitar class shares characteristics with

- gym class: movement, breathing, and recreation
- art class: creativity, graphic design of music diagrams, calligraphy, individual expression, and communication
- choir, band, and orchestra: practice strategies, music theory, breath management, etc.
- history class: most songs have a historic or geographical significance
- math class: music reinforces the ability to subdivide, count intervals, and process numerical relationships between fingers, frets, and strings
- English class: practice speaking and writing about music

Guitar Lesson Format: The Six S's

Use the Six S's to remember the elements of guitar lesson planning: salutation, strength, scales, sight reading, songs, and skills. Figure 1.4 provides you with a form for planning each daily lesson. Due to time restraints, you may not be able to address all six

Name:_____

Date:_____

Grid and Staff Worksheet

Number Completed:

Figure 1.1: This sheet may be photocopied for classes or other groups within purchaser's institution only. This provision does not confer any other rights to the purchaser or his or her institution.

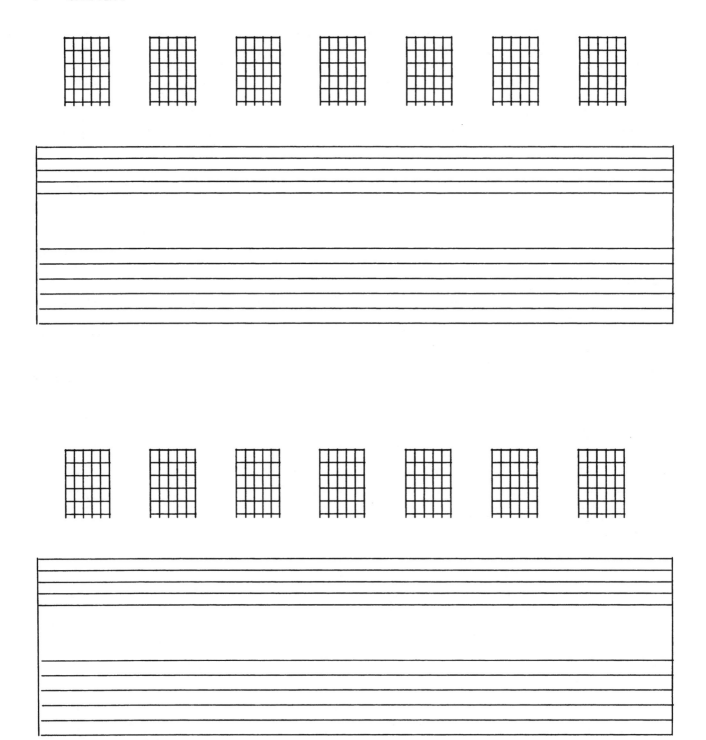

Figure 1.2: This sheet may be photocopied for class or other groups within purchaser's institution only. This provision does not confer any other rights to the purchaser or his or her institution.

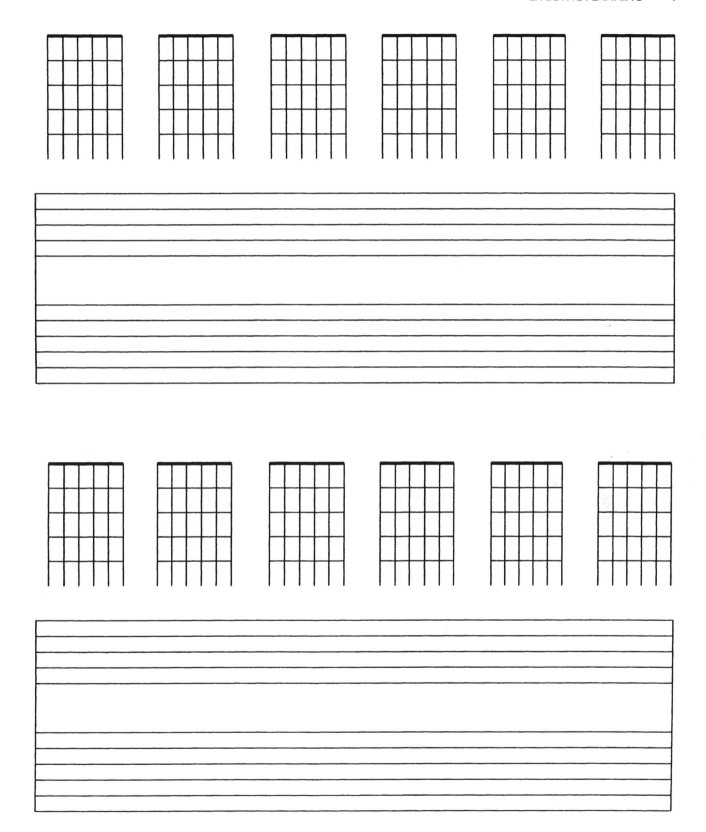

Figure 1.3: This sheet may be photocopied for class or other groups within purchaser's institution only. This provision does not confer any other rights to the purchaser or his or her institution.

LESSON PLAN WORKSHEET

Date:

Class Level:

Proficiency Unit Skill:

Salutation/Anticipation:		
Songs:		
Scales:		
Reading:		
Skills:		
Independent Practice, Circulation, Feedback, & Assessment Activities:		
Looking Ahead: Other:		

Figure 1.4: This sheet may be photocopied for classes or other groups within purchaser's institution only. This provision does not confer any other rights to the purchaser or his or her institution.

categories in each lesson. The core daily elements are scales, sight reading, and songs.

Salutation and Agenda. The beginning of the class is a good time to share a word of encouragement, to inspire, or to pose a thought or question. Circulate throughout the class to greet students one-on-one. If there is not time to circulate, be sure to welcome your students as a class.

Strength. This includes all the exercises discussed in chapter 10. Strength and motion exercises are especially important during the first semester.

Scales and Slurs. The term *scale* is used to include material such as scales, mini-scales, scale patterns, intervals, triad scales, power-chord scales, and barre-chord scales. Part of scale practice may include variations using hammer-ons and pull-offs, formally referred to as *slurs*. Challenge students to substitute a rest for important reference notes as a way to keep them engaged.

Sight Reading. After working on scales, music reading should be practiced. As a preliminary, use your overhead projector to point to notes, in the context of the natural-note scale, that are contained in the music you are about to play. This technique provides students with an important connection between the scale fingering and the printed note. (Note: In addition to locating notes, you may build chords and intervals using the same technique.) Reading activities include playing melodies from your method book, melodic dictation, rhythm drills, and playing ensembles. As part of your routine, offer mini-reading opportunities to introduce new chords, arpeggios, and other skills.

Skills and Techniques. Skills include accompaniment styles, improvisation, slurs, right-hand arpeggios, singing, and strumming. Skills can lead into songs, or, the reverse, songs can lead into skills. On Fridays, when playing songs for fun, you may need to introduce and practice a skill in order to be successful with the song. Strive to make the connection between guitar techniques and playing songs.

Songs. Songs can be presented at the beginning of the workout to warm up the hands, release energy, increase circulation and breathing, and have fun. As mentioned, songs are the best way to present skills in a meaningful context. Songs include singing and strumming, ensembles, guitar solos, and melodies with accompaniment from your method.

Individual Practice Time and Assessment Activities. After ingraining a skill as a class, I like to give the students a few minutes to review each skill on their own and really absorb it. Individual practice time must be handled with care so that the students stay on task. Be sure to model the practice material. Check to see that the music is on the stands and open to the correct page. Personal

experience has taught me that too many transitions reduce retention of information. Instead of rushing into new material, take a practice pause. When you take a practice pause, announce the page number of the next exercise. Many students will preread this material. Use practice time to meet with and assess individuals or small groups. Use a checklist or index cards to be sure you don't miss anybody.

Grand Finale. When time permits, it is a good idea to end the class with a grand finale to send students on their way humming.

GENERAL LESSON STRUCTURE

Here is a generally accepted lesson structure that applies to all disciplines. It is important and useful for guitar as well.

- List which national or state standard is being addressed.
- List the daily and unit goals.
- Create anticipation.
- Provide a demonstration.
- Provide group instruction.
- Provide independent guided practice time.
- Evaluate student understanding and skill, and use the information for future planning.
- Provide a closing to each lesson.

STUDENT CHOICES

To facilitate different skill levels and interests, you may present students with multiple proficiency choices. For the first chord proficiency some students might prefer Johnny Cash's "I Walk the Line," while others might prefer "The Lion Sleeps Tonight." For note reading some might prefer Beethoven's "Ode to Joy," while others might prefer "Yankee Doodle." One instructor I know assigns "any song on a given page." I have provided you with a semester planning sample with song ideas (figure 1.5) and a semester proficiency planning worksheet for you to sketch out ideas (figure 1.6). I also encourage you to study my list of suggested guitar songs by skill proficiency level, artist, and key (figure P.1 in the preface) so that you have a ready repertoire of popular songs that you feel will work best in any given situation.

OVERLAPPING AND FORESHADOWING SKILLS

Allow proficiency skills to overlap. For instance, you could start the song for proficiency #4, "Hotel California," while you are working on proficiency #3,

SEMESTER ONE - PLANNING SAMPLE

Prof. #	Date Due	Song Choices	Skill/Techniques	Note Reading Method Pg. #	Ensemble	Assessment Type	Worksheet Type
1		Lion Sleeps Tonight I Walk the Line	C, F, G chords	String 1,2 Pg.			
	9/18	Amazing Grace Yellow Submarine	G, C, D chords 3/4 Time				
2	10/9	Leaving on a Jet Plane Jambalaya	D, G, A chords	String 3,4			
		Blue Suede Shoes What I Say	E, A, B7 chords Blues Form				
3	10/23	Wayfarin' Stranger El Condor Pasa	Emin, Amin	String 5,6			
4	11/6	Hotel California	Amin, Dmin				
5	11/20	Joy to the World Twist and Shout	Power Chords G, C, D				
6	12/4	Sunshine of Your Love	Riff Embellishment Improvisation				
7	12/18	Colors of the Wind Let it Be Theme from Titanic	Finger Picking				
8	1/15	Thunderstruck	Hammering On				
9	1/22	Leroy Brown Proud Mary	Barre Forms R6 Barre Forms R5				

Figure 1.5: This sheet may be photocopied for class or other groups within purchaser's institution only. This provision does not confer any other rights to the purchaser or his or her institution.

SEMESTER PROFICIENCY PLANNING WORKSHEET

Prof. #	Date Due	Songs	Skill/Techniques	Note Reading Method Page #	Ensemble	Assessment Type	Worksheet Type
1							
2							
3							
4							
5							
6							
7							
8							
9							

Figure 1.6: This sheet may be photocopied for class or other groups within purchaser's institution only. This provision does not confer any other rights to the purchaser or his or her institution.

which is "Wayfaring Stranger." This gives students more time to master each song and creates variety during the class period.

SEMESTER PLANNING

Reading

Your method book will be arranged chronologically. In the table of contents, pencil in dates next to page numbers to create your goals. Be prepared to modify the dates as needed.

Songs

Songs are what make the guitar program attractive to students. The song list that I have provided lists songs by skill level. I also have provided you with a sample of songs that I have found to work well at the high school level. Each song addresses a different skill and proceeds in a logical sequence. I have provided you with a blank planning form to fill in your own choices.

Techniques

Your method may or may not include the breadth of techniques necessary to interest your class. For this purpose I have published four levels of techniques that I have found to work well. (Visit www.guitar musicman.com for more information on *Guitar Techniques, Levels One, Two, Three, and Four.*) I have provided you with a list of the techniques in figure 1.8.

CURRICULUM OVERVIEW

Skill	Semester 1	Semester 2	Semester 3	Semester 4
Scales	• Natural note scale • C major & A minor • F# • Pentatonic scale on one string • Pentatonic scale using two string patterns • Diagonal pentatonic • Motion/posture/tuning	• Natural notes up to the 12th fret on all strings • Major scales in 12 keys ---Thirds in open position in keys of C, G, D, A • Diagonal pentatonic scale, with slurs • Triad scales	• Diatonic intervals in key of C, G, D, A, E • Second Position scales in C & G • Intervals in second position	• Chromatic octaves • Chromatic intervals • Thirds, sixths, and tenths up the neck • Modes
Chords	• Open position chords • Open position and moveable power chords • Intro to barre forms • I, IV, V Theory/Blues Form	• Chords w/ color tones: min7, maj7, sus4, add9 • Chord families • Inversions (G/B) • Applied barres • Introduction to triads	• Introduction to moveable jazz forms with roots on strings 5 & 6 • Barre chords in chord families	• Application of jazz forms • Writing and reading notated chord forms • Four note ukulele-style chords
Voice and Accompaniment	• Introduction to voice and vocalizations • The pick • Basic strumming patterns • Basic syncopation • Bass patterns	• Singing and playing • Embellished strumming • Bass runs • Frailing • Capo Theory	• Singing and playing • Sixteenth note accompaniment rhythms • Applied triad accompaniment	• Singing and playing • Embellished triads
Reading and Rhythms	• Basic rhythms and rhythm figures • Simple ensembles	• Eighth notes and syncopated rhythms • Ensembles	• 16th note patterns • Ensembles embellished with vocals, improvisations, etc.	• 16th note syncopations • Higher level ensembles
Right Hand Arpeggios and Solo Guitar	• Introduction to finge picking • Root-bass patterns • "Für Elise"	• Applied finger picking patterns • Travis picking • Scale played over a bass • Two-part solos (melody and bass) • "Blackbird"	• Performance of written guitar solos in open position • Finger picking two chords per measure • Solos with melody, bass, and fill tones • "Pachelbel Canon"	• Expand repertoire of solos • Solos using higher positions • "Greensleeves"

Figure 1.7: This sheet may be photocopied for class or other groups within purchaser's institution only. This provision does not confer any other rights to the purchaser or his or her institution.

FIGURE 1.8:

GUITAR TECHNIQUES AND ENSEMBLES

Level One

The Open Strings,
The B/C E/F Rule, Understanding the Neck
The Seventeen Natural Notes
Skill Builders
Blues Progression in Eight Keys
Rhythm Reading
Rhythm Reading (part 2)
Strumming Patterns
Finger Picking Patterns
Open Power Chords
Moveable Power Chords,
Natural Notes Up the Neck
Blues Bass Line (The 1-3-5-3 Arpeggio)
Barre Forms Based on String 6 (E Type)
Barre Forms Based on String 5 (A Type)
E minor Pentatonic Scales
A minor Pentatonic Scales
Hammering on and Pulling Off
Blues Training Riff in E
Blues Training Riff in A
Blues Training Riff in C
Triad Study
CHORD CHART
CHORD QUIZ
PLAY BY EAR
SING ALONG LIST

Level Two

Rhythm Reading
Notes on All Six Strings
Speed Patterns
Pentatonic Scale Review
Capo Theory
Major and Minor Jazz Blues
Triad Scales for Picking Practice
Triad Inversions for Picking Practice
Diatonic Chord Families
Diatonic Chord Families—Minor Keys
Chord Progressions Using "Slash Chords"
Chord Formulas in Open Position
Strumming Patterns:
Bolero, Rhumba, 3/3/2, 6/8, Rock
Bass Runs: Key of C, D
Bass Runs: Key of G, Minor Chords
Banjo "Frailing" Patterns
Fingerpicking Patterns:
    Travis Style, Click Picking,
    Alberti, and Pinch with Alternation
Hammering On and Pulling Off

Alternate Picking and Speed Patterns
Pentatonic Patterns for Improvisation:
    Open Position
Pentatonic Patterns for Improvisation:
    Moveable Forms
Cycle of Fifths
Major Scales in 12 Keys
Diatonic Chord Progressions using Barre Forms and
    Triads
Barre Review

Level Three

Slur and Strength Study
Rhythm Reading: Sixteenth Note Figures
Intervals:
    Thirds, Sixths, and Tenths Up the Neck
Intervals: Tenths across the Neck
Interval Study: Third - Octaves
The Natural Notes on All Six Strings
Right Hand Variations and Speed Patterns
Natural Note Fingerings:
    Three Notes Per String
Major and Minor Blues (four strings)
Jazz Blues
The II/V Progression and Diminished Chords
Voice Leading Triads
Root 3 & 2
Voice Leading Triads
Root 1 & Root 3 Minor
Voice Leading Triads
Minor Root 2 & 3
Triad Progressions
Second Position—Root 5
Intervals as Preliminary for Chord Study
Second Position
    Root 5—Major and Minor
Second Position
    Root 5—Sevenths and Diminished
Second Position
    Root 5—Altered Sevenths and Misc.

Level Four

Chromatic Octaves
Second Position
    Interval Study Key of G
Second Position
    Root 6—Major and Minor
Second Position
    Root 6—Sevenths and Diminished
Second Position
    Root 6—Altered Sevenths and Misc.
I #I II V Progression Root 6, 5, 4
Arranging for Solo Guiar
Arpeggios for "Melodization"

Modes (Parallel)
Modes (Relative)
Improvisation—Triplet Study—Root Six
Improvisation—Triplet Study—Root Five
Counterpoint – Scale Over a Bass
Natural Notes in the Fifth Position

Ensembles

Warm Ups and Jam Sessions

Bingo Variations
Blues Jam in E
Blues Jam in G
Blues Jam in D & C
"My Cat Toby" Jam in A minor
Pachelbel Canon

Traditional Music

Amazing Grace
Ash Grove
Aura Lee
Celtic Melody
Danny Boy
Down By the Sally Gardens
Flow Gently Sweet Afton
Hymn Tune
Rising Sun
Scarborough Fair
Shenandoah
Cruel War
The Water Is Wide
Sea Shanty
Shady Grove
Waters of Babylon

Classical Selections

Gavotte, Bach
Bianco Fiore, Renaissance
O Solo Mio

Little Waltz, Carcassi
Bouree, De Visee
Minuet in D, De Visee
Minuetto, De Visee
Preludio, De Visee
Greensleeves
Kemp's Jig
Minuet, Purcell
O Mio Babbino Caro, Puccini
Song of Joy, Beethoven
Siciliano

Christmas

Away in A Manger
Carol of the Bells
God Rest Ye, Merry Gentlemen
It Came Upon A Midnight Clear
Jingle Bells
O Little Town of Bethlehem
Silent Night

Solos and Duets

Away in a Manger
The Friendly Beasts
Jingle Bells
March of the Toy Soldiers
O Come Emmanuel
What Child Is This?
Theme from Bonanza
Reading Warm-Ups
Dueling Banjos
Flight of the Bumble Bee
Star of the County Down
Vocal Warm-Up
Rhythm Exercise
Reading Warm-Up (beginners)
Chorales
Building Chords – Root 5
Building Chords – Root 6
Reading Reference Tones

FIGURE 1.9

GUITAR SONGS AND SKILLS, FOUR SEMESTERS

LEVEL ONE

Techniques

Chord Reference Chart: Alphabetical
Chord Reference Chart: Quick Start
Scale Workout: Seventeen Natural Notes
Pentatonic Scales for Improvisation
Plectrum Study
Fingerstyle Picking Patterns
Voice Exercises

Songs:

The Lion Sleeps Tonight – Key of C, Rhythm Values
Folsom Prison Blues – Key of G, Root-Strum
Jambalaya – Key of D, Double Stops
Kumbaya – Key of A, Power Chords
Blue Suede Shoes – Key of E, Stop Time
Wayfaring Stranger – Key of E minor, Finger Arches
Hotel California – Key of A minor, Pinch Accents
Joy to the World – Power Chords, Pentatonic Scale,
Twist and Shout – Power Chords, Triads
Sunshine of Your Love – Riff Embellishment
Colors of the Wind – Finger Picking
Let It Be – Finger Picking, Combo
Theme From the Titanic, Piano-Style Picking, Combo
Thunderstruck – Hammer-ons and Pull-offs
Ensemble: *Bingo Variations*
Ensemble: *Amazing Grace:* ¾ Time
Solos: *Fur Elise, 32 Moonlight Sonata*

LEVEL TWO

Techniques

Chord Reference Chart: Chord Families
Major Scales 12 Keys
Natural Notes on All Six Strings
Root 5 and Root 6, Diagonal Pentatonic Forms
Plectrum Study
Fingerstyle Picking Patterns
Voice Exercises

Songs:

Landslide – Travis Picking, Chord Family in C
Dust in the Wind – Travis Picking, Variable Treble
Annie's Song – ¾ Time, Passing Chords in C
I Walk the Line – Bass Runs and Frailing
City of New Orleans – Frailing and Passing Chords

Layla – Barre Review, Improvisation in D minor
In A Gadda Da Vida – Riff Embellishment
Ghost Riders in the Sky – Bolero Strum
Heart of Gold – Funk Strum
Tequila Sunrise – Rhumba Strum
I Can See Clearly – Triads, Barre Review
My Girl – Triads, Major Pentatonic Scale
La Bamba – Triads, Major Pentatonic Scale
Yesterday – The sus4 Chord, Combo
Walk Don't Run – Scale Running, Surf Guitar
Arkansas Traveler – Scale Running, Bluegrass Guitar
Ensemble: *Good Cheer*
Ensemble: *Ash Grove*
Solos: *Bouree in E minor, Blackbird*

LEVEL THREE

Techniques

Second Position—Moveable Chords, Root 5
Second Position—Moveable Chords, Root 6
Review Notes on all Six Strings
Root 5 and Root 6, Diagonal Forms
Fingerstyle Picking Patterns
Picking Patterns with Chord Families
Voice Exercises

Songs:

Hallelujah – Finger Picking Review
Your Song – Passing Chord Review
While My Guitar Gently Weeps – D minor
Fire and Rain – Funk Strum, Passing Chords in G
Blackbird – Travis Picking and Passing Chords
Puff the Magic Dragon – Travis Picking
Blues with Jazz Chords – 3 Jazz Chords
Cold, Cold Heart – 3 Jazz Chords, Texas Swing
Black Magic Woman – 3 Jazz Chords, Triad Review
I Shot the Sheriff –4 Jazz Chords, Funk Strum, Riff
Susie Q – 4 Jazz Chords
Summertime – 6 Jazz Chords
So Lonesome I Could Cry – ¾ Time, 6th and Maj7
Don't Know Why – Major Seventh Chords
Ring of Fire – Bo Diddly Strum
Rocky Top – Bluegrass Strum
Ensemble: *God Rest Ye Merry Gentlemen*
Ensemble: *Carol of the Bells*
Solo: *Pachelbel Canon*
Solo: *Malaguena*

LEVEL FOUR

Techniques

Chord Families with Arpeggios

Chromatic Octaves
Thirds, Sixth, and Tenths
Scales: Three Notes Per String
Modes
Plectrum Study
Fingerstyle Picking Patterns
Voice Exercises

Songs:

Moondance – 5 Jazz Chords

Light My Fire – 7 Jazz Chords
Europa – 10 Jazz Chords
Somewhere Over the Rainbow – 10 Jazz Chords,
Jazz Blues – 10 Jazz Chords
Satin Doll – 12 Jazz Chords
Embraceable You – 14 Jazz Chords
Ensemble: *Waters of Babylon*
Ensemble: *Sea Shanty*
Ensemble: *Bianco Fiore*
Solo: *Star Spangled Banner*
Solo: *Greensleeves*

MAXIMS ON THE CLASS ENVIRONMENT

- Group instruction requires the ability to make transitions from exercise to exercise seamlessly and logically. This skill takes time to develop. Be patient with yourself.
- Use continuity from day to day.
- Use a balance of routine and surprise, predictability and variation.
- Stay on track: Teach students to hold their personal questions for appropriate breaks in the workout. When a student asks a question unrelated to the whole class, tell the student you will meet individually to discuss it. *Never* allow students to highjack the class—*you* are the pilot.
- Rule: Everyone must succeed at some level. Students should be encouraged to adapt class activities in such a way as to ensure successful participation.
- Use students' problems to plan tomorrow's lesson.
- Use a balance of intrinsic and extrinsic motivation.
- Create situations and ask questions that encourage students to learn through intuition and discovery. Some people refer to this as the *constructivist* approach to learning—students construct their own learning and meaning. What they learn on their own, they really learn.
- "Always ride a horse in the direction it is going." —Cowboy wisdom
- Present students with thought-questions and problems for them to grapple with and insist that they really make an effort to solve them. Avoid spoon feeding every morsel of information.
- Believe in your students. Never underestimate their sophistication.
- Find ways for students to connect with other students. Use student mentors.
- Help the students feel safe to err, experiment, personalize, and question.
- Bring in guest performers from the community or from other classes.
- Students learn at different rates and at different times. Empower students to succeed by providing materials that match their varying abilities.
- Relate learning to your students' lives. Find music that is relevant to their interests.
- Use modeling and enthusiasm to create interest in new and unfamiliar music.

MAXIMS ON DISCIPLINE

- Make every effort from the beginning to ensure that students do not fall behind. Because when students do fall behind, your job will be made more difficult, since you will be dealing with discipline problems and remediation efforts.
- Involve families in a planned Family Night, complete with sing-alongs, demonstrations, and refreshments. Parents and siblings should be encouraged to bring instruments.
- Call all parents routinely, twice a semester.
- Make it clear that you do not allow interruptions. When necessary, take an impromptu practice point, talk with the student, and move them to another location.
- Use the principal and/or discipline referral forms when necessary. That is their job.
- Explain to students that you are absolutely committed to their success; tell them specifically what they need to do to reach their goals.
- Consistency is critical.

- Let students know that you will not let them fall behind or disturb others.
- Convey the idea that it is fun to be good at what you do. Instill pride in self-development.
- Know what you want to accomplish, and move forward calmly and firmly.
- Be sure the climate of your classroom reflects the competent guidance of a professional (you), not the manipulation of adolescents or children.

② Assessment Techniques

The successful guitar instructor will:

- use of a variety of assessment methods
- have an organized filing and information-retrieval system
- be able to share the information with students, parents, and administrators
- be able to detect problems, diagnose their causes, suggest adjustments, and monitor student progress
- have set criteria for determining grades
- use assessment information in planning
- inform students precisely what they will do to earn a grade of A, B, C, D, or F.

OVERVIEW

In the following chapter I outline a variety of assessment methods and provide you with custom guitar papers for creating your own. I share a useful filing system and provide ideas for determining grades. Students and parents should know in advance the answers to the questions that follow.

What is the scope of the class content? Minimum competency goals should be clearly defined in writing, but they should never limit a student's potential.

What are the testing procedures, and how often are tests administered? Students benefit from knowing that a formal assessment occurs on a regular basis. I prefer a two-week (ten class periods) assessment cycle. Students should be informed that they are observed daily. This is known as *embedded assessment*. Worksheets, writing assignments, creativity, and "song collecting" are also factors in grading. Write the proficiency skills and learning goals clearly on the white board at the beginning of the unit so there is a specific target for the students to work toward. For example:

Proficiency skill: "The Lion Sleeps Tonight"
Learning goals: Smooth the transition between the C, F, and G chords; strumming in rhythm; and strumming from the roots of each chord

You may then plan your lessons to include the preliminaries necessary to achieving the learning goals.

On what criteria are grades based? Grading philosophies vary from department to department, teacher to teacher, and school to school. Several of the worksheets that I provide have built-in numerical grading systems. The following is an excerpt from my course syllabus (figure 2.1). Many thanks to my colleague and bandmaster Allen Slater for assistance with this information.

FIGURE 2.1

SYLLABUS—GUITAR CLASS, 2008–2009

INSTRUCTOR, STEVE ECKELS

Telephone: 751-3617
email – eckelss@sd5.k12.mt.us

SECURITY: The school cannot take responsibility for the security of instruments. Please be sure your name is clearly marked on the case. Many students decorate their cases in creative ways, which individualizes them. If possible, keep your case locked.

COURSE OBJECTIVE: To stimulate life-long, mental, physical, and social growth through the joyful creation of music on the guitar.

COURSE OUTLINE: (See Attachment)

Classroom Expectations

BE PREPARED

- Be in class each day, on time, with *your* guitar, ready to play.
- Bring a pencil to class every day.

FOLLOW INSTRUCTIONS

- Listen to instruction and play only when instructed. (Mute strings when instructor is talking.)
- Stay at the same speed as everyone playing.
- Play at a moderate volume (not too loud and not to soft).

APPLY KNOWLEDGE AND SKILLS DURING CLASS

- Warm up with scales, skills, and techniques, while waiting for the class to start.
- Use class time/practice pauses to improve the needed skill.
- Sing or speak the words in vocal songs to improve rhythm

BE A POSITIVE PARTICIPANT IN THE CLASS

- Chip in and help clean the room and organized.
- Develop a positive line of communication with others.
- Be a mentor.

GRADES ARE CALCULATED BASED ON:

Instructor observation of practice and rehearsal work in class;

Student demonstation of proficiency skills;

Accuracy on written tests, worksheets, and writing essays; and

Self- and peer-assessment final project: song portfolios assessment.

GRADING RUBRIC

A   Proficient in assigned playing skills and written evaluations, positive and productive daily work.

B   Approaching proficiency (not consistently proficient), uses class time wisely

C   Novice: rudimentary demonstration of skills, partial understanding evident in written evaluations, lacking in good daily work skills

D   Nearing Novice: struggles to adequately demonstrate playing or written skills, poor daily work

F   Failure to exhibit required skills and/or complete assignments and/or excessive absences.

EXTRA CREDIT: Credit is awarded for performance of music beyond what is required. This includes class demonstrations, lunch concerts, Friday open stage, riff-exchange, consultations outside of class time, playing in other groups, etc. Documentation of extra work must be provided to instructor.

Final Project: Students will create an heirloom quality, keepsake portfolio of songs that they will be able to enjoy for a lifetime.

Portfolio production checklist:

____Sing-and-strum lyric sheets, guitar solos, and other music (minimum twenty- five songs).
____Published songbooks you have purchased.
____Cover design of original artwork, collage, or graphics; name, date, and place.
____List of contents and/or sections.
____Section dividers.
____Artwork, graphics, and music from class assignments.
____Photos of yourself and friends.
____Rugged, archival quality, three-ring binder and sheet protectors.

DAILY CLASS STRUCTURE:

1) Tune and review before class starts.
2) Direct instruction: daily scales; sight reading; songs and skills.
3) Individual practice and consultations
4) Final song performance.
5) Dismissal by instructor.

IMPORTANT ACCESSORIES: Guitar strap, electric tuner, music stand, capo, picks, three-ring binder for music portfolio.

WORKBOOKS AND TEXBOOKS: The school provides materials necessary for classroom use. The text is available at local music stores for optional purchase.

SUPPLEMENTAL BOOKS: Are available from the library for checkout.

GUITAR STORAGE: Students are welcome to store guitars in the guitar room, which is open before school and at lunch. Students are required to provide their own guitars. The school cannot take responsibility for the security of instruments. Please be sure your name is clearly marked on the case.

IMPORTANT DATES: Family guitar nights offered once per month on the second Tuesday of every month. The time is 7:00, and the place is in room G110.

DIFFERENTIATED INSTRUCTION: Instruction in which differences between students' readiness and interest are addressed by providing various learning methods, materials, and requirements.

THE EIGHT HABITS OF SUCCESS: These famous habits are transferable to all areas of success and were published by Stephen Covey.

Begin with the end in mind	Visualize the goal.
Be proactive	Take action, find answers, don't wait, make things happen.
Put first things first	Prioritize, learn time and project management.
Seek first to understand, then to be understood	You learn more by listening than by talking.
Synergize	Work with a team where people compliment each other.
Think "win-win" or no deal	Find ways to reach mutual goals without sacrificing your own needs and identity.
Sharpen the saw	Find a teacher and improve your skills following their guidance.
Find your own voice, and help others to find theirs	"Voice" is where your gifts and passion meet the need of society.

FORMULA FOR SUCCESS:

Achievement
Respect
Fun
Freedom

CLASSROOM EXPECTATION ASSESSMENT

Name: _____
Class Period: _____ Date: _____

Fill in the blanks on a scale of 1–5 with 5 being always and 1 being never. Then total your score at the bottom.

1. ____**Being Prepared** – in school every day, on time to class, with *your* guitar and a pencil

2. ____**Following Instructions** – play only when instructed, listen to instructions, stay at class speed on exercises, play at a moderate volume.

3.____**Applying Knowledge and Skills** – do warm-ups before class, apply skills during class, use practice pauses to improve ability, sing or speak along with songs

4.____**Positive Class Member** – develop good lines of communication, speak one at a time, listen politely to others, help pick up room organize materials, mentors.

Student Score_____ **Teacher Score**_____

CLASSROOM EXPECTATION ASSESSMENT

Name: _____
Class Period: _____ Date: _____

Fill in the blanks on a scale of 1–5 with 5 being always and 1 being never. Then total your score at the bottom.

1. ____**Being Prepared** – in school every day, on time to class, with *your* guitar and a pencil

2. ____**Following Instructions** – play only when instructed, listen to instructions, stay at class speed on exercises, play at a moderate volume.

3.____**Applying Knowledge and Skills** – do warm-ups before class, apply skills during class, use practice pauses to improve ability, sing or speak along with songs

4.____**Positive Class Member** – develop good lines of communication, speak one at a time, listen politely to others, help pick up room organize materials, mentors.

Student Score_____ **Teacher Score**_____

CLASSROOM EXPECTATION ASSESSMENT

Name: _____
Class Period: _____ Date: _____

Fill in the blanks on a scale of 1–5 with 5 being always and 1 being never. Then total your score at the bottom.

1. ____**Being Prepared** – in school every day, on time to class, with *your* guitar and a pencil

2. ____**Following Instructions** – play only when instructed, listen to instructions, stay at class speed on exercises, play at a moderate volume.

3.____**Applying Knowledge and Skills** – do warm-ups before class, apply skills during class, use practice pauses to improve ability, sing or speak along with songs

4.____**Positive Class Member** – develop good lines of communication, speak one at a time, listen politely to others, help pick up room organize materials, mentors.

Student Score_____ **Teacher Score**_____

CLASSROOM EXPECTATION ASSESSMENT

Name: _____
Class Period: _____ Date: _____

Fill in the blanks on a scale of 1–5 with 5 being always and 1 being never. Then total your score at the bottom.

1. ____**Being Prepared** – in school every day, on time to class, with *your* guitar and a pencil

2. ____**Following Instructions** – play only when instructed, listen to instructions, stay at class speed on exercises, play at a moderate volume.

3.____**Applying Knowledge and Skills** – do warm-ups before class, apply skills during class, use practice pauses to improve ability, sing or speak along with songs

4.____**Positive Class Member** – develop good lines of communication, speak one at a time, listen politely to others, help pick up room organize materials, mentors.

Student Score_____ **Teacher Score**_____

Figure 2.2: This sheet may be photocopied for class or other groups within purchaser's institution only. This provision does not confer any other rights to the purchaser or his or her institution.

PHILOSOPHY

Using a variety of assessment techniques provides a more in-depth learning experience and contributes to better student engagement. Including some form of informal assessment on a daily basis keeps students on their toes. Having a formal assessment on a routine schedule gives students concrete goals to work toward.

One of the goals of assessment is to ensure that you do not allow students to fall behind. It is critically important that you identify, assist, and make adaptations for students *before* they become lost. Teachers must insist that students learn how to grapple with ideas and how to solve problems. By using their own constructive thinking processes, students can experience the rewards of self-discovery and become better independent learners.

Be alert for students who are tired or lethargic. Seek out and address the root causes. When appropriate, inspire, encourage, prod, and push them to think. In some cases, students may be suffering from depression or other mental-health problems. Work with parents and your school counseling staff to know and understand your students' behavior.

Guitar classes are comprised of students at varying levels of proficiency, so it is important that you present assessment opportunities that match the needs of *all* the students. In Montessori education, students are grouped into three levels: observers, active participants, and mentors. It is likely that any guitar class will contain some students at all three of these levels. Students at each level need to be appreciated, respected, and integrated into a learning community where everyone is a learner and everyone is a teacher in some way.

FILING STUDENT WORK

Students in guitar class should produce a number of written work samples, including worksheets, dictation exercises, essays, graphic organizers (designs), and the like. The teacher must be able to retrieve this work in order to share it with parents and administrators. Furthermore, the materials will be included in the student's portfolio/practice kit. I recommend placing hanging file boxes on a table near the exit of the room. Every student will have a file with his or her name on it. As students complete written work, they will show it to you and then place it in the file. They will also store song sheets and other written materials in their files. At the end of the semester, students can retrieve the work for their portfolios.

PROFICIENCY SLIPS

When it is time to assess a student's grade, you need to have a tangible record of the student's performance. Consider using a proficiency slip—a piece of paper passed out to students on which they fill out their name and the list of performance skills under examination. As each student performs, circle the number that reflects the student's work. All students who are working to improve should be encouraged and inspired, and for this reason I frequently use grading that is nonpunitive. In this case the feedback, on a scale of four to one, is (E) Expert, (P) Proficient, (MA) Moving Ahead, and (NY) Not Yet. For the sake of school grade systems, the four levels may align with the letter grades A, B, C, and D. Your personal philosophy will guide you in choosing the grading symbols that work best for your situation. I thank my colleague Julie Blakeslee for this excellent idea.

The feedback categories on the proficiency slip may include right- and left-hand form, rhythm, and any other parameters you wish to include. Another variation is to grade based on the *quantity* of the piece performed. For example, playing all of the piece by memory would be an A, 75 percent of the piece a B, 50 percent of the piece a C, and an excerpt a D. I carefully save the slips so that when I'm entering grades I have proof each student's achievement. I have provided you with two types of proficiency slips: individual proficiency and extra-credit proficiency (figures 2.3, and 2.4). Feel free to design your own.

The following assessment techniques can be used as your situation merits. I have divided them into two categories, performance assessment techniques and written assessment techniques.

PERFORMANCE ASSESSMENT TECHNIQUES

The Daily Five-Second Observation

By monitoring students' progress daily, you not only improve your lesson planning but also remind students that they will be carefully observed as they learn each new skill introduced in class. This is a very powerful strategy that can be used at the beginning of class or during a practice pause.

Here's an example of how to employ the five-second observation at the beginning of class: Suggest that the students warm up by looping the natural notes from G-0/3 to G-3/1. Circulate from student to student and provide them with approximately five seconds to demonstrate their skill. If a student is not

STUDENT PROFICIENCY FEEDBACK SLIP

Name: _____
Date:_____ Period: _____

Skill/Song Title: _____
Left Hand Form: 4   3   2   1
Right Hand Form: 4   3   2   1
Flow: 4   3   2   1
Evidence of Extra
Practice: Yes
Comment:_____

Name: _____
Date:_____ Period: _____

Skill/Song Title: _____
Left Hand Form: 4   3   2   1
Right Hand Form: 4   3   2   1
Flow: 4   3   2   1
Evidence of Extra
Practice: Yes
Comment:_____

Name: _____
Date:_____ Period: _____

Skill/Song Title: _____
Left Hand Form: 4   3   2   1
Right Hand Form: 4   3   2   1
Flow: 4   3   2   1
Evidence of Extra
Practice: Yes
Comment:_____

Name: _____
Date:_____ Period: _____

Skill/Song Title: _____
Left Hand Form: 4   3   2   1
Right Hand Form: 4   3   2   1
Flow: 4   3   2   1
Evidence of Extra
Practice: Yes
Comment:_____

Name: _____
Date:_____ Period: _____

Skill/Song Title: _____
Left Hand Form: 4   3   2   1
Right Hand Form: 4   3   2   1
Flow: 4   3   2   1
Evidence of Extra
Practice: Yes
Comment:_____

Name: _____
Date:_____ Period: _____

Skill/Song Title: _____
Left Hand Form: 4   3   2   1
Right Hand Form: 4   3   2   1
Flow: 4   3   2   1
Evidence of Extra
Practice: Yes
Comment:_____

Figure 2.3: This sheet may be photocopied for class or other groups within purchaser's institution only. This provision does not confer any other rights to the purchaser or his or her institution.

EXTRA CREDIT RECORD & FEEDBACK SLIP

Name: _____

Date:_____Period: _____

Skill/Song Name: _____
| | | | | |
Flow: 4   3   2   1
Left Hand Form: 4   3   2   1
Right Hand Form: 4   3   2   1
Evidence of Extra
Creativity: Yes
Form: Full Song   Excerpt
Comment:_____

Name: _____

Date:_____Period: _____

Skill/Song Name: _____
Flow: 4   3   2   1
Left Hand Form: 4   3   2   1
Right Hand Form: 4   3   2   1
Evidence of Extra
Creativity: Yes
Form: Full Song   Excerpt
Comment:_____

Name: _____

Date:_____Period: _____

Skill/Song Name: _____
Flow: 4   3   2   1
Left Hand Form: 4   3   2   1
Right Hand Form: 4   3   2   1
Evidence of Extra
Creativity: Yes
Form: Full Song   Excerpt
Comment:_____

Name: _____

Date:_____Period: _____

Skill/Song Name: _____
Flow: 4   3   2   1
Left Hand Form: 4   3   2   1
Right Hand Form: 4   3   2   1
Evidence of Extra
Creativity: Yes
Form: Full Song   Excerpt
Comment:_____

Name: _____

Date:_____Period: _____

Skill/Song Name: _____
Flow: 4   3   2   1
Left Hand Form: 4   3   2   1
Right Hand Form: 4   3   2   1
Evidence of Extra
Creativity: Yes
Form: Full Song   Excerpt
Comment:_____

Name: _____

Date:_____Period: _____

Skill/Song Name: _____
Flow: 4   3   2   1
Left Hand Form: 4   3   2   1
Right Hand Form: 4   3   2   1
Evidence of Extra
Creativity: Yes
Form: Full Song   Excerpt
Comment:_____

Figure 2.4: This sheet may be photocopied for class or other groups within purchaser's institution only. This provision does not confer any other rights to the purchaser or his or her institution.

able to play, make a note of it and keep moving. Ask them to confer with a peer and make a point of talking with them at the end of class.

Another way to use the five-second observation is in the middle of class: Announce that the next song you play requires a D7. Place the D7 on the overhead, and circulate, observing everyone finger the D7. I particularly like asking the students to preread a melody from the method book. Circulate with your method in hand and point to *one note or one measure* and have the students play it. This is a quick flashcard test.

Spot Quizzes

A spot quiz puts students "on the spot." It also assists in monitoring student understanding. The objective of the spot quiz is for each student to demonstrate an understanding of class instruction.

Administer a spot quiz by announcing something like the following: "Let's check and see if everyone knows the B7 chord." Have everyone finger the chord silently. Next, point to each student, saying their name out loud, and observe their B7. If a student needs assistance, assign him or her to a mentor nearby. Using spot quizzes regularly keeps students on their toes. Intrinsic motivation is the ideal for all students; however, some students respond better to extrinsic motivation. Spot quizzes are an example of mild extrinsic motivation.

Informal One-on-One

The objective of the informal one-on-one is for the instructor to assess each student's progress daily by observing the student's practice. There is no substitute for immediate, one-on-one assessment *and* feedback. The informal one-on-one assessment occurs daily, during practice pauses.

Practice the informal one-on-one in the following way: After a skill has been introduced, announce a practice pause for the students to fully absorb the skill. Circulate through the room to observe their practice. For example, say, "Lets take a practice pause to work on the first four measures of 'Amazing Grace.'" You can save time by instructing students to continue practicing as you move by them. This way they can continue practicing and you can initiate conversation where necessary. You can also address more than one student at a time. The goal is for them to demonstrate and for you to observe, assess their understanding, and provide feedback. One method of ensuring that you don't miss anybody is to use index cards or a student-assessment checklist mounted on a clipboard (figure 2.5).

The Formal One-on-One

The objective of the formal one-on-one is for the instructor to provide specific feedback and suggestions while giving the student an opportunity to ask questions.

Proceed with the formal one-on-one in the following way: Have each student perform the proficiency skill, observed by the instructor, who provides guidance when necessary. It is extremely important that the student leave the session knowing *how to practice* and improve. During the individual assessments, the rest of the class can be working on combos or ensembles or can be practicing individually. The disadvantage of formal one-on-ones is that they take lots of time. One way to expedite the process is to meet with students in pairs or small groups. Encourage students to meet with you during lunch or after school for one-on-one work. (See figures 2.6 and 2.7.)

Small-Group Consultations

The objective of small-group consultations is for students to observe and interact with peers while the instructor provides assessment and suggestions. Meeting in small groups is a good way to ensure contact with every student within a reasonable period of time. The advantage of this method is that the instructor does not have to repeat a common explanation for every student.

Proceed with small-group consultations in the following way: Sit with a small group of students. Have each student play an excerpt while the others observe. When a student is especially successful, ask the student to share learning insights and methods.

Small-Group Unison Performances

This is a technique that I learned from my colleague Eileen Iams, who teaches middle school orchestra. Its objective is to help students feel the security of playing in a group, rather than as a soloist. The entire class gets to hear the performance and the feedback.

To use a small-group unison-performance evaluation, have a group of approximately five students play an excerpt of a piece while you record their score. You may also give them proficiency slips to record their own scores, which they then turn in to you as they leave the classroom.

Individual Performances of Excerpts

The objective of this assessment is to allow the students to hear the proficiency skill repeatedly and

INFORMAL OBSERVATION ASSESSMENT CHECKLIST

Student/Date Proficiency #	1	2	3	4	5	6	7	8	9

Class Period _____   Class Level _____

Figure 2.5: This sheet may be photocopied for class or other groups within purchaser's institution only. This provision does not confer any other rights to the purchaser or his or her institution.

PROFICIENCY SCORING WORKSHEET

Guitar for Instructor or Peer Assessment

Name:
Date:
Class:
Piece Performed:
Scoring: Total points divided by 700 = Score   Final Score:_____

1. Motion and Positioning

| 0 | 10 | 20 | 30 | 40 | 50 | 60 | 70 | 80 | 90 | 100 |

Comments:
_____

2. Tuning

| 0 | 10 | 20 | 30 | 40 | 50 | 60 | 70 | 80 | 90 | 100 |

Comments:
_____

3. Right-Hand

| 0 | 10 | 20 | 30 | 40 | 50 | 60 | 70 | 80 | 90 | 100 |

Comments:
_____

4. Left-Hand

| 0 | 10 | 20 | 30 | 40 | 50 | 60 | 70 | 80 | 90 | 100 |

Comments:
_____

5. Musicality, expressiveness, tone, and vibrato

| 0 | 10 | 20 | 30 | 40 | 50 | 60 | 70 | 80 | 90 | 100 |

Comments:
_____

7. Improvement

| 0 | 10 | 20 | 30 | 40 | 50 | 60 | 70 | 80 | 90 | 100 |

Comments:

Figure 2.6: This sheet may be photocopied for class or other groups within purchaser's institution only. This provision does not confer any other rights to the purchaser or his or her institution.

PLAYING TEST

Name: _____

Date: _____

Song or Technique: _____

Skill	Possible Points	Points Earned
Playing Position	5	_____
Left Hand Form/Motion	10	_____
Right Hand Form/Motion	10	_____
Correct Notes/Fingerings	20	_____
Rhythm and Tempo	20	_____
Phrasing, Style, and Dynamics	10	_____
Tone Quality	15	_____
Intonation	10	_____

Comments:

Total: _____   Grade: _____

Figure 2.7: This sheet may be photocopied for class or other groups within purchaser's institution only. This provision does not confer any other rights to the purchaser or his or her institution.

to perform segments appropriate to individual skill levels. This technique provides several advantages to teacher and student alike. For the student, the advantages include hearing and observing the proficiency skill performed and critiqued many times. For the teacher, it provides a closely managed classroom environment. The disadvantage of this technique is that some students may be frightened at the thought of playing in front of their peers. For this reason, I suggest introducing this technique later in the semester. Consider providing nervous or shy students the option of playing for you in private. It is also helpful for the students to rehearse the music informally for a peer or the instructor the day before the assessment.

Procede with the individual performance of excerpts by having the students assume the muted rest position. Then call students by name to perform an excerpt of the proficiency piece. Using an excerpt allows students of varying skill levels to show what they know. For example, a remedial student may play only a few measures, whereas an advanced student mentor may demonstrate an entire piece. Keeping the excerpts short avoids boredom. Furthermore, it doesn't take very long to assess the student's skill level.

Combo Performances

This assessment focuses on a student's ability to rehearse and perform with a group. This process can be highly enjoyable and engaging when carefully organized. Combos are discussed in more detail in chapter 26.

To assess your students using combo performances, have small groups perform written ensemble music or sing-and-strum pieces in front of the class. Success is based on technical accuracy and creativity. Successful combos can be invited to perform outside of class for your guitar concert evening. A less formal option is to take the class "on tour" to perform for another classroom or the office staff.

Extra-Credit Performances

These performances allow students to demonstrate their ability to generate and perform their own musical projects. Students should be encouraged to work independently, so be sure to give credit. Creativity and personal artistic expression are an important part of the guitar experience. Independent performers educate and inspire others. Encouraging students to apply skills to music that is personally relevant to them is one of the keys to tapping intrinsic motivation.

Assess extra-credit performances by having students perform their own music for you or for the entire class. Students may be asked to teach the music to peers or to the instructor. A Friday "riff exchange" is an enjoyable way to let students demonstrate popular music. Give students time to think about what they play for fun. Circulate through the class and find students who are willing to share. After a reasonable practice period, invite students to share their music with the class. If space permits, sit in a circle.

WRITTEN-ASSESSMENT TECHNIQUES

Written assessments can provide students with important writing and thinking practice and offer parents and administrators evidence of student achievement. Use written worksheets, exercises, and assessments to lead into and reinforce musical material that you are working on. Written assessments and worksheets can be organized into individual student hanging folders placed near the exit. Teach students to place their work into the folders as they exit the class. Stand near the door and inspect the work before it is filed. Depending on the age of the students and school policies, those who finish first may be dismissed. The files provide you, the parents, the administration, and the students a way to view student progress at a glance.

Timing Written Exercises

Some written exercises can be made more effective when timed. For example, if students are writing the fingerings for a melody of sixteen measures and you determine that it should take only ten seconds per measure to complete the task, then allow only 160 seconds for the assessment. If a student completes fourteen measures, the grade can be recorded as 14/16, which means that fourteen of sixteen measures were completed in the allotted time. If you use the same process repeatedly, the students can work to improve their scores each time. This is sometimes referred to as *formative* assessment, which means charting progress over time. Students enjoy the intensity and the brevity of this method. At your discretion, you can add extra minutes after the score has been recorded for students to continue working. Proficient students who finish should have

extra material to work on and may end up with a score such as 20/16.

General Music Worksheets

Instructors may use materials from general music classes to reinforce learning. Learning guitar consists not only of learning the instrument but also of learning the fundamentals of music that are universal to all instruments.

Assess guitar students' progress using their general knowledge of music. Music-theory and music-reading worksheets drill students on their understanding of the staff, rhythms, musical terms, and other music-theory concepts.

Melodic Dictation

This assessment technique allows students to demonstrate their ability to listen to and notate music. For more details, see chapter 14 on music reading.

Proceed in the following way: As always with notation exercises, have students begin by creating their own notation reference chart of the seventeen natural notes in open position. The chart consists of the note heads, their names, strings number, and fingering numbers. Over time, students will be able to create the chart in less than a minute. Play short examples that are derived from proficiency skill material. Provide the first note, and instruct the students to write out the rest of the example. If necessary, prompt the students by asking whether the pitches move up or down or by step or skip. Provide the answers immediately on the overhead projector. After working through the examples, have the class play them.

Short, frequent melodic dictation maintains students' interest and improves their skill. To save paper, cut your staff paper in half or thirds. Be sure the staff is large enough to allow comfortable writing. I have provided you with a staff template for reproduction (figure 2.8). Melodic dictation is effective, enjoyable, *quiet*, and highly recommended. Have students grade their work as proficient, approaching proficiency or needs help. Near the end of class, have the students show you their papers and then place them in their individual files, which, of course, are placed in a box near the door.

Writing Frets and String Numbers for Notated Music

This exercise assesses each student's preparedness for music performance by identifying note names and locations.

Figure 2.8: This sheet may be photocopied for class or other groups within purchaser's institution only. This provision does not confer any other rights to the purchaser or his or her institution.

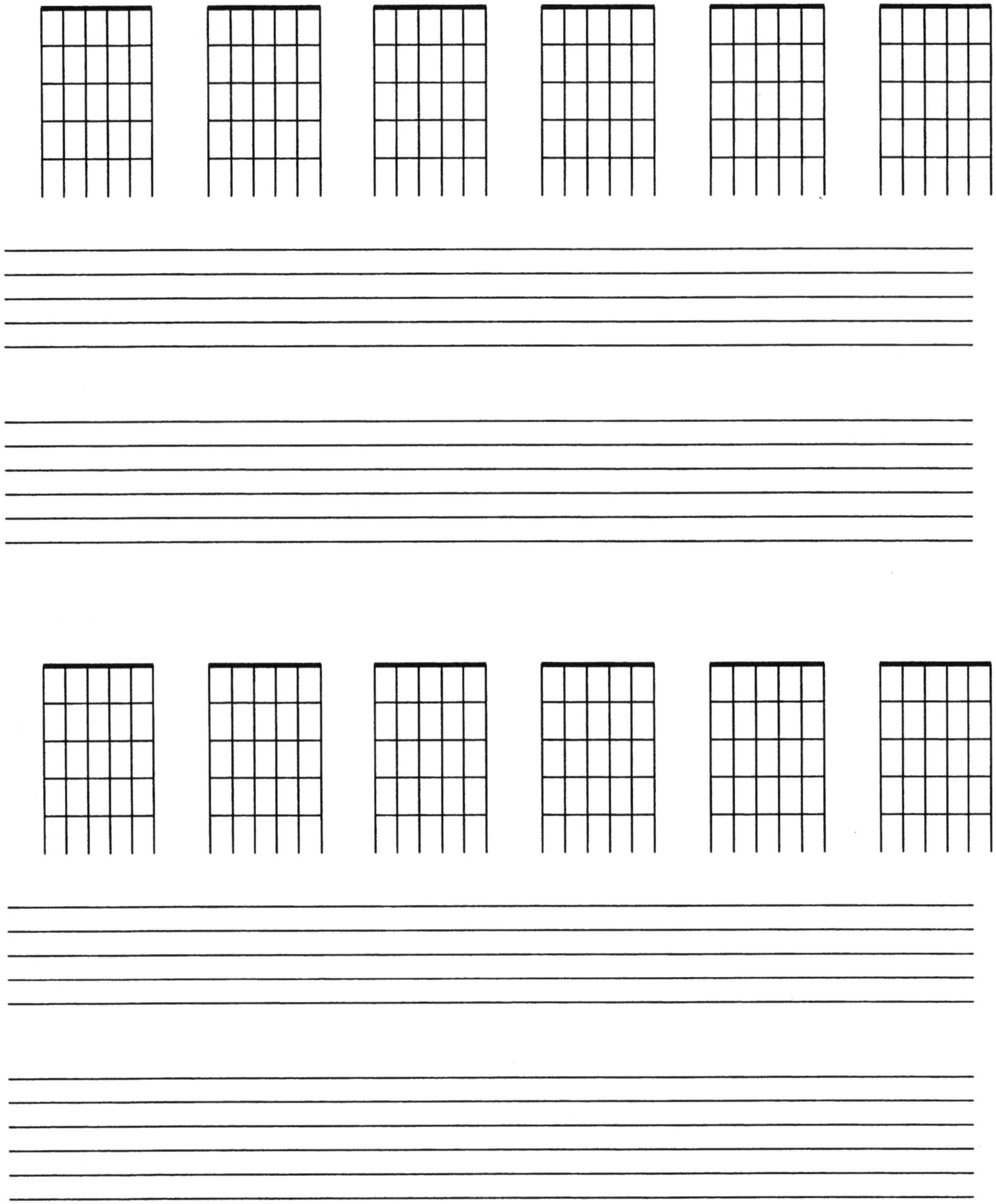

Figure 2.9: This sheet may be photocopied for class or other groups within purchaser's institution only. This provision does not confer any other rights to the purchaser or his or her institution.

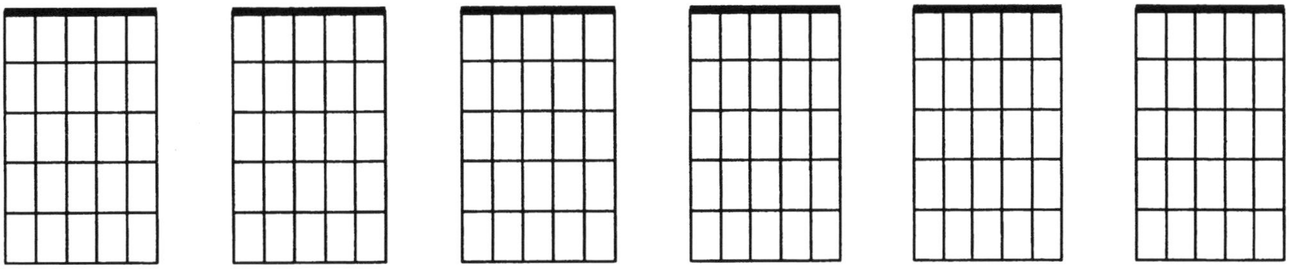

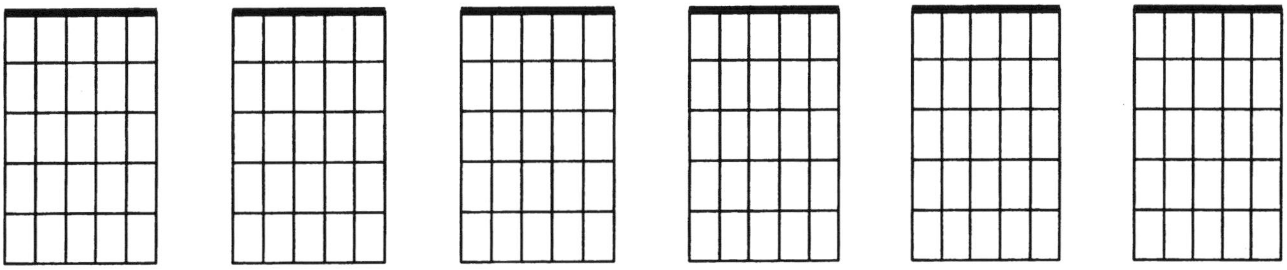

Figure 2.10: This sheet may be photocopied for class or other groups within purchaser's institution only. This provision does not confer any other rights to the purchaser or his or her institution.

Notation Into Tablature Conversion

Figure 2.11: This sheet may be photocopied for class or other groups within purchaser's institution only. This provision does not confer any other rights to the purchaser or his or her institution.

Proceed with the assessment by having each student create a notation/fingering reference chart. Pass out copies of the notated music that the class is working on. Have students indicate the fret and string numbers and the note name for each note. This may be done using *classical* nomenclature or by using *fraction notation*. For example, the fraction for the first fret on the second string is 1/2 (fret/string). In classical nomenclature, the string is written in a circle above or below the note, and the finger is written to the left of the note head. Time the exercise based on the number of measures in the example. Have students show you their work and file it as they exit class.

This exercise is highly recommended and works especially well when preparing ensemble pieces.

Combining Grids, Staff, and Tablature

This exercise assesses each student's ability to convert guitar diagrams into notation or notation into a diagram. Use one of the papers that I have provided (such as the small grids and staff paper used in chapter 1). Following are a number of drills you can administer that allow you to assess a student's grasp of specific skills.

- Provide chord diagrams for students to identify.
- Provide a blank fingerboard diagram, and have the students fill in the chord or scale fingering.
- Provide a fingerboard diagram of a note, and have the students write it on the staff.
- Provide a note, chord, or scale on the staff, and have the students write it in the fingerboard diagram.
- Provide a chord diagram, and have students spell the chord on the staff. For example, the C chord is spelled C-E-G-C-E.
- Convert any note, chord, scale, or finger-picking pattern from any of the three modalities: tablature, staff, and grids.

I have provided blank paper templates for you to create the assessment relevant to your lesson (figures 2.9, 2.10, 2.11).

FIGURE 2.12

FINAL ASSESSMENT: GUITAR PRACTICE PORTFOLIO ASSIGNMENT SHEET

Objectives:

- Students will gain experience organizing and archiving materials for future use.
- Students will evaluate current musical culture and events to create a "time capsule" of the school year.
- Students will gain experience being the "curator" of a museum exhibit on the popular culture during the school year. Another way of looking at it is to create a musical year book.
- Students will create an heirloom quality keepsake of songs that they will play and continue to develop for a lifetime.
- Students will have materials organized and on a music stand for practice at home.

Format:

- A rugged, archival quality, three-ring view binder.
- Plastic sheet-protectors.

Organization:

- Cover design of original artwork, collage, etc.
- Name, date, and place.
- Artwork and graphics from class assignments.
- Photos, clippings from magazines or newspapers.
- Photo of self and friends.
- Table of contents.
- Section dividers.
- Sing & strum lyric sheets. Copies available from class songbook.
- Recording or videos of student performances.
- Assignments, worksheets, hand-outs, etc.

Grading is based on:

- Amount and quality of materials collected.
- Organization.
- Archival-quality (durability over extended time).
- Creativity, personality, communication, impact.
- Use of color, design.
- Development on a weekly basis. Ability to use the binder during the semester.

Graphic-Arts Exercise

With these exercises, students reinforce and communicate key concepts by designing a sample textbook page.

Proceed by having students imagine that they are applying for a job at a music publisher. As part of the application, they have been asked to create a sample page communicating a key concept. Pass out markers or colored pencils and paper for students to design a textbook page. They are to use illustrations, diagrams, and text to convey the key concept, such as musical symbols.

The Portfolio

This assessment tool has students create their own songbooks or practice kits for life-long enjoyment (figure 2.12). In order to enjoy guitar for a lifetime, students need access to technical exercises and a repertoire. Building a portfolio ensures that students will have music to play in the future.

Proceed in developing student portfolios by having the students save class handouts and collect songs and songbooks during the course of the semester, archiving them in a three-ring binder. Each student binder should include a table of contents, name, date, and cover sheet. Stress the idea of compiling the portfolio to enhance their enjoyment of guitar well into the future.

Teach the idea of archival storage and of creating a time capsule. Imagine being a museum curator fifty years in the future who creates an exhibit of the present school year. Include clippings of current popular culture and photos of the student and class.

The portfolio is a required and helpful indicator of the student's investment in the class. Facilitate the collection of materials by having extra song sheets and materials on display for students to take.

Reading and Writing: The Written-Response Essay

The written-response essay assesses each student's grasp of key concepts through read and written exercises. This is often referred to as a *constructed-response test* (CRT). I simply call it a *written-response essay*. Students who struggle with hands-on performance may excel in the area of reading and writing. Furthermore, the written essay makes a good *pretest*. An essay on an upcoming unit can create anticipation and provide a foundation for future lessons. For example, if you are learning new chords, as a preliminary to the unit you may ask students to read an essay on practicing and retaining chords. The essays and completed answers should be saved and included in each student's portfolio. I have provided you with a sample essay (figure 2.13)

FIGURE 2.13

SAMPLE WRITTEN RESPONSE ESSAY

"Overview of Guitar—Level One"

Questions:

Why do we use famous "hit" songs in guitar class?

What is our goal regarding life-long learning?

List the eight key terms in level one guitar.

Why is singing such an important part of guitar class?

What is the alternative to singing that the instructor developed as a teenager?

Explain how reading music can make learning go faster.

Define musical improvisation.

What is jamming?

What is a riff?

What psychological barriers do you need to overcome in order to succeed on an instrument?

How can you obtain individual instruction from the teacher?

What is meant by the phrase, "The grades are written in pencil."

To succeed on guitar, during class instruction you need to_____.

To really gain skills on the guitar, how much practice at home is best?

What are the six steps of the scientific method as applied to learning guitar?

"Overview of Guitar—Level One"

Essay:

In level one guitar we develop a positive attitude about personal growth and potential, with the goal of pursuing independent life-long learning. The skills that we learn can be applied to songs of many styles, from different historical periods. Since popular music changes from year to year, we use famous guitar "hit songs" that emphasize techniques. These techniques may be used to play popular *modern* songs that you are interested in. In each level of guitar there are only a few fundamental skills that, when mastered, have many benefits. Our emphasis is on mastering these skills, which are communicated by the following eight vocabulary terms. They are:

Chords:
>   Open position chord forms
>   Power chords
>   Barre chords

Scales:
>   The natural note scale
>   The pentatonic scale

Accompaniment:
>   Arpeggios
>   Strumming

Music Reading:
>   The staff

Since there are eighteen weeks in the semester, you will have time to develop skill in each of these areas, and to set the meaning of these terms into your long-term memory.

Many of the skills you learn in the first semester may be used to accompany singing. Your guitar instructor will share with you information on the voice and how to practice it. Singing is a very important way to reinforce your musical skills. It is an indispensable learning aid, whether you sing in front of people or not.

For most teenagers, singing alone can be an intimidating experience. For me it was. To compensate for not singing as a teen, I learned to play solo guitar. During the first year of guitar you too will learn how to play guitar solos.

Music reading will be an important part of guitar class for many reasons. I believe that the most important reason is that music reading provides you with a *visual* way to understand how music is *constructed*. Understanding how music is constructed improves your ability to *recognize*

what you hear. Improving your hearing makes learning faster.

An important part of guitar is the creative ability to improvise. To improvise means to invent music while it is happening. This is often referred to as *jamming* or *lead guitar*. You will learn about scales, and how to practice them. You will also learn short melodies called *riffs* that are used by lead guitar players. You are encouraged to write songs using improvisation as a starting point.

One of your first steps in learning a new subject of any kind is to overcome *fear and doubt* about your ability. If you follow the activities done in class you will succeed. For best results, you should sit near the front of the class. There you get the best view, and the instructor can give you the most personal feedback. Although much of what we do in guitar class is as a group, you are encouraged to seek out individual instruction. The instructor will be available to work with you individually at your request.

Grading in guitar is done a little differently than in other classes. Since we build on your strengths, there is more of an emphasis on your successes than your failures. The grades are written in pencil so to speak, which means that they can be changed when you are ready to change them. Grades are not given—they are earned. In other words, you are empowered to obtain the grade that you desire. Students learn at different rates, so you are encouraged to demonstrate your successes as you achieve them. Of course, they success will only come with concentration and focus in class, and even faster with practice at home. For the best results, I personally practice between one and two hours a day.

What is a good practice method? It is similar to the *scientific method.*

1. *Ask Questions*—How can I reach my goal?
2. Do Background Research—*Observe others* and how they succeed.
3. Construct a Hypothesis—Make an educated guess at several approaches to reaching your goal.
4. *Experiment*—Try the different approaches.
5. Draw a Conclusion—Carefully *observe* the results of your experimentation.
6. Develop a habit of success by repeating your practice method and teaching it to others.
7. Develop a good relationship with your instructor.
8. Have fun, play, ask questions, and help others.

Attribution Assessment

Students build self-esteem by stating their strengths and accomplishments and by planning their own progress.

Proceed with the attribution assessment by having your students affirm their musical ability by listing and describing their significant guitar accomplishments, completing the statement, "My greatest strength is. . . ." Part of the goal is to gain practice in technical writing. Students should describe the accomplishment in detailed, descriptive writing. They should create diagrams where helpful. Additionally, students provide written examples of how their accomplishment is related to specific songs. They conclude by reflecting on what comes next in their guitar study—for example, specifying what they would like to accomplish in the next two weeks.

Descriptive Technical Writing Summaries

These summaries help the students practice and improve their writing skills by describing guitar techniques in written form.

Proceed by modeling descriptive summary. Then, instruct students to describe a skill, how they practiced it, and the level of proficiency attained. Students should include diagrams and artwork where appropriate.

Skill Self-Assessment

Self-assessment helps students learn that grades are earned, not given. Students are in control of their grades, based on their participation in the learning process. Students assess their own progress based on a carefully constructed grading system. See sample self-assessment forms in figures 2.14, 2.15, and 2.16.

Class-Participation Assessment

Students assess their participation based on a carefully constructed grading system. This is also an excellent way to teach classroom rules and procedures. See the sample class-participation self-assessment form in figure 2.17.

Generative Assessment

Generative learning is also referred to as *engaged learning* because it involves the students in the selection and evaluation of music relevant to their own lives. Students are motivated to solve problems and reflect on their learning because the music has personal meaning to them. Engaged learning often involves small groups or teams of two or more students. The role of the teacher is less of an information giver and more of facilitator and guide. Often the teacher also is a colearner and coinvestigator with the students. I have included a generative performance assessment form in figure 2.18.

Assessment of Instructor

Students assess the instructor based on a carefully constructed survey and grading system. This provides you with feedback useful for planning lessons that meet the needs of all your students. See the sample survey in figure 2.19.

ASSESSMENT OPTIONS, AT A GLANCE

Performance

- spot quizzes (all class members)
- one-on-one (informal; circulate the classroom)
- one-on-one (formal; with performance test form)
- small-group/sectionals
- small-group unison performance
- individual performance of excerpts
- combo performances

Written (File for Portfolio)

- parent interview*
- skill self-assessment*
- skill self-reflection*
- portfolio of songs and materials*
- class-participation assessment*
- staff/grid conversion*
- staff/grid/tab conversion*
- writing/identifying chord grids*
- generative performance assessment*
- written-response essays (CRT)
- general music worksheets
- writing fret and string numbers for notated music
- melodic dictation
- chord-grid identification
- graphic-arts illustrations and text
- self-affirmation (attribution assessment)
- generative performance assessment*
- technical-writing summaries and illustration

* indicates that forms are included

SELF ASSESSMENT AND REFLECTION FORM

Name:_____ Period:_____ Date:_____

Rubric:

4 – Proficient
3 – Approaching Proficiency
2 – Lacking Proficiency
1 – Incomplete

Instructions: Give yourself a grade between 1 and 4 for each of the categories below. Use the numbers to calculate a score.

Song or Skill:	Right Hand	Left Hand	Memorization	Effort	Total
Totals:					

Scoring – Total Points/Total Possible x 4 = Score (1 Skill = 16 Points; 2 Skills = 32 Points)

Score_____

Essay Instructions: Use the following thought questions to write an essay reflecting on your learning experience. Write on the reverse side of this form. These questions will help you get started.

1. Write a letter to a friend describing what you're learning. Use diagrams, notation, and pictures if applicable. Dear Friend: . . .
2. Describe how, where, and when you practice.
3. What are the benefits of learning the proficiency skills?
4. What are your guitar goals for the next two weeks? Six months?
5. What new songs, photos, newspaper clippings, or artwork have you added to your guitar portfolio?
6. What are you playing for your own enjoyment?
7. Think hard, and generate a musical question. What would you like to know more about?
8. What was your favorite in-class activity during the last two weeks?
9. What is your philosophy of life, and how does music play a part?
10. What music have you listened to recently?
12. What is your warm up routine? If you don't have a routine, invent one now.

Figure 2.14: This sheet may be photocopied for class or other groups within purchaser's institution only. This provision does not confer any other rights to the purchaser or his or her institution.

SKILL SELF-ASSESSMENT

Scoring: 4=Highest; 1=Lowest

Proficiency Skill:_____

Points	1	2	3	4
1. I practice approximately 30 minutes per day at home.				
2. I can play the skill from start to finish without hesitation.				
3. At home, I practice scales for at least five minutes per day.				
4. At home, I practice reading music for at least ten minutes per day.				
5. At home, I practice the proficiency skill for at least fifteen minutes per day.				
6. I have added new material to my portfolio this week.				
7. My portfolio is open and on a music stand at home.				
8. In the past week, I have learned new music from a friend.				
10. In the past week, I have been a mentor to someone.				
11. In the past week, I have made an effort to personally talk with the instructor.				
12. In the past two weeks I have learned a new song of my choice.				
13. I understand the relationship between singing and ear training.				
14. I practice singing on a regular basis.				
15. I have clear musical goals. (list on reverse)				
16. I have a guitar strap and use it.				
17. My instructor would say that my posture aids efficient movement.				
18. I have memorized one song in the last month.				
19. I am proficient at tuning the guitar.				
20. I have scanned the class song list and have a to-learn list.				
Sub Totals				
Grand Total:				
Scoring: Grand Total divided by 80 x 4 =				
Final Score:				

Name: _____   Date: _____   Class Period:_____

Figure 2.15: This sheet may be photocopied for class or other groups within purchaser's institution only. This provision does not confer any other rights to the purchaser or his or her institution.

GUITAR CLASS SELF ASSESSMENT (GUITAR 1)

Scoring: 1=Novice, 2=Nearing proficiency, 3=Proficient, 4=Advanced; Last column (T) is for teacher scoring which may agree or disagree with student	1	2	3	4	T
1. Tuning my guitar					
2. My playing position (body and left hand)					
3. My knowledge and use of basic Major chords (i.e., G, C, D, Easy F, E)					
4. My knowledge/use of basic Minor chords (i.e., Emin, Amin, Dmin)					
5. My knowledge and use of Dominant 7 chords (i.e., D7, G7, A7, B7)					
6. Use of barre chords (i.e., F)					
7. Use of power chords (i.e., E, G, D)					
8. My tone quality on chords (how good is my sound)					
9. Use of strumming patterns (other that straight quarter notes)					
10. Ability to identify and emphasize the root tone of a chord					
11. Ability to play natural note scale and scale with F# (by memory)					
12. Ability to read music (melodic patterns on strings 1, 2)					
13. Ability to read music (melodic patterns on strings 3, 4)					
14. Ability to read music (melodic patterns on strings 5, 6)					
15. My tone quality on individual pitch reading (how good is my sound)					
16. Using a steady rhythm					
17. My use of time while waiting for class to start					
18. My daily class participation					
19. My practice skills outside of class					
20. Playing my guitar outside of class for enjoyment					
Other strengths					
Other weaknesses					

Name: _____   Date: _____   Class Period: _____

Figure 2.16: This sheet may be photocopied for class or other groups within purchaser's institution only. This provision does not confer any other rights to the purchaser or his or her institution.

CLASS PARTICIPATION SELF ASSESSMENT

Scoring: 4=Maximum; 1=Minimum

Points	1	2	3	4
1. When I see litter or books on the floor, I pick it up.				
2. I stay inside the classroom until the bell rings or the instructor dismisses class.				
3. I do not play when the instructor is talking.				
4. I am working to my full potential.				
5. My participation in rehearsals and discussions enhances the class environment.				
6. When appropriate, I ask questions for clarification.				
7. I help keep the guitars neatly organized.				
8. I treat all school materials with care.				
9. I bring a pencil to class every day.				
10. I bring my guitar to class every day.				
11. I sit forward and concentrate during class.				
12. I sit where I have a clear view and can hear the lesson.				
13. I come to class on time.				
14. I warm up with scales and techniques while waiting for class to start.				
15. Students sitting near me would say that I am helpful and thoughtful.				
16. I regularly discuss guitar with my parents and play for them.				
17. I have visited the instructor's website and am familiar with his publishing and recording career.				
18. I put first things first and work on technique as well as songs.				
19. I mute my guitar and listen quietly while the instructor is talking.				
Subtotals				
Grand Total:				
Scoring: Grand Total divided by 80 x 4				
Final Score				

Name: _____   Date: _____   Class Period:_____

Figure 2.17: This sheet may be photocopied for class or other groups within purchaser's institution only. This provision does not confer any other rights to the purchaser or his or her institution.

GENERATIVE PERFORMANCE ASSESSMENT

Name:
Date:
Period:

	Possible Points	Points Earned
1. (Description) Name the piece, describe the accuracy of the performance, and grade the accuracy your of performance.	10	_____
2. (Reflection) Why did you choose this piece?	10	_____
3. (Diagnosis/analysis) What challenges or problems did you encounter?	10	_____
4. (Problem solving/analysis) How did you overcome or respond to the challenges? What was you practice methodology?	10	_____
5. (Analysis) What guitar skills were necessary to perform the piece?	10	_____
6. (Reflection) How does this piece represent progress for you?	10	_____
7. (Reflection) What might be your next step, or piece?	10	_____
8 (Reflection) What issues or challenges still remain?	10	_____
9. (Reflection) What are your goals for improving?	10	_____
10. (Reflection) What questions do you have for the instructor or to be self-answered?	10	_____

Total Points_____ Grade_____

Figure 2.18: This sheet may be photocopied for class or other groups within purchaser's institution only. This provision does not confer any other rights to the purchaser or his or her institution.

INSTRUCTOR FEEDBACK FORM

Your feedback is used to improve the class. The information here is anonymous, but feel free to take part in designing the class by communicating your ideas and suggestions.

Rubric: 4 = strongly agree; 3 = agree; 2 = neither agree nor disagree; 1 = disagree
Scoring: Calculate the total points, divide by 80 and multiply by 4.
Final Score_____

	4	3	2	1
1. The instructor told us how we would be graded.				
2. The instructor made the goals and requirements clear.				
3. My grade is fair and reflects my effort and progress.				
The instructor:				
4. Was well prepared for the class.				
5. Made good use of class time.				
6. Provided individual assistance when asked.				
7. Made students feel comfortable asking questions.				
8. Made good use of teaching aids such as films, guests, etc.				
9. Was well informed and knowledgeable				
10. Stressed creativity as well as facts.				
11. Recognized and nurtured my strengths.				
12. Was enthusiastic.				
13. Was available for consultation outside of class.				
14. Treated students with tolerance, patience and respect.				
15. Related this course to other subjects.				
16. Related this course to my personal interests.				
17. Maintained order in the classroom.				
18. Made learning enjoyable.				
19. Was inspiring.				
20. Was fair regarding discipline				
Total points:				

Figure 2.19: This sheet may be photocopied for class or other groups within purchaser's institution only. This provision does not confer any other rights to the purchaser or his or her institution.

3

Applying the National Standards for Music Education

What better way to get a feel for history than to hear it?

The National Standards for Music Education were developed by the Consortium of National Arts Education Associations (*What Every Young American Should Know and Be Able to Do in the Arts*, MENC, 1994). The standards provide guideposts for improving the quality of your teaching. Guitar class has the potential to meet the broad challenge of these standards because it can include all of the following: singing, playing, improvising, composing, arranging, notating, discussing, reading, listening, and exploring different cultures. The purpose of this chapter is to review the standards and take a look at how they relate to guitar class.

The standards follow:

- singing, alone and with others, a varied repertoire of music
- playing on an instrument, alone and with others, a varied repertoire of music
- improvising melodies, variations, and accompaniments
- composing and arranging music within specified guidelines
- reading and notating music
- listening to, analyzing, and describing music
- evaluating music and music performances
- understanding the relationships between music, the other arts, and disciplines outside the arts
- understanding music in relation to history and culture

Singing, Alone and with Others, a Varied Repertoire of Music

Guitar class provides students with daily opportunities for singing and playing guitar accompaniment. Guitar class provides you with the opportunity to model good singing and/or to share vocal concepts. (See chapter 23 for more information on singing.) Learning about the voice promotes healthy breathing. Popular songs used in guitar class provide an incentive to sing. Although most singing is done as a group, individuals will sing and play as they get comfortable with the classroom environment. As a quick-start, encourage students to hum, chant, or mouth the words in rhythm. Another idea is to have them sing the song and strum muted strings.

Playing on an Instrument, Alone and with Others, a Varied Repertoire of Music

Guitar combines the aspects of the violin's lyrical potential and the piano's harmonic potential. It is useful as a solo instrument and as an instrument to accompany singing.

Many guitar students get their start playing solo guitar by playing intros to rock classics such as Led Zeppelin's "Stairway to Heaven," others by learning finger-picking accompaniments. There are others still whose goal is to learn solo guitar from the start. Once students have established their skills and interest for solo playing, you may inspire them further by sharing recordings, videos, and guest performances of classical guitar artists. There are many good choices of music available for solo guitar. I have written several books expressly for this purpose—namely, *A Modern Method for Fingerstyle Guitar*, *The Guitar Christmas Encyclopedia*, and *Fingerstyle Classics Made Easy*.

Performing with others in guitar ensembles provides good motivation for students to improve their reading skills. My compilation of guitar ensembles specifically for classroom guitar, *Guitar Ensembles, Vols 1 and 2*, provides reading warm-ups, jam sessions, and arrangements of songs from a variety of genres. (For more information, visit www .guitarmusicman.com.)

In addition to playing formal solos and ensembles, students will form their own combos based on their interests. Playing an instrument supports students whose learning styles are in the *kinesthetic* or *psychomotor* domain. Playing in an ensemble supports the *affective* (relationships) domain.

Improvising Melodies, Variations, and Accompaniments

Many students come into guitar class with improvisation a top goal. By learning a five-note pentatonic scale on one string, such as "Flaming Ice Cube," students can begin to improvise during the very first day of instruction. The simplicity of guitar lends itself to exploration or learning through discovery (*heuristics*). One of my former students told our class, "I try a lot of things and remember what I like."

There are many famous guitar riffs that are constructed using the *blues scale*, such as Cream's "Sunshine of Your Love." Once students learn the riff, they can improvise by varying the rhythm and the order of notes. I like to refer to this as *scrambling the riff*. My book on the subject of improvisation, *Blues for the Young Beginner* (Mel Bay Publications), comes with its own backup tracks.

Composing and Arranging Music within Specified Guidelines

The attitude of discovery that is developed in guitar improvisation is a perfect lead into arranging and composing. Arranging is the process of constructing a song form that consists of multiple sections. Playing songs in class provides the instructor and students opportunities to discuss and create interesting extended arrangements.

A sample song arrangement might take the following form:

1. muted string percussion
2. introduction: instrumental melody
3. two verses with singing
4. instrumental embellished melody
5. two verses with singing
6. instrumental improvisation
7. one verse with singing
8. ending: repetition of the last eight measures and slowing down at the end

Here's a tip: find ways to arrange and extend the simple songs presented in your method book.

Jam-session rhythmic episodes provide an opportunity to explore musical-arranging concepts such as building from soft to loud and from simple to complex. A good jam session consists of a series of rhythmic episodes that build from one section to the next. Here is an example of one way to develop *rhythmic terracing* in a jam session:

1. half-time feel
2. standard song groove
3. double-time feel
4. jam-session ending riff (composed by students)
5. back to song

Accompaniment and Arranging

Another way to incorporate arranging into guitar class is to vary the guitar accompaniment styles. One verse might consist of strummed whole notes, which leads to a verse of finger picking, to a verse of strumming, to a verse of embellished strumming, and so forth.

Composing

Reading exercises can provide guitar students with opportunities to get started composing. Students may be asked to compose and perform a sequence of quarter notes. As they gain skill, the instructor may add a variety of rhythmic, melodic, and structural parameters.

Reading and Notating Music

Writing is so valuable in supporting music reading that music writing exercises should be included in your lesson regularly—perhaps once a week. Writing music supports students whose learning strengths are in the *cognitive domain*.

Here's a brief summary of an effective music-reading sequence (I have included more details in part 3 of the book, *Music Reading*):

1. *Hear.* Students listen to the instructor's examples and become familiar with the music.
2. *Play.* Students play short skill-building exercises, consisting of three to five notes, by echoing the instructor.
3. *Write.* Melodic dictation: After creating a *notation reference chart*, students write examples (note heads only) by listening to the instructor play short examples (see pp. 100, 103).
4. *Read.* Students read and play what they have written. Now they are ready to read music from your method book.

Listening to, Analyzing, and Describing Music

There are many opportunities for listening to and analyzing music in guitar class. By attaching your computer to your stereo system, you can have quick access to a great deal of quality music using iTunes. Writing and drawing assignments provide an excellent opportunity to play "background music." If students wish to bring in samples of their own popular music, or would like to talk about a concert that they have attended, you can use an interview format to practice analyzing and describing music. To assist you with this interview, I have provided interview questions for concerts and listening in the appendix.

Evaluating Music and Music Performances

You can help students evaluate music through carefully guided questions. Was the music in tune? Interesting? Innovative? Was there enough unity and variety? Was the performance precise? Did the music successfully fulfill its goal of entertaining, educating, or uplifting the intended audience? How would you describe the melody, harmony, rhythm, form, and texture? Challenge your students through well-crafted leading questions.

Understanding the Relationships between Music, the Other Arts, and Disciplines outside the Arts

Find out who in your class studies art, dance, athletics, theater, speech, and the like.

Use your student's hobbies and activities as a way to compare disciplines. Explore questions such as "what motivates you?" and "how do you practice?"

Here is what a member of the softball team shared with our class and the correlation we made to the study of guitar:

1. "First we start with stretches." Guitar class should include *finger stretches*.
2. "Next we run laps." In guitar class we *run scales* as part of the daily routine.
3. "Then we do drills on specific skills, such as throwing, catching, and batting." In guitar class we drill chord progressions, strumming and finger-picking patterns, improvisation, and reading skills.
4. "After these warm-ups we play a scrimmage game." Playing songs in class is the equivalent of a scrimmage.
5. "Eventually, we play a game in front of the public." In guitar class, this would be giving a public performance.
6. "We practice for two hours every day." Imagine what your music students could accomplish if they practiced for two hours each day.

One of the most enjoyable parts of teaching classroom guitar is that it is about more than just the instrument. Guitar class is a general music class that happens to use guitar. It is about music theory, music history, the creative process, composition, improvisation, philosophy, aesthetics, biomechanics, motion, geometry, mechanics, physics, physiology, graphic design, calligraphy, singing, spirituality, ear training, technical and creative writing, family, world cultures, American culture, community service, and more.

Understanding Music in Relation to History and Culture

Guitar instruction provides a fertile opportunity to broaden students' understanding of the relationship between music, history, and culture. The guitar's tradition and repertoire are closely linked to Hispanic and Afro-American culture. Guitar is often associated with the American West and cowboy culture. Electric guitar has played a very important role in American popular culture from the 1950s to the present. Playing and singing songs from different places and time periods provides opportunities for discussing historical periods and geographical locations. Frequently the words to a song provide explicit educational insights. Be sure to have a world map on your wall that you can refer students to. If you are interested in further study of world cultures, I recommend *World Music, a Global Journey* by Terri Miller and Andrew Shahriari. It contains two CDs of examples and is written in an enjoyable style.

Ask your students to interview their parents and grandparents regarding the songs that they grew up with and those that they currently listen to. This activity expands students' perspective as it relates to their family history and ethnic heritage. I have provided a parent interview in the appendix.

4

Your Strengths as an Educator

If you are new to teaching classroom guitar, or if guitar is not your primary instrument, you may be concerned about your limited guitar skills. I like the term *learning edge* more than *limitation*. Before we look at the specific teaching strategies for guitar, let's acknowledge what you already know and can bring to the class. Guitar class is a general music class that happens to use guitar, and what you already know is valuable.

Your existing strengths as a music educator include the following:

- how to teach music reading
- music theory
- music history and culture
- your own life experiences
- musicianship and practice strategies
- human growth and development
- discipline and classroom management
- your principal instrument
- your favorite songs and a repertoire of material
- aesthetics of music
- assessment techniques

Some hidden advantages of not being a guitar specialist include the following.

- Your students will be good music readers, and therefore they will be good independent learners.
- You can model humility, curiosity, determination, and humor as you colearn with the students.
- Your limitations will keep the class focused.
- You get to be challenged and invigorated by learning something new.
- By diversifying, you increase job security and improve your resume.

- You can put your students to work helping each other.

SHARE YOUR SPECIAL INTERESTS AND TALENTS WITH MORE STUDENTS THROUGH GUITAR CLASS

Think of guitar class as a good opportunity to share your interests and specializations with a larger group of students. For example, if you are choir director, teach your students how to sing. If you are a band or orchestra director, develop a guitar ensemble using your rehearsal and conducting skills. Your students can become strong note readers, which in turn promotes independent and accelerated learning. If you are a general music teacher, teach your guitar students about the elements of music, music history, world cultures, and repertoire. If you are a string player, share you knowledge of hand movement, phrasing, and musicality. Play along with the class on your violin. Which do you think is the better scenario in the classroom: a great guitarist who doesn't understand classroom teaching or someone with limited ability on the guitar who is a superb music educator?

THE THREE PILLARS OF INSTRUMENTAL EDUCATION

"We don't use music to play the violin; we use the violin to play music."

—Isaac Stern

To learn any instrument, one must develop three pillars of knowledge: art, music, and the instrument. If you are just starting to teach guitar, you already know about art and music. Only guitar remains.

Expect to enjoy teaching classroom guitar. The music teachers I know who are specialists in other areas all have a wealth of musical knowledge to offer their students. With this book as a resource, you will find the answers to guitar questions as they arise.

II

PRELIMINARIES

5

Preparations

The goal is to make music as soon as possible.

You've been asked to teach a guitar class, and you know almost nothing about the guitar. Now what? The following is a checklist of skills you should practice as soon as you can. Your method book will contain most of the information you need to get started. *Teaching Classroom Guitar* will provide you with ample teaching strategies as you need them.

You need to know the following in order to teach the first semester of guitar:

- the names and numbers of the open strings
- the basic parts of the instrument: nut, bridge, neck, fret, sound hole, and tuning knob
- how to tune
- how to hold the instrument
- fret, finger, and string numbers, so you can give instructions
- how to play a melody on one string (I recommend "Amazing Grace" on the G string)
- how to hold the pick
- how to strum with the right hand
- the three notes on the first string
- the easy C, F, and G chords
- learn one or two sing-and-strum songs using the C, F, and G chords (I recommend "The Lion Sleeps Tonight," "Jamaica Farewell," or The Beatles' "Obladi Oblada"; for younger students, songs with only two chords may be better, such as "Rock My Soul," "Marianne," or "He's Got the Whole World"; and for very young students, think of songs with only one chord, such as rounds—"Row, Row, Row Your Boat" or "Hey, Ho, Nobody Home."

QUICK-START SKILLS

The Open Strings: E, A, D, G, B, E

To help remember the names, use the acronym "Elephants and donkeys grow big ears." Better yet, to get a hands-on experience of the string names, put a new set of strings on your guitar. The open strings are reference pitches for everything to come and are the basis for learning scales and note reading.

The Parts of the Guitar

There should be a diagram of the guitar in your guitar method book. I have also provided a diagram of the essential parts of the guitar used for putting on strings in chapter 6, figures 6.1 and 6.2.

Tuning

I strongly recommend obtaining a clip-on electric tuner to simplify your tuning process. Practice your tuning skills until you can tune a guitar in fifteen seconds or less.

You can also tune by ear using "The Tuning Song." The intervals for tuning a guitar are:

fourth, fourth, fourth, third, fourth

or

E–A, A–D, D–G, G–B, B–E

"The Tuning Song" is based on "Amazing Grace." Sing and play as follows:

A-maze (E–A), A-maze (A–D), A-maz-ing (D–G–B), A-maze (B–E).

In short, here is "The Tuning Song":

E–A—, A–D—, D–G–B—, B–E—

Quick-Start Chord Forms

Exercise: Learn the Easy F, C, and G Chords

Objective: To play songs, and achieve success as soon as possible.

Process: The three chords of F, C, and G are nearly identical in shape and are easy to learn. Here are the fingerings:

F	xx321x
C	x32010
G	320000

Notice that the third and second fingers simply move across the neck *without changing their relative shape.*

Strumming Chords

To get you started strumming you should know:

- where the main bass note (root) is located and
- how many strings to strum.

The Root Rule

The root is the lowest fingered note of a chord, unless you're playing an E, A, or D chord. In this case the root is the corresponding open string E, A, or D. The strum always begins on the root of the chord.

Exercise: The Root-Strum pattern

Objectives: To be able to hear the root of the chord and the length of a measure, and to avoid bass strings that are not part of the chord.

Process: In four/four time the pattern is:
Root-strum-strum-strum
The roots for the G, C, and F chords are the sixth, fifth, and fourth strings. The strumming motion is similar to flicking water off of your right hand. Use the least amount of motion necessary, and stay loose. Most people use too much motion and are too stiff at first. Imagine Jell-O.

Exercise: Natural-Note Scale

Objective: Knowing the natural-note scale enables you read music, develop finger technique, and find the main bass notes of chords.

Process: The natural-note scale is played by placing your fingers on the following frets: Start from the sixth string: 013/023/023/02/013/013. Practice this every day until it flows freely and without hesitation.

- Recite the *alphabet letters* forward and backward as you ascend and descend the scale: E, F, G / A, B, C / D, E, F / G, A / B, C, D / E, F, G.

- Practice short segments of the scale in *loops* that get faster and faster. For example: E, F, G, F, E, F, G, F, E . . . F, G, A, G, F, G, A, G, F. . . . Begin with four repetitions per note, then three, then two, and then one.

Exercise: Melodies on One String

Objective: To make music as soon as possible.

Process: Using echo imitation, teach "Amazing Grace" on the G string. Using the G string places the song in the key of C, which is a good key for singing and strumming. Sing, and demonstrate the fret numbers for each phrase as follows:
0-5, 9-9, 7-5, 2-0, 0-5, 9-9, 7-12; 9-12, 9-5, 2-5, 2-0, 0-5, 9-9, 7-5.

- Have students figure out "Happy Birthday," "Jingle Bells," and other simple songs on one string on their own.
- Invent rock-style bass patterns on the low E string. For example, "Flaming Ice Cube" consists of the notes in the minor pentatonic scale and goes like this:
0, 0, 12, 12, 0, 0, 10, 10, 0, 0, 7, 7, 5, 5, 3, 3.
Have students rearrange the notes to make their own riffs and improvisations.

Exercise: Collect a Repertoire of Your Favorite Songs for Strumming and Singing

Objective: To use songs that you are familiar with to lead the class in singing and strumming.

Process: In the preface to this book I have provided you with an extensive list of songs to choose from. Highlight the songs you would enjoy using. Start a collection of sing-and-strum music of your favorite songs.

SUMMARY OF SKILLS NEEDED TO COMPLETE THE FIRST SEMESTER

To complete the first semester, you will need to acquire a few more skills. You can learn them with the students as you go:

- the natural-note scale
- the open-position chords in alphabetical order: A, Amin, A7, Bmin, B7, C, D, Dmin, D7, E, E min, E7, F, and G
- open and moveable power chords, which are the foundation of barre chords
- barre fingerings for the E, Emin, A, and Amin chords. A *barre fingering* is a chord played

with the index finger behind the nut. Barre chords enable students to play sharp and flat chords (see chapter 24).

- how to play barre chords by transposing the barre fingerings. If you struggle with these chords, don't worry; most level-one students will not achieve full proficiency with barre chords until the end of their second semester.
- one or more moveable pentatonic riffs, such as "Sunshine of Your Love" by Cream.
- the basic finger-picking patterns, which are the ascending and circular arpeggios

- you should have a method book you are comfortable with

CONCLUSION

Encourage the students to have a sense of curiosity, discovery, and adventure. Encourage students to learn from one another. Introduce students by name, and ask them to demonstrate what they have learned before they joined the class. Have experienced students teach you a riff. Everyone will enjoy learning together.

6

Quick Start: Your First Week

Allow your fingers to settle into the strings
like your head settles into a pillow.

To the extent possible this book will guide you toward ease of play. Your students should know that the techniques and concepts you are sharing have evolved with the concept of making the field of hand acrobatics easier. Think how restful it is to have your head sink into a soft pillow at the end of the day. Now imagine that the guitar strings are pillows, and let your fingers peacefully settle into them like your head sinks into a pillow. Naturally, this is a slight exaggeration, but it offers an important image.

The topics covered in this chapter follow:

- the learning environment
- tuning
- noise management
- playing positions
- the open strings
- left-hand mobility
- frets
- the first song and success
- playing, writing, and reading notes on the first string

THE LEARNING ENVIRONMENT

Guitar Class in the Context of the School Day

Providing guitar students with physical activity during the school day is a positive contrast to more sedentary classes. Physical education, relaxation, breathing, stretching, and emotional expression are all products of strumming, singing, swaying, and other aspects of playing. You should take advantage of physical motion as an important tool for classroom management.

Communicate an Absolute Commitment to Students

During week one and every week following, remind your students that your commitment to their success is *absolute*. Part of this commitment is building background knowledge about your students as human beings. Another part of this commitment is taking responsibility for being in charge. If you must correct or scold a student, make sure they understand that it is in the context of your absolute commitment to their individual success and the success of the class as a whole. Have guitar-related reading materials on hand for students who don't have a guitar on a given day.

Some Housekeeping Tasks

You will need to explain:

- grading and tests
- guitar storage and security
- labeling the guitars
- how to mute the guitar strings during instruction (Think, "stop, mute, and rest.")
- what they will accomplish by the end of the semester
- procedures, materials needed, and positive character qualities
- introduce yourself and tell personal stories

Communicating the Daily and Unit Goals of Your First Days of Teaching

The goals of the first days are to generate anticipation and excitement and to provide students with their first successful guitar experience. It is very important to let the students know what they will be doing during the daily lesson and where it is leading in regard to testing. List the assessment goals and dates in writing, in clear view, on the chalkboard or dry-erase board, and explicitly direct their attention to it. Distinguish between the proficiency assignment and the learning goal.

Here is an example of what you might say: "Today we will learn how to hold the guitar and have our first jam session on the famous riff 'Flaming Ice Cube.' The learning goal of 'Flaming Ice Cube' is to learn fret numbers and the pentatonic scale on the first string. By the end of next week, we will also play a melody using note reading and we will sing and strum your first song."

Bring the class to order by moving to your teaching station and asking students to shift gears by muting their strings and assuming the rest position. Model the position. Use your teaching station as a nonverbal cue that class is about to start.

ORGANIZE A TUNING BREAK

Instruct the students that you will need to take a few minutes to tune their guitars. To the extent possible, tune the guitars for students as they arrive. While you are tuning, instruct them to browse through the method book and find songs that are of special interest to them. If you have students who have electric tuners or know how to tune put them to work as *tuning monitors*, tuning the guitars of their friends. Over time, all students should tune their own guitars and begin warming up before class starts.

TEACHING POSITIONS

The Rest Position: Noise Management

Explain to the students that in order to have a successful class they should play only when instructed to do so. Rule 1 states that *students should play only when instructed to do so.* Failure to stop playing during group instruction wastes time. The guitar is an irresistible manipulative, so teaching, practicing, and modeling the rest position helps students avoid the temptation of playing while you talk.

Exercise: The Rest Position

Objective: To provide students with something to do with their hands while you are teaching.

Process: Students place their left hand completely over the strings of the guitars as if they were going to grip the neck. They place their right arm over the strings near the sound hole (photo 6.1).

When to use:

- At the beginning of class, when you direct them to stop playing, ask them to begin by reviewing the rest position.
- If students play when you are talking, ask the class to practice the rest position.
- At the end of songs or exercises, as a routine, I always ask students to use the rest position by saying, "Stop, and mute, and rest."

Exercise: Ending a Song

Objective: To help students make a transition from playing to listening.

Process: Announce that you will be practicing how to end songs. During the last measure of a song you may say, "And one, and two, and three, and stop, and mute, and rest." As you say rest, model the rest position, make eye contact, and be sure the students assume the rest position. Taking a deep breath contributes to calming down.

Exercise: The Desk Position

Objective: To give students a writing surface during times when there will be written work or extended listening.

Process: Have the students flip their guitars so the strings are face down on their lap.

Teaching Playing Positions

The goal of a playing position is ease of movement. Put another way, it is the reduction or elimination of

Photo 6.1: Rest position

Photo 6.2: Posture using guitar strap

Photo 6.3: Posture using a footsool

muscular interference. Since the hands are constantly moving, the concept of a static posture is misleading. Instead, we should encourage the study and exploration of movement—biomechanics and kinetics.

Demonstrate Sitting with the Guitar Strap and Footstool. Find ways to bring the guitar to your hand, rather than reaching for the guitar. The *guitar strap* and *footstool* are two devices that that are useful for holding the guitar steady when playing (photos 6.2 and 6.3). Footstools can be purchased at your local music store, or you can have your woodshop make them for you. If you construct footstools, make the measurements a little different for each side of a cube, and the student will be able to rotate the cube according to what feels best. My recommendation is about 6″ x 7″ x 8″. Some instructors require that students purchase their own footstools. Guitar straps have the advantage of allowing the guitarist to stand up and are easy to fold up and put in the case.

Home Position and Movement Exploration. Since everyone's hands are different, neutral home position will vary from person to person. Finding neutral home position is a matter of self-exploration. Encourage your students to explore a full range of positions in order to find the one that allows them to

- hold the guitar relatively still,
- reach the strings with minimum effort,
- be sufficiently free to move the arms and hands with ease, and
- be sufficiently relaxed to awaken an awareness of gravity.

Exercise: Model Neutral Sitting Position

Objective: To communicate body positioning that leads to efficient movement.

Process: Have one student come to the front of the class. Work with the student to achieve a comfortable position. Have other students adjust their guitars using mirror imitation.

Variation: Sit in clear view of the students and go through the following checklist:

1. *Guitar Neck Elevated.* The elevated guitar neck should be about a foot from your eyes; use a ruler to demonstrate. Use a strap or footstool, sit cross-legged, or place one foot on top of the other to get the neck elevated.
2. *The Left Hand.* The thumb of the left hand should be near the center of the neck. The

fingers should look like a spider. I also like the image of four skaters on a skating rink.

3. *The Right Hand.* Rest the right elbow on the edge of the guitar (the bout). Curl the fingers, and extend the thumb for strumming.

TEACH AND PRACTICE THE NAMES OF THE OPEN STRINGS

In order for students to understand your instructions, they must know the names of the strings and fingers. The names of the strings are easier to remember with the use of an acronym. I use, "Elephants and donkeys grow big ears." Practice the names of the strings using the following open-string drill. (Also refer to figures 6.1 and 6.2.) The entire neck can be understood by using the open strings as reference points. I cannot overstate the importance of knowing the names of open strings. One good way of learning string names is to encourage students to restring their guitars as soon as they can.

Exercise: Positioning the Thumb of the Right Hand

Objective: To establish a thumb position that creates a good tone and allows free movement of the fingers. The fingers and elbow are used as a gentle brace.
Process:

- Place the thumb on the sixth string. It should be nearly parallel to the string.
- Place the remaining fingers on the high E string to *brace the hand.*
- Check to see that *the elbow* is resting on the bout of the guitar.
- Rotate the right forearm until the fingers are tilted toward the bridge and the thumb is well in front of the fingers. A common error is for the fingers of the right hand to be pointing toward the neck. If this occurs, rotate the forearm counterclockwise until the fingers are pointing toward the bridge.

Exercise: Open-String Drill

Objective: Students memorize the names of the opens strings and play them with the thumb.
Process:

- Using their thumbs, have the students play the open strings in repeated quarter notes following your verbal cues:

E E E E, A A A A, D D D D, G G G G, B B B B, E E E E.
- Call out random strings, and have students find them.

Variation: Use string numbers 6 6 6 6, 5 5 5 5, 4 4 4 4, etc.
Memory Tip: The larger the string, the larger its number.

LEFT-HAND MOBILITY

Exercise: The Spider

Objective: The students will position their thumb so that the fingers will be positioned on their tips.
Process:

- Demonstrate and explain that the thumb and the fingers work together as a team. Holding their left hand in front of them, have the students repeatedly touch their thumb to their middle finger. A variation is to have the students hold a pencil between their thumb and middle finger. With the pencil held between the thumb and middle finger, have them lift various fingers to develop balance and independence.
- Make a finger spider with the left hand by having students set their fingertips on their leg, and allow the fingers to find their natural/neutral curve. When the spider has its legs, the fingers will be resting on their tips. Have students imitate a spider running on their leg.
- Place the spider on the neck of the guitar, and make the spider run around the neck freely without any predetermined targets. Run until there is a slight warm feeling in the arm. (If you prefer, have the four skaters skate on the ice.)

Exercise: Backing Onto the Neck

Objective: Students develop thumb positioning, finger relaxation, and mobility.
Process:

- Have students wrap their fingers around the neck as they do in the rest position. Notice that the wrist is arched and that the thumb lies behind the fingers, toward the lower half of the neck.
- From this position have students back onto the neck by slowly allowing all four fingers to move over the low E string.

Guitar Strings Worksheet

Name:_____   **Class Period:**_____   **Date:**_____

Instructions: Add strings to this guitar. Connect them to the proper tuning peg in the proper direction. Label the parts of the guitar, and the label strings by their pitch name and string number.

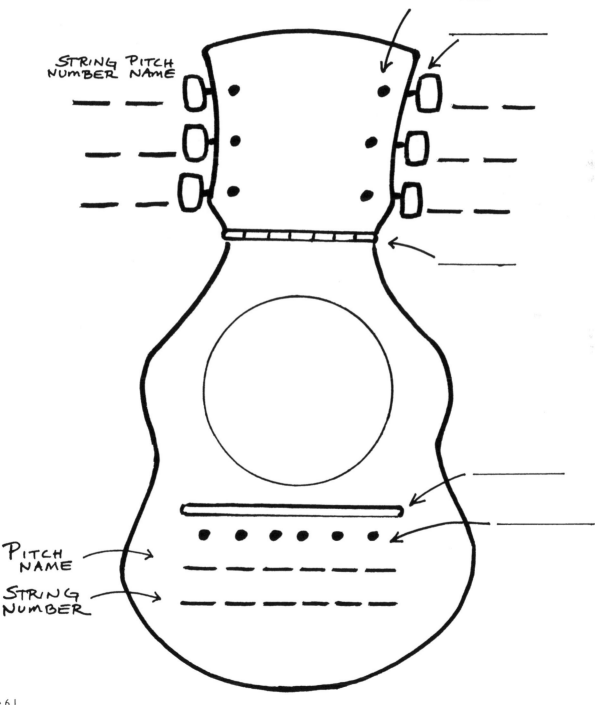

Figure 6.1

Guitar Strings Guide

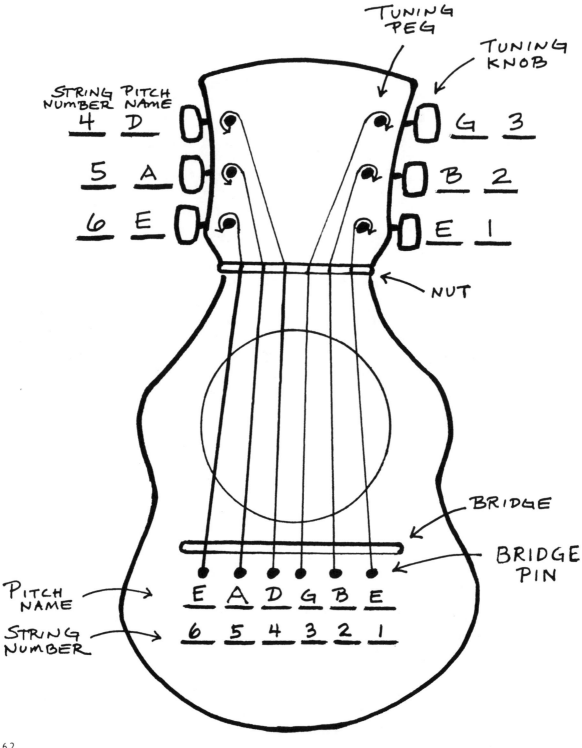

Figure 6.2

- Have them rest their fingers on the E string without pushing. The end result should look like four arches resting on the sixth string. I call this the *keyboard position.*
- Fingers should be parallel to the neck with space between the knuckles.

Note: This is only one of several finger postures. Keyboard position is particularly useful for reading single-note melodies.

Exercise: *Teaching the Finger Numbers of the Left Hand*

Objective: The teacher will be able to give verbal instructions by using finger numbers.

Process: Explain that numbers of the fingers of the left hand are:

first finger (1)	index
second finger (2)	middle
third finger (3)	ring
fourth finger (4)	pinky

- Hold your left hand out in front of you, and have students mirror your movements and echo what you say.
- Wiggle your first finger and say "One."
- Repeat with random fingers.
- Wiggle random fingers, and have students identify the finger with the correct number.

Exercise: *Active and Passive Fingers*

Objective: Students will develop finger independence, review finger numbers, and exercise the extensor muscles in the forearm and hand.

Process:

- Rest the four fingers of the left hand on the sixth string, fingers arched, palm parallel to the neck, thumb toward bottom side of neck.
- Have students lift one finger at a time while the others remain resting on the string. Use the finger numbers to give instructions. The moving finger is the *active finger*, and the resting fingers are the *passive fingers*.
- Have students try to keep the passive fingers resting on the string.
- Repeat on the first string.

Exercise: *Gauging the Pressure and Distance*

Objective: Students will identify and memorize the body sensations of pressure and distance necessary to

play a note (drop a finger). They will use this information to conserve energy and motion in their technique.

Process:

- Place all the fingers on the sixth string as in the previous exercise
- Tell the students to leave all their fingers at rest except their first finger. With the first finger, have them gently push the string toward the neck to gauge the distance and pressure. The other fingers must remain passive and at home position. Instead of pushing the finger, you may prefer the idea of allowing the finger to settle into the string.
- Pulse the finger repeatedly with attention to distance and the pressure used.
- Repeat this procedure with each finger in turn, and then randomly.
- Practice on other strings.

FRETS

Exercise: *Teach the Fret Numbers by Playing the Chromatic Scale*

Objective: Students will be able to locate frets when hearing verbal instructions.

Process:

- Demonstrate the *chromatic scale* for one *octave* on the low E string. Use only the index finger. Recite the fret numbers as you play: 0 0 0 0 1 1 1 1 2 2 2 2 3 3 3 3, etc.
- Remember to let the fingers settle into the strings like your head settles into a pillow.
- Point out the dots on the neck and their importance as reference points. Ask your students to determine which frets the dots are on and to memorize them.
- Explain that when you reach the twelfth fret the notes start over and that this is called an *octave.*
- Point out that at the fifth fret, the note matches the next string. This is called the *unison point.*
- Have the students play the chromatic scale up to the twelfth fret and back down, using only the first finger of the left hand, and the thumb of the right hand. Have them recite the fret numbers as they play.
- Check the passive fingers. Surprise them by saying "Freeze" at a random fret. When they freeze, have them check the passive fingers (2, 3, 4). They should be no more than a half inch from the strings, and nearly parallel to it.

- Repeat the chromatic scale using other fingers, and freeze again to check the passive fingers.
- Have the students locate random frets as they continue to play repeated notes. Continuing to repeat notes minimizes stopping and starting, which improves classroom management.

TEACH STUDENTS THEIR FIRST SONG: "FLAMING ICE CUBE"*

> Whenever possible, create anticipation for daily activities by using words, recordings, or demonstration.

The fastest way to get started playing songs is to teach riffs or melodies that can be played entirely on one string. There are many skills that can be emphasized and improved by playing riffs on one string. This is covered in detail in chapter 34.

Part 1 of "Flaming Ice Cube"

"Flaming Ice Cube" is composed with the Emin pentatonic scale played in constant quarter notes, on the low E string. Melodies played on one string accomplish several important objectives:

- fret numbers and location
- position shifting
- point of contact of left fingers with the frets
- quick success
- being on one string, and in constant quarter notes, makes it easy to teach using verbal instructions:
  0-0-12-12-0-0-10-10-0-0-7-7-5-5-3-3

Exercise: Teaching "Flaming Ice Cube"

Objectives: Students gain quick success, learn the fret numbers, attune their ear to the minor pentatonic scale, and gain experience improvising.

Process: Use echo imitation to teach phrases.

- You play and say
  0, 0, 12, 12
  and have the students echo you by playing and saying the same. Repeat this process until they know all of part 1.
- Here is the song in constant quarter notes:
  | 0,0,12,12,| 0,0,10,10,| 0,0,7,7, | 5,5,3,3 |
  repeat.
- Practice each four-note phrase in echo imitation.
- Play the entire riff as a class.
- Add a drum machine to help hold the beat and add excitement.

Variation:

- Play the riff on the first string.
- Have students improvise by rearranging or *scrambling* the order of the notes while you provide a steady low E bass note or other accompaniment pattern.
- One measure before the end, say "One, and two, and three, and stop, and mute, and rest."

Advanced Variation:

- Have advanced students play the song without looking at their hand.
- Increase the tempo each day for a week or two.

Part 2 of "Flaming Ice Cube"

Part 2 of "Flaming Ice Cube" is played on the fifth string with the low E repeating as a *drone*. It is also played in constant quarter notes.

Exercise: "Flaming Ice Cube," Part 2

Objective: Students are able to pluck the sixth and fifth strings at the same time.

Process:

- Using their thumb or a pick, have students practice plucking the sixth and fifth strings at the same time. The thumb or pick may bump the fourth string but not play it.
- Teach the fifth-string part using echo imitation as before. Here are the frets:
  7,7,7,7,7,7,7,7,7 | 5,5,5,5,5,5,5,5,5 | 3,3,3,3,3,3,3,3,3 | 5,5,5,5,5,5,5,5
- Remember to have them pluck both the sixth and fifth strings, using the low E as a drone.
- Play part 2 four times.
- Play the entire piece.
- Have a jam session by having one group play the low E as a drone, while the other improvises using the notes of "Flaming Ice Cube" on either the sixth or first string. Give a demonstration of what an improvisation might sound like.

Exercise: Creating a New Riff

Objective: Students gain experience creating original music.

Process:

- Working as individuals or in pairs, have students create their own riffs using the same notes as those in "Flaming Ice Cube."

- Suggest compositional ideas such as:
    o Keep the rhythm, but scramble the order of the notes.
    o Keep the order of the notes, but create a new rhythm.
    o Use repetition and varied repetition of musical ideas.
- Identify students who are having success, and have them demonstrate their new songs.

PLAYING, WRITING, AND READING NOTES ON THE FIRST STRING

Teach Music Reading on the High-E String

To set the tone for the semester, I like to have students read music every day and to begin as soon as possible. Begin with a brief discussion of why they should learn to read music. Be sure students know that they benefit from reading music. As music readers they are more independent learners, and they can learn more quickly.

Exercise: The Notes E, F, and G on the High E String

Objective: Students read music using only three notes, E, F, and G.

Process: Teach the notes E, F, and G on the first string using fret numbers to communicate finger positions.

- Demonstrate 0 0 0 0, 1 1 1 1, 3 3 3 3
- Explain that this is a small scale that can be played over and over like running laps on a track. Therefore it is called a *scale loop*.
- Have students play the repeated-note scale loop using only frets 0, 1, 3, 0, 1, 3, etc. Use four repetitions per note.
- Continue repeating, using only three repetitions per note, then two, then one.
- When they play the scale with one note at a time, have them accelerate until they can go no faster.
- Explain that speed is important. The finger motion should be light, automatic, and without wasted motion. A scale is like a road: the road must be smooth in order to be drivable.
- As soon as possible, students should practice these frets without looking at their fingers.

Exercise: The Note Names of E, F, and G on the First String

Objective: Students learn the note names for E, F, and G on the first string.

Process:

- Once the students can play the scale loop 0, 1, 3 smoothly, teach them the note names E, F, and G. Demonstrate E E E E, F F F F, G G G G. Explain that notes move in alphabetical order.
- Have the students play and say the note names as they play a scale loop using four repetitions per note. Use progressively less repetitions.
- Do four-note echo imitation. For example, play E F E F, and have the students echo the same. Do this using various combinations.
- Perform echo imitation again, but this time, sing *doo* on each note. Have the students echo you by playing and saying the appropriate note name E, F, G. For example, sing doo (E) doo (F) doo (G) doo (E), and have the students echo you by playing and saying the same.

Exercise: Intuitive Reading

Objective: Students use logic to learn to read music.
Process:

- Write four measures of music on the overhead projector using only E, F, and G.
- Perform random measures, and have students identify which measures you are playing.

Variation:

- Write one measure of music using only E, F, and G.
- Play two examples, one of which matches the example and one that does not. Students determine which performance example matches the written example.

Exercise: Writing Music

Objective: Students become familiar with the staff by writing simple examples using E, F, and G.
Process:

- Pass out staff paper. (Tip: Cut a piece of staff paper so each piece has three staves. This saves paper and allows you to do short written exercises more frequently.)
- Show students what E F G looks like on the staff.
- Have students practice drawing the note heads for E F G on an entire line of paper. For example: E F G, E F G, E F G, etc. Do not worry about rhythms yet.

- Have the students label the note heads with alphabet letters.
- Tell the students you will be playing some short phrases for them to notate.
- Provide students with the first note, E.
- Play a short phrase using only E, F, and G. The students may watch your hands if they wish.
- Have the students write the notes that you played.
- After you have played it twice, provide the answer, and have them check their work and make any necessary corrections.
- After writing a number of examples, have the class play them. This is important. (Tip: If there are any students who get lost, instruct them to simply play the open string. This tells you how well the class is doing.)
- Congratulate them on reading and writing music.

Read Music from your Method Book

Most method books will start note reading on the first string. If you have preceded the method book with the previous readiness exercises, students will find reading music easy, since they have already played the notes and written them. Be sure to take advantage of intuitive learning. For example, play two versions of the first measure and ask which version is correct, or play one of the measures in the first line, and ask them to identify which measure you are demonstrating.

If you have advanced students who already read music, have them play and write the E, F, and G on the second string at frets 5, 6, and 8.

Vocabulary

"Flaming Ice Cube" is an example of an *oxymoron*. Discuss the meaning of *oxymoron* using examples such as *Skydiving Fish* and *Iron Butterfly*, and have students invent some oxymoron song titles themselves.

Constructed-Response Tests

As you determine what is important for students to know, write your own short essays and use them as reading and writing assignments. Your essays should be followed with questions that require the students to read and write in complete sentences and use higher-level reasoning when possible. I have provided you a sample essay, "An Overview of Guitar, Level One," which can be found in chapter 2. In "Knowing Your Instructor," you might write, "I attended the University of _____, where my main area of specialization was vocal music." The students then answer these questions in writing: Where did your instructor attend college? What was his/her area of specialization? What are the benefits of attending a university in your home state? Similarly, an essay pertaining to rules and procedures might state that "Books should be stored on the music stands. Picking up books and materials from the floor is an example of maturity." The related questions would be, Where is the proper place to store books at the end of the period? Leaving books on the floor exhibits what personality trait?

Exercise: Write Two Short Essays: (1) Rules and Procedures and (2) About Your Instructor

Objectives: Communicate important information in writing to provide students with practice reading and writing answers.

Process: On separate days, have students read your essays and then answer the essay questions on a separate sheet of paper. Discuss the answers as a class. The students keep the essay for their *portfolio*. *They should show you* their work before filing it in the student files near the door.

7

Hand and Body Positions: Learning How to Learn

Guide students through a series of motion experiments so they learn how to discover hand and body positions for themselves.

When playing the guitar, the body and hands are in constant motion. The idea of a statuesque posture is misleading. Instead, emphasis should be placed on enhancing motion by reducing physical and mental interference. It is more important to teach the principals of motion than to memorize a set of statuesque posture rules.

The best playing positions are ones in which the skeletal and muscular systems organize themselves in a cooperative manner, which enables the student to attain results with the least amount of effort.

Body positions will vary depending on what music being played and the physical characteristics of the player. Students may use an informal posture for strumming a folk song but will need a formal classical-guitar posture to meet the technical demands of a more complex piece. In any case, the guitarist should change positions often enough to avoid repetitive motion injuries.

STUDENTS HAVE VARYING NEEDS

Some students sit naturally in a way that allows for relaxed, unrestricted movement of the forearms and hands. For others will need you to manually adjust their hands into a more efficient position. Be prepared to continue reminding them repeatedly until relaxed efficient movement is achieved. Some students may be awkward, rigid, or stiff. In this case, your job will be to help them relax, build their confidence, and make them laugh, smile, and have fun.

HELPFUL AIDES TO STABILITY AND ELEVATION OF THE GUITAR

The neck of the guitar needs to be elevated so that the left arm can move without unnecessary reaching or bending.

Footstool: Traditional Classical Position

Position the left leg on a footstool. Place the guitar on the left leg. This technique is the traditional classical stance and provides the advantages of stability and elevation of the neck. The disadvantages are that such a position may create a slight twist in the spine, and the footstool is an extra gadget to carry around or stumble on. If a footstool is not available, students can experiment using their guitar case to elevate the left foot.

Guitar Strap

I recommend that all my students use a strap because it is effective in elevating the neck and creating stability. I use a strap and a footstool, even when playing concert pieces. With a trip to the local craft store, students can make a strap and decorate it.

Chair

The bottom of the guitar may rest on the corner of a chair to elevate the neck and create stability.

Foot

One foot may rest on top of the other to elevate the leg upon which the guitar rests.

Use of a Ruler

To make a strong visual point, use a ruler to demonstrate the distance from your eyes to the fingers of your left hand. The distance for me is less than a foot.

Computer Keyboard

An old computer keyboard can be used to demonstrate finger position. Hold it for the student at the location and angle where the left hand would be placed on the guitar neck. Have the student wrap his left hand around the keyboard and play it as if he were playing the guitar. This demonstrates the similarities between keyboarding and left-hand fingering.

Exercise: Teaching by Using the Wrong Way

Objective: Students discover for themselves which positions make playing easier or more difficult. Positions that impede movement are the wrong way.
   Process:

- Have students try to finger a C chord in the following extreme positions, and then compare these positions to the generally accepted neutral or home position.
- Wrong way #1: Let the neck sag down to the left leg.
- Wrong way #2: Tilt the guitar so that the soundboard is almost facing the ceiling.
- Wrong way #3: Wrap the thumb of the left hand around the neck on the bass-string side.
- Conclude by fingering the C chord using the right position, and notice how much better it feels. Checklist: thumb behind the neck approximately opposite the middle finger; neck elevated sufficiently so the hand is approximately a foot from the eyes; the body of the guitar tilted slightly—only enough to see the fingerboard.

USING A CHECKLIST TO FIND NEUTRAL POSITION

Students can use the checklist as a starting point for their own exploration. Neutral position is the starting position that enables the guitarist to move in any direction based on the needs of the music.

Checklist

Feet

Feet should be separated enough to create balance and security. Place a footstool underneath the left foot to elevate the guitar. If the student has a strap, place both feet flat on the floor, and shift weight to the left and right until a balance point is found.

Spine

The back of a chair may be used to support the spine, or the student may prefer to sit forward on the edge of the chair. The spine must be free to move in cooperation with the shoulders, arms, and hands. The pelvis should be tilted slightly forward, which in turn will slightly arch the back. The arched back elevates and opens the rib cage for easier breathing.

Left Elbow

The left elbow must be free to move in cooperation with different hand requirements. A neutral starting position is one in which the elbow hangs close to the body and in a vertical relationship to the floor. The left arm should be loose enough so the student may sense gravity. I like the image of a hanging clothesline that might sway to the slightest breeze.

Right Elbow

The right elbow will rest near where the bout (side of the guitar) meets the soundboard. The forearm and elbow should be free to move in coordination with the right hand.

The Palm of the Left Hand

The palm of the left hand will either be parallel to the neck or at an oblique (diagonal) angle. The angle of the palm should be free to move in coordination with the requirements of the left hand.

Presenting the Fingers to the Neck

The angle of the left palm needs to vary from being parallel to the neck, for chords like C, to being at an oblique angle, for chords like B7. When the hand is parallel it is described as the *longitudinal presentation* of the fingers. When the hand is oblique it is described as the *transversal presentation* of the fingers.

Finger Dropping

The fingers of the left hand drop down, or settle, into the string when playing a note. As an experiment, hold the left hand in front of you in neutral or home position. With the right hand, lift one of the fingers of the left hand slightly, then release it, and watch it flick back to home position. This is finger dropping.

The Right Hand

The thumb of the right hand may serve as a brace, as a mute, or to stroke the string. In most cases it is nearly parallel to the string. The fingers should rest on the treble strings with the fingertips pointing toward the bridge. Experiment rotating the forearm until a triangle appears between the index finger and the thumb. The goal is freedom of movement, minimum friction, and a pure tone. As a variation, insert the pick (plectrum) between the thumb and index finger from this position. As an experiment, open and close the fingers of the right hand so the fingers close into the palm. Notice that the fingers do not collide with the thumb. There are many nuances of right-hand finger movement related to tone and expression. They are covered in more detail in chapter 21, which discusses finger picking, or in a good classical-guitar method book.

The Head

Position the neck of the guitar so that it is about a foot from the student's face, such that the head should be able to rotate in coordination with the movements of the elbows and shoulders.

The Body-Mind

An alert body position reflects an alert mind. Physical fitness enhances mental fitness. Let's make a comparison to athletics. Imagine the intensity of a professional wrestler or gymnast in their ready position, mentally and physically ready to grapple with the demands of their sport. Inspire students to sit in a ready position that reflects mental alertness and quickness.

Exercise: Finding Balance; Cantilever Motion

Objective: Students discover how pelvic motion creates a chain reaction that extends to the head and feet.
   Process:

- Have students practice rocking the pelvis forward and backward, and notice the corresponding motion of the spine, head, shoulders, and feet. When the pelvis rocks forward, the spine arches backward. This reciprocal chain reaction of the pelvis and spine is referred to as a *cantilever motion.*
- Practice rocking the pelvis to the right and left, and notice the corresponding cantilever motion of the spine, head, and shoulders.

Exercise: Full-Body Warm-Up

Objective: Students observe how the body parts move in a chain reaction.
   Process:

- Sit comfortably without the guitar. Extend the forearms and hand in front of you as if to pantomime playing the guitar. Elbows should hang at your side. We will start with the large muscles and progress to the small muscles. Pay attention to how one motion affects the others.
- Arch the spine gently and subtly, forward and backward. Notice the corresponding motion in the pelvis, head, and feet.
- Arch the spine gently and subtly to left and right. Notice the corresponding motion in the head, pelvis, and feet.
- Roll the head in a small circular motion. Notice the corresponding motion in the shoulders.
- Roll the shoulders in small circular motions. Notice the corresponding motion in the elbows.
- Roll the elbows. Notice the corresponding motion in the wrists.
- Roll the wrists. Notice the corresponding motion in the fingers.
- Move the fingers at random, as if to pantomime guitar playing.
- Pick up the guitar, and assume the neutral position. Notice the cooperative motion of the body parts as you begin to play.

Exercise: Swinging the Left Palm; "The Gate"

Objective: Students gain understanding of the various angles of the palm of the left hand.
   Process:

- Have the student place the palm of the left hand to the side of the neck in parallel position as if the student were going to play a C chord. The thumb will remain behind the neck.
- Have the student imagine that the base of the index finger is a hinge of a gate. Swing the palm of the hand from parallel position to oblique position and back. Opening and closing the gate in this manner teaches the range of motion necessary to support different chord forms.
   General Rule: Chords that have two or more fingers on the same fret use the oblique angle. Practice changing from a D chord to a C chord, and observe the difference between the oblique and parallel palm positions.

Exercise: The Master-Class Demonstration

Objective: One student receives a lesson on posture at the front of the class, while the rest of the class observes.

Process:

• Have a volunteer sit with you at the front of the class.
• Have him sit naturally, without the guitar.
• Have him place his left foot on the footstool.
• Have him place his right foot flat on the floor. The distance between the feet should be far enough to create stability.
• Once the feet are positioned, have the student relax his shoulders and move his forearms and pantomime guitar playing. Since he is not actually holding the guitar, this will feel and look almost effortless. The back and head will be straight and relaxed, the arms and elbows hanging close to the body.
• From this position you will place the guitar into the student's arms with the bout resting on his left leg.

• Adjust the strap and/or footstool so that the guitar stays in this position after you let it go.
• The guitar should be positioned so that the student's hands naturally fall onto the instrument with little or no extra reaching or effort.
• For younger students with shorter arms and fingers, place a capo on the third or fifth fret to eliminate reaching. Use a larger footstool to support their feet.
• Demonstrate the five points of contact. Using your baton as a pointer, direct the students' attention to the guitar's five points of contact with the body. They are the right leg, left leg, right elbow, left hand, and sternum.

FEMALE POSTURE

Females may benefit from the use of a footstool rather than a strap, because the footstool supports the guitar further away from their upper body.

8

The Right Hand: Using the Thumb and the Pick

> The down-up motion of the pick provides a clear image of the downbeat and upbeat.

Guitarists should be able to play with or without a pick. Teachers differ on whether to start with the pick or fingers. This is a personal preference that is based in part on the instructor's skill and background information. Take advantage of your personal strengths. My recommendation is to start with the thumb because it is simpler and it is a preliminary to playing solo guitar.

The advantages of playing with the thumb follow:

- Playing with the thumb is a natural preliminary to playing solo guitar.
- There is no extra gadget (pick) to distract the student from the guitar itself.
- If you require students to use the pick, some students will not have one because they have lost it.
- For younger children, the pick can be something that is a reward after mastering the thumb.

The advantages of using a pick follow:

- The down-up motion of the pick provides a clear image of the downbeat and upbeat.
- For strumming, the pick provides additional volume and a percussive quality.
- For improvisation, the pick allows for more speed.

THUMB POSITION

Use the fingers as a brace to obtain better control of the thumb. To do this, rest the index, middle, and ring fingers on the treble strings 3, 2, and 1. Rest the thumb on the sixth string so it is almost parallel to the string. The student should experiment and find a position where the thumb can move with minimum friction and achieve the best possible tone. The easiest way to pluck a melody on one string is with the thumb. Using the fingers requires more time and thought and should not be attempted until later. If a student naturally plays with the fingers, allow them to do so. Try playing "Twinkle, Twinkle, Little Star" by ear, using the thumb to pluck it on one string.

Exercise: Exploring Thumb Motion

Objective: Students discover the weight of the string and the motion of the thumb.

Process:

- Brace the fingers on strings 3, 2, and 1.
- Place the thumb on the sixth string. Lift the thumb off and on several times, without looking, to develop a sense of location.
- Press down on the string. Explore the tension of the string by wiggling it without plucking. Also explore the spring action of the string.
- After pressing the string, allow the string to slide off the thumb, creating the sound. This is referred to as *releasing the string* or the *stroke*.
- Return to home position. After releasing the string, allow the thumb to spring back to starting position. Learn to allow the muscles to spring back automatically to their neutral starting position.

Summary: Place the thumb, press the string, release the string, and spring back to home position. Recite the phrase, "Place, press, release, and spring back."

Variation: Place the thumb on the sixth string as a brace, and repeat this four-step process using each finger.

USING THE THUMB FOR STRUMMING

The thumb strums the strings in downward and upward directions. The down and up strums correspond to the downbeat and upbeat, which makes the guitar an excellent instrument for teaching rhythm. The down and upward motion may be referred to as *alternate strumming*.

Exercise: Forearm Rotation and Alternate Strumming

Objective: Students develop rotary forearm motion.
  Process:

* Have your student hold her right forearm in front of her with her hand hanging freely.
* Allow the fingers to curl naturally. Let the thumb and index finger touch as if they were holding a pick.
* Have the student wiggle her hand in a pendulum motion, alternating from left to right. Think Jell-O.
* Shake the hand as if flicking water off.
* Have her blow on her hand and allow it to sway with the breeze.
* Mute the guitar strings with the left hand, and practice simple down strokes on the muted strings. I call this *string percussion*.
* Keeping the same beat, add the up-strokes, and perform constant eighth notes.
* Try accenting the up-strokes.
* Guide the students through various quarter-note and eighth-note patterns using echo imitation.
* Reinforce the instructions with vocalizations such as "down, down, down-up, down" or "walk, walk, run-ning, walk" or "one, two, three-and four."

DOWNBEATS AND UPBEATS

This is a good time to explain that music consists of pulses know as *beats*. Explain that every beat consists of two parts, the downbeat and the upbeat.

Exercise: Downbeats and Upbeats

Objective: Students use vocalizations and physical motions to understand down- and upbeats.
  Process:

* Have students count aloud, "one and two and three and four and."

* Add foot tapping to the counting, and notice the down-up motion of the foot.
* Add a down-up conducting motion with the right hand.
* Have students imagine a string connected from their foot to their conducting hand. Every time the foot moves down the hand moves down, and when the foot moves up the hand moves up.
* Mute the strings with the left hand, and convert the conducting motion into strumming on the muted strings.
* Perform echo imitation and overlapping imitation using a variety of rhythms of your choice. Include vocalizations of your choice: down-up, one-and, walk-run, or boom-chick. (Overlapping imitation: Once students get started on one rhythm, have them maintain that rhythm while you overlap a contrasting rhythm. When you say *switch*, they switch to your new rhythm.)

SELECTIVE STRUMMING

Strumming the guitar rarely includes all six strings. Strumming begins with the root of the chord and continues across the strings. Students must be able to strum six, five, or four strings depending on the chord they are playing. Here are the roots for the chords in the key of C: G is root 6, C is root 5, and F is root 4.

Exercise: Selective Strumming

Objective: Students gain the ability to strum various numbers of strings.
  Process:

* Have the students mute the strings with their left hand.
* Play quarter notes on the first string using down strokes.
* Add the second string, third string, etc., until the class is strumming on all six strings.

Tip: It is sometimes easier to aim *between* the strings rather that for the target string. For example, if you want to start the strum on the D string, aim for the *space* between the D string and the A string.

HOLDING THE PICK

Professional guitarists hold the pick in different ways (see photo 8.1). Here are some guiding principles:

- Think of the pick as an extension of the hand.
- Keep the hand and fingers relaxed to facilitate natural movement.
- Thicker (heavy) picks produce a fuller sound for melodies.
- Thin picks produce a slapping percussive sound that some like for strumming.
- Hold the pick at a diagonal angle to the string to allow the pick to stroke the string with less friction.
- For scales, melodies, and improvisations, use only the tip of the pick, and practice small movements over the string.
- Axiom: The less movement involved, the more speed.

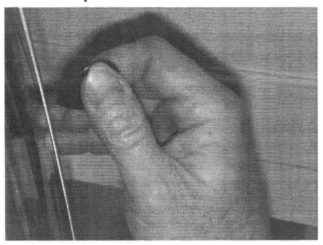

Photo 8.1: Holding the pick

Exercise: *Placing the Pick in Your Student's Hand*

Objective: Students practice holding the pick.
   Process:

- Hold the right forearm parallel to the floor and in front of the guitar. Rotate the wrist counterclockwise so that the fingers are facing to the left, and parallel to the floor.
- Place the pick so it balances on the tip of the index finger of the right hand. The fingers of the right hand should remain curled in their neutral position. Imagine that the pick is an extension of the finger. Some people find that resting the pick on the middle finger feels more balanced. The tip of the pick should look and feel like an extension of the finger.
- Place the thumb across the index finger so the thumb is perpendicular to the tip of the finger.
- Now let the hand hang from the wrist, and swing it to the right and left in a pendulum motion. Pretend to shake water droplets off of the hand. Blow on the hand, and let it sway

in the breeze. This motion is called *forearm rotation*.

Exercise: *Fanning the Fingers*

Objective: Student gain awareness of subtle finger motion when using a pick.
   Process:

- Hold the pick as described in the previous exercise.
- Practice moving the fingers as a group in toward the palm and back to home position. This is known as *fanning*.

Exercise: *Relating the Pick to the Thumb and Fingers*

Objective: Students experience the relationship between of the thumb and fingers, and the down- and upstrokes of the pick.
   Process:

- Play downstrokes with the thumb on the D string.
- Play upstrokes with the index finger on the G string.
- Alternate the thumb and the index finger on the D and G strings.
- Alternate both the thumb and the index finger on the G string.
- Place the pick between the thumb and the finger, and play alternating down- and upstrokes on the G string.
   Variation: Use the middle finger instead of the index finger.

Exercise: *Minimum Movement*

Objective: Students develop speed through the economy of picking motion.
   Process:

- Place the pick on top of the first string. It should be at a slight diagonal angle to the string. The side of the pick that contacts the string is a personal preference. Some prefer the front side, and others the back side of the pick as the contact point.
- Slowly move the pick so that it slides over the string without ever losing contact with the string.
- Notice that the other side of the pick is now in contact with the string.
- Repeat this motion of gliding over the string, with out losing contact, to get the idea of minimum movement.

• Gradually increase speed.

ABOUT TREMOLO

• Tremolo is a fundamental picking practice technique for the right hand.
• Tremolo is a rapid succession of down- and upstrokes.
• Tremolo is an important technique for producing the effect of a sustained pitch and should be practiced with crescendo and decrescendo.
• Students enjoy tremolo because it give them the opportunity to play as fast as possible.
• Tremolo of the right hand should eventually be synchronized with trills of the left hand.
• Mandolin players frequently use tremolo.

Exercise: Tremolo

Objective: Students practice minimum motion of the pick and flexibility of the forearm and fingers.
  Process:

• On the muted high E string, play down, up, down, up, starting very slowly. Check to see that the volume of the downstrokes and the upstrokes is even.
• Gradually speed up until the sound is continuous, like a mandolin.
• Gradually slow down.
• At the fastest point of the tremolo, experiment getting louder and softer.

Exercise: Synchronizing the Left Hand with Tremolo

Objective: Students gain accuracy when combining the right and left hands.
  Process:

• On the high E string have students repeatedly play the note E with a downstroke, and the note F with an upstroke.
• Accelerate this combination while keeping the right and left hands synchronized. The goal is to alternate any two notes, such as E and F, in perfect synchronization with the tremolo.
  Variation: Synchronize the tremolo with combinations of three or four notes (E-F-G or E-F-G-F).

Exercise: Matching Downbeats and Upbeats with Down and Up Picking Strokes

Objective: Students make a visual and sensory connection between the downbeats and upbeats and the motion of the pick.

Process:

• Write out a measure with the numbers *1 + 2 + 3 + 4 +*.
• Have students conduct using a simple down-up motion of the wrist while reciting "one and two and three and four and."
• Write out a simple rhythm that is placed over the appropriate numbers.
• Above the rhythm, write the symbols for downstrokes. These are the same symbols used for violin bowings. The symbol for down stroke looks like a staple, and the upstroke looks like a V. As a memory aid recite "staple down." Any note above a number gets a downstroke, and any note above a + sign gets an upstroke.
• Resume conducting, and add the vocalizations "down and up," synchronized with the rhythm. For example, *1 , 2+, 3, 4+* would now be vocalized, "down, down-up, down, down-up." Recite again using the numbers 1, 2+, 3, 4+.
• Practice the rhythms using string percussion (muted string using either one string or all the strings).

HOW TO REMOVE A PICK FROM INSIDE THE GUITAR

Inform your students that if their pick falls into the guitar, they must leave it there until a suitable break in the period to get it out. Here's how to get it out:

• Hold the guitar flat in front of you with the sound hole facing up.
• Jiggle the guitar until the pick is visible directly beneath the hole.
• Using a quick motion, flip the guitar, and the pick should drop out of the hole after a try or two.

Written Exercise: Write an Open-String Picking Etude

Objective: Students locate the open strings without looking at their fingers.
  Process:

• On a piece of staff paper, have each student create her own reference chart of the open strings:
  Bass   E A D
  Treble   G B E
• Have each student write several open-string etudes: (1) the treble strings, (2) the bass strings, (3) all the strings. Use steady quarter notes.

- Have each student perform the exercise using the thumb and/or the pick.
- Bracing:
  - o When picking the bass strings with the thumb, the fingers serve as a brace by resting on the treble strings.
  - o When picking the treble strings with the thumb, the fingers may serve as a brace by resting on the guitar.

❾

The Left Hand

Playing guitar requires many different left-hand fingerings and, therefore, many different hand positions.

Because of this variety, it is better to have students explore and discover principles of movement rather than to teach a static posture.

MOVEMENT-AWARENESS EXERCISES

The objective of the following exercises is for students to discover how one part of the body affects the motion of other parts.

Exercise/Exploration: The Wrist and Fingers

Objective: Students discover finger elongation.
Process:

- Hold the left forearm in a vertical position in front of you.
- Tilt the forearm slightly to the right, and allow the wrist to fall to the right in a limp manner. Notice that the fingers elongate as the wrist arches (extends).
- Next, tilt the left forearm slightly to the left, and allow the wrist to fall to the left in a limp manner. Notice that the fingers curl as the wrist falls backward. To achieve elongated fingers for guitar playing, the wrist will frequently be in a gently arched position.

Exercise/Exploration: The Forearm and the Wrist

Objective: Students learn to present the fingers of the left hand to the neck in the elongated position.
Process:

- Practice allowing the wrist to fall to the left and to the right as in the previous exercise.

- Slowly rotate the forearm clockwise and counterclockwise with the fingers in both the elongated and curled position.
- With the fingers in the elongated position, rotate the forearm until the left hand is in a position for playing guitar.

Exercise/Exploration: Relationship of the First Knuckle to Finger Elongation

Objective: Students discover finger elongation.
Process:

- Hold the left hand in front of you, with the fingers held straight, pointing toward the ceiling.
- Bend the first finger at the middle joint.
- Next, test the distance you can bend the first knuckle while the finger remains bent at the middle. It will move very little.
- Return to the starting position, and this time keep the first finger straight, and bend it from the first knuckle. Notice how much more it bends.
- For the final experiment, start with your first finger bent at the middle knuckle, but as you begin to bend the first knuckle forward, allow the finger to elongate. Notice how the bones organize themselves.
- Repeat, using all of the fingers at the same time.

MOTION EXPLORATIONS

Before beginning any of the following explorations, have students sit in the ready position, with the guitar neck at a diagonal, and the fingerboard about a foot from their eyes.

Exercise/Exploration: Neutral Position the Thumb

Objective: The student discovers the connection between the forearm, hand, and fingers.
Process:

- Wrap the fingers of the left hand around the neck at about the fifth fret.
- Notice the angle of the wrist and the location of the thumb.
- Slowly back onto the sixth string so all four fingertips rest on the string. The fingers should remain in their naturally arched position. Allow the thumb to move freely with the hand.
- Next, move all the fingers from string to string, and allow the palm and thumb to move with the fingers.

Exercise/Exploration: The Keyboard Position

Objective: The student discovers the similarity between the guitar and the keyboard.
Process:

- Wrap the fingers of the left hand around the neck at about the fifth fret.
- Slowly and evenly, back the fingers onto the sixth string, and let all four fingers rest on the string without pushing.
- Align each finger with a consecutive fret. I refer to this as *keyboard position* because each finger is aligned with a fret, similar to aligning each finger to a key on a keyboard. The fingers need to be on their tips in order to avoid bumping the adjacent string.

Exercise/Exploration: Gauging the Pressure of a String

Objective: The student develops an awareness of finger pressure, string distance, and sense of touch.
Process:

- With the fingers aligned over the string in keyboard position, experiment with the string's spring action by pressing and releasing the first finger while the others remain relatively still.
- Gauge the pressure with each of the fingers independently.

TRANSVERSAL AND LONGITUDINAL PRESENTATION OF THE FINGERS

The formal guitar term for diagonal position is *transversal presentation* and for parallel position is *longitudinal presentation*. By keeping the palm, wrist, elbow, and shoulder loose, the palm can shift angles without muscular interference.

Exercise: Hinge Action of the Palm; "The Gate"

Objective: Students practice shifting the palm from parallel to diagonal position.
Process:

- Place the palm of the left hand so it is parallel to the neck. The neck should contact the palm just beneath the first knuckle.
- Leaving the base of the index finger in contact with the neck, rotate the hand and wrist in a gate-like motion from a parallel to a diagonal angle with the neck.
- Notice that in diagonal position there are still double contact points—the first knuckle of the index finger and the thumb are in contact with the neck. Double contact points are important for bracing and as reference points.
- Repeat.

Exercise: The Diagonal and Parallel-Palm Exercise

Objective: Students discover the relationship between left-hand fingering and the parallel or diagonal palm positions.
Process:

- At the fifth fret, place fingers 1, 2, 3, and 4 all on the first string. The palm must be parallel to the neck.
- At the fifth fret, place fingers 1, 2, 3, and 4 on strings 4, 3, 2, and 1 (frets 5, 6, 7, 8). The palm of the hand must be at a diagonal angle to the neck.
- At the fifth fret, place fingers 1, 2, 3, and 4 on strings 1, 2, 3, and 4 (frets 5, 6, 7, 8). The palm of the hand must be parallel to the neck.
- Place fingers 1, 2, 3, and 4 *all* on the fifth fret—on strings 4, 3, 2, and 1. The palm must be extremely diagonal to the neck. The fingers will all be touching each other in an overlapping manner that I call *nesting*.
- Alternate between each of the preceding positions, and allow the elbow and forearm to move freely.
Variation: Using the previous positions, gauge

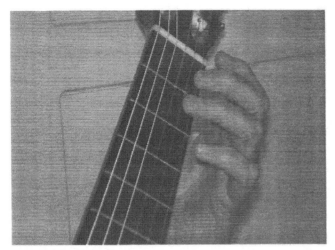

Photo 9.1: Parallel palm

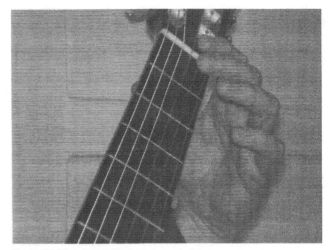

Photo 9.2: The diagonal palm

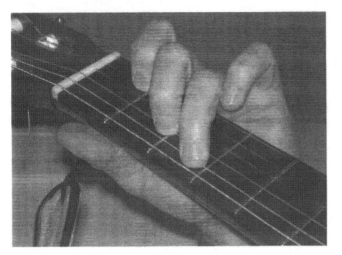

Photo 9.3: The C chord—parallel palm

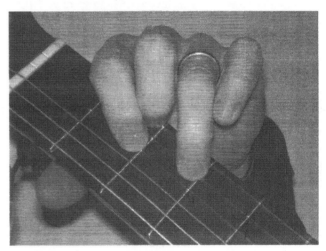

Photo 9.4: The D chord—diagonal palm

the pressure and distance for each finger independently.

Exercise: The Diagonal and Parallel-Palm Exercise Using Chords

Objective: Students learn when to shift from a parallel position to diagonal position using chords.
  Process:

- Finger a C chord. Notice that the palm needs to be parallel in order to reach the frets (photo 9.3).
- Finger a D chord. In order to play the D, which has two fingers on the same fret, the palm must be diagonal (photo 9.4).
- Finger a B7 chord. Since several fingers are on the same fret, which position is necessary to play this chord?
  Axiom: When more than one finger is on the same fret, the diagonal position will be used.

THE CONTACT POINT

The point at which the finger contacts the string, in relation to the fret, is called the *contact point*. It is a good idea to make a habit of placing the fingers close to the frets because:

- it gives you a definite target,
- the closer to the fret you push, the less pressure you need, and
- string buzz is caused when a finger is not close enough to the fret; the third finger is particularly prone to buzzing.

Exercise/Exploration: The Contact Point

Objective: Students learn to *feel* the fret and use it as a reference point when playing notes.
  Process:

- Place the finger on any note.
- Nudge the finger toward the fret until you can feel the fret.
- Finger any chord. Nudge the fingers until you can feel the frets with each finger.
- Visualization: Imagine a thread passing through the center of your finger and being connected to the fret.

Exercise/Exploration: *The Arches of the Fingers*

Objective: Students observe the connection of body parts involved with finger arch.

Process:

- If a student needs more arch in his fingers to avoid bumping the adjacent string, have him adjust the thumb toward the bottom side of the neck.
- As the thumb moves, so will the wrist, elbow, and shoulder in a chain reaction.
- Any muscle interference (tension) from the hinges of the wrist, elbow, and shoulder must be eliminated in order for these hinges to move freely.

Exercise: *Using a Computer Keyboard to Teach Hand Position*

Objective: Students make a connection between keyboard technique and guitar playing.

Process:

- Hold a computer keyboard in front of a student, and have them type a sentence. Notice the finger arches and the use of the fingertips on the keys.
- Next, hold the keyboard so that it lies directly on the neck of the guitar and on top of, and parallel to, the strings.
- Have the student reach around the neck as if to play the guitar, but instead have her "play" the keyboard.

Exercise: *The Left-Hand Roll*

Objective: Students experience the sensation of playing on their fingertips. Fingernails must be extremely short in order to play on the fingertips.

Process:

- Have the students place all four fingers on the third string. The palm should be parallel to the neck, the knuckles slightly spaced, and the fingers arched.

- Curl the fingers, and roll the wrist outward until the entire first phalange is resting flat on the strings. Rolling into this position will force the thumb to move toward the bottom of the neck.
- Slowly, relax the hand, and roll the fingertips back into the neutral starting position.
- Repeat several times on other strings.
- Axiom: It is not unusual for the first phalange to be tilted toward the sixth string.

Exercise: *The Left-Hand Water Spider*

Objective: Students gain the sensation of relaxed, rapid motion.

Process:

- On the back of the guitar, or on their left leg, have the students make an imaginary spider with their left hand. Have the spider run around freely. Be sure the spider feet are on the tips of the finger, near the nail.
- Bring the spider to the neck of the guitar to run around freely. Be sure the spider uses all four fingers and that the hand retains the spider shape.
- Move the fingers as quickly as possible as the spider runs up and down the neck.
- Imagine that the spider is running on water.
- Be sure all four fingers are in contact with the fingerboard.
- Continue for thirty seconds until you feel warmth in the forearm.

Exercise: *The Finger Buddy System*

Objective: Students learn to rest passive fingers on the strings to conserve motion and to support the active finger.

Process:

- Have students place their first finger on the fourth fret of the first string. The first finger stands on its own, and the passive fingers hover an eighth of an inch above the string.
- Leave the fourth-fret finger in place, and drop the second finger on the fifth fret. The second finger is now supported by the first finger, which remains resting on the string. The second finger has one "buddy."
- Continue the process by adding the third and fourth fingers and always leaving the passive fingers resting on the string.
- How many buddies does the third finger have? (Two)

• Summarize: Play repeated notes on the fifth fret, and switch fingers every four beats. Here is the finger pattern: 1 1 1 1, 2 2 2 2, 3 3 3 3, 4 4 4 4, etc. The first finger should never leave the string; each finger in turn will play the fifth fret.

SUMMARY

When your students learn how to experiment with motion, and how to notice the subtle body sensations, they will discover better motion and hand placement for themselves. The general axioms for the left hand follow:

• Less distance equals more speed.
• Lightness of touch equals more speed.
• The palm must be free to hinge in a gate-like manner from the parallel to diagonal positions on the side of the neck. To do this, the wrist, elbow, shoulder and head must be free to move.
• The palm usually touches the neck when playing on the sixth string,
• The palm usually moves away from the neck when playing on the first string.
• When the wrist is arched outward, the fingers become elongated. As the wrist arches inward, the fingers become curled.
• Whenever fingers 2, 3, or 4 of the left hand are used, the passive fingers serve as buddies by resting on the string.

THOUGHTS ON BEING LEFT-HANDED

Left-handed students may benefit from a left-handed guitar, which should be available through your favorite music store. Have the student experiment with both the standard guitar and left-handed guitar to see which works best.

⑩

Strength and Motion

Playing guitar is an athletic activity.

Students who are involved in sports are already familiar with practice routines that develop motor skills. The process of developing muscle memory for golf or baseball is similar to that in guitar. Students who do not participate in organized sports still can relate to the practice routines of skateboarding, snow boarding, skiing, ballet, debating, or other extracurricular activities. Have the students in your class describe practice routines from their other activities, and explicitly point out the similarities between those activities and guitar practice.

Athletic training involves strength, stretching, speed, and mental alertness. Hand exercises work especially well for developing specific muscles that are used in playing the guitar. Strength exercises are especially useful at the beginning of the year for developing strength needed for playing.

Categories of guitar strength exercises include:

- isometric-strength exercises
- stretching and elongation
- digital-independence patterns
- fixed-finger exercises
- contrary-motion exercises
- parallel intervals

Exercise: The Pancake Stretch

Objective: Students increase the distance between their fingers.
Process:

- Place the guitar in playing position with the fingerboard elevated by using a footstool or a strap.
- Students hold their left hand in front of themselves, with their palm facing them, as if they were playing.

- The students slowly stretch the fingers as wide as they can go. I call this *the pancake* because the hand is as flat as a pancake.
- Lay the pancake on the strings of the guitar with the thumb gently touching the lower side of the neck.
- Adjust the hand so the tips of the index and pinky are on the A string.
- Count the number of frets that the fingers can span from this position. High-school students should be able to span five to six frets in this position.

Exercise: The Pancake Stretch with Finger Groupings

Objective: Students separate fingers into different combinations.
Process:

- With the palm facing you, stretch the fingers to create the pancake.
- Separate and hold the fingers in the following positions: 1-2 3 4, 1 2-3 4, 1 2 3-4.
- Perform these finger combinations on the fingerboard with the fingers lying on the strings in the pancake position.

Exercise: The Wrist Clock

Objective: Students gain familiarity with forearm rotation.
Process:
- Have students hold the left forearm vertically in front of them.
- Allow the wrist to hang freely. Find the most neutral position. Let's call this *twelve o'clock.*
- Gradually rotate the wrist and forearm counterclockwise through the eleven o'clock posi-

tion, and then ten o'clock position. Gently stretch. Return to home position.

- Gradually rotate toward the clockwise through one, two, three, four, five, and six o'clock. Move slowly, with awareness of all the corresponding movements of the elbow and arm.
- Repeat, and gently stretch in each direction.

Exercise: Lateral Motion of the Fingers

Objective: Students develop strength and coordination to separate the fingers.
  Process:

- Place the fingers of the left hand flat on a tabletop or the back of the guitar. Separate the fingers into the pancake position.
- Slide the first finger alternately to the right and to the left while the other fingers remain still.
- Repeat the previous motion using the other fingers.
  Variation: Practice these finger combinations using arched fingers (the spider position).

Exercise: Separating the Knuckles

Objective: Students exercise muscles that assist finger separation. This exercise is from Yehudi Menuhin's book *Violin and Viola—Practical Guide by Two Masters* (coauthored by William Primrose, New York: Schirmer Books, 1976).
  Process:

- Begin with the fingers of the left hand all resting on the first string in playing position.
- Place the fingertips of the first and second fingers so they are touching.
- While the tips remain touching, separate the knuckles of the fingers. This may feel odd at first because it is an unusual movement. Success will be based on mental concentration.
- Repeat several times.
- Allow movements of the hand, wrist, and forearm to facilitate knuckle separation.
- Repeat using fingers 2-3, and 3-4.

INDEPENDENCE EXERCISES

Since all the body parts are connected, there is no such thing as complete independence of the fingers. Every movement involves a chain reaction of the parts. Nevertheless, a certain amount of independent finger control is necessary to play guitar. Learn

the following terms to help provide students with instructions:
  Knuckle one–joint closest to the palm
  Knuckle two–middle joint
  Knuckle three–joint closest to the fingertip
  Phalange–the segment of the finger between two joints
  First phalange–the section between knuckle one and the palm
  Second phalange–the middle section of the finger
  Third phalange–the section that is closest to the fingertip

Exercise: Knuckle Independence

Objective: Student gain independence of motion with all of the joints of the finger.
  Process:

- Have the students hold their left hand in front of them as if they were playing guitar. Note that in the neutral position, the fingers are gently arched as if they were sleeping.
- Stretch the fingers until they are straight, into the pancake position.
- While retaining the pancake position, slowly bend the first finger from the second joint, and return to starting position. Keep the remaining fingers straight. Repeat ten times. Bring your attention to the muscles in the forearm, and notice their connection with the movement of the fingers. Keep the other fingers straight.
- Do the same thing with fingers two, three, and four. (Only a few people can bend their pinky exclusively from this joint.)
- Next, have students bend combinations of two fingers at a time, while the others remain straight. Here are combinations of two fingers to bend: 1-2, 2-3, 3-4, 1-3, 2-4, 1-4.
- Repeat the previous exercise using the first joint, near the palm.

Exercise: The Clock and Forearm Rotation

Objective: To free the wrist and forearm from habitually being locked in one position.
  Process:
- Hold the left forearm in the vertical position in front of you. Rotate until the wrist is facing you, as if playing the guitar.
- Let the wrist hang forward, and then let it flop backward. In the backward position, the fingers will be curled, and in the forward position they will be elongated. Let's refer to the for-

ward position as six o'clock and the backward position as twelve o'clock.
- Next, rotate the forearm both clockwise and counterclockwise while flopping the wrist forward and backward.
- Discover a playing position that feels best.

Exercise: Elbow Awareness

Objective: Students observe the relationship between the elbow position and the position of the hand.
Process:

- Place the left forearm in vertical position with the left hand hanging forward on top of the forearm. Rotate the forearm so the wrist is in playing position.
- Leaving the hand at rest, rock the elbow progressively forward, then backward. Notice how the elbow motion affects the hand movement.
- Variation: Swing the elbow from left to right.

Exercise: Thumb Isometric

Objective: Students gain strength in the thumb necessary to play barre chords.
Process:

- Students squeeze and hold their left thumb against the knuckle of the index finger for approximately ten seconds. Relax and repeat.
- Notice that the muscle between the thumb and the hand will bulge. Develop this muscle.

Exercise: Fist Isometric

Objective: Students gain strength in their forearm and awareness of extension, flexion, and rest.
Process:

- Begin with the fingers of the left hand extended into the pancake stretch.
- When the fingers are extended in this fashion, notice the muscles in the forearm that are being used. This is *extension*.
- As slowly as possible, allow the fingers to return into their curled natural position as if asleep. This is *neutral position*.
- Continue curling the fingers into a fist, and notice the muscles in the forearm that are being used. This is *flexion*.
- Relax by gently shaking the hand. Repeat. This exercise strengthens the forearm muscles, which are connected to the fingers.

Exercises: Digital Patterns

Students can accelerate their learning process by practicing numeric finger patterns referred to as *digital patterns*.
Objective: Student will develop use of all the fingers, especially the third and fourth fingers of the left hand. Digital patterns also exercise the mind.
Process:

- Play each of the following patterns several times on the high E string, and then cross to the next string, and the next, etc. When working in a classroom setting, it best to begin with repeated notes, and then progressively reduce the repetitions.
  - Alternate between the following finger groups of two: 1 2 1 2, 1 3 1 3, 1 4 1 4, 2 3 2 3, 2 4 2 4, 3 4 3 4
- An example of using repeated notes would work like this: 1 1 1 1 2 2 2 2, 1 1 1 2 2 2, 1 1 2 2, 1 2 1 2, and then repeat the next sequence.

Stretching Variation: There is a difference between stretching and lengthening. The ability to reach wider distances is related more to hand, thumb, and wrist placement than actually stretching the muscles. A more accurate way to refer to increasing distance between fingers is *lengthening and elongation*.
Process:
Using the proceeding digital patterns, increase the number of frets between fingers. For example, use fingers 1 and 2 to play frets 1 and 3. Use any two fingers, and increase the number of frets the hand can reach. Experiment with hand and thumb placement to reach greater distances. Generally greater distances require a lower thumb position. In extreme cases, the thumb will be placed all the way on the bottom side of the neck.
Triplet Variation: Triplet patterns can be played as follows, with the slash representing a movement from string to string: 1 2 1 / 2 1 2 / 1 2 1, etc.

- Here are the other finger combinations to be practiced in the same manner as above: 1 3 1 / 3 1 3, 1 4 1 / 4 1 4, 2 3 2 / 3 2 3, 2 4 2 / 4 2 4, 3 4 3 / 4 3 4, etc.
- In a group setting it is easier to start with repeated notes and progressively reduce the repetitions.
Slur Variations: Play these patterns using slurs. See chapter 31 on hammering-on (slurs), which are commonly referred to as *hammer-ons* and *pull-offs*.

DIGITAL PATTERNS USING ALL FOUR FINGERS

Independent control of all four fingers makes playing most music easier. The following four-finger combinations work especially well on one string. For an extra challenge, the fingers may be placed on different strings.

Groups of four: 1 2 3 4, 4 3 2 1, 1 3 2 4, 4 2 3 1
Combined groups of four: 1 3 2 4-4 2 3 1
Asymmetric groups: 1 2 4 2, 1 3 4 1; 4 3 1 3, 4 2 1 4

Remember to start with repeated notes and progressively reduce the repetitions.

GRAY (MUTED) TONE VARIATION

Gray, or muted, tones help to develop lightness of touch by allowing the mind to focus on location rather than power. To develop lightness, play the preceding digital patterns, but only push the string down *halfway* to the fingerboard. This produces a muted or gray tone. Since gray tones do not require strength, students will notice a more graceful hand position. By alternating gray and clear tones you can develop a lighter and faster touch. For example, play gray tones on frets 1, 2, 3, and 4, then clear tones on frets 1, 2, 3, and 4, then gray tones on frets 2, 3, 4, and 5, and then clear tones on frets 2, 3, 4, and 5, etc.

Exercise: Digital Patterns Using Barre Forms

Objective: Students use digital patterns to develop barre technique. Note: This is a powerful preliminary for learning moveable barre forms.
Process:

- Have the students lay their first finger across the fifth fret, creating a barre.
- Begin by dropping the second finger four times on each string. Next, practice dropping the third and then the fourth fingers in the same manner.
- Practice combinations of two fingers moving across the fingerboard. While maintaining the barre, alternate fingers 2 and 3, 2 and 4, and 3 and 4 on each string.
- Include the first finger (barre finger) as part of the digital pattern: 1 2, 1 3, 1 4, etc.
Variation: Add slurs to the above patterns.

FIXED-FINGER EXERCISES

Fixed-finger exercises are exercises in which one or more fingers remain anchored or fixed while the remaining fingers perform a motion. Beginners who are learning to play chords may use a fixed-finger exercise to learn a new chord form.

Exercise: Fingers Out, Up, and In

Objective: Students learn chord forms while developing finger independence
Process:

- Silently finger the C chord. Let's call this *home position.* Cover the strings with the right arm to keep them quiet.
- Leave fingers 2 and 3 fixed on their home position, while finger 1 independently performs the following six-step sequence: out-home, up-home, in-home. Here is the explanation:
Out Extend the first finger *out* away from the palm until it almost lays flat on the fingerboard. (Remember the other two fingers must remain fixed.)
Home Return the first finger to its home position in the C chord.
Up Lift the first finger up as if you were pointing away from the fingerboard.
Home Return the first finger to its home position in the C chord.
In Curl the first finger in toward the palm.
Home Return the first finger to its home position in the C chord.
- Repeat the process using the second and third fingers.

Exercise: Contrary Motion

Objective: Students develop the ability to move the fingers in two different directions at the same time.
Process:

- Students place the first finger on the first fret of the D string and the second finger on the second fret of the G string.
- Simultaneously have the fingers switch strings. As always, use repeated notes and progressively reduce the repetitions.
- Progressively, add more distance between the fingers. For example, exchange fingers 1 and 2 between the A and the G strings.
- Continue increasing the distance between strings until the student can shift fingers 1 and 2 between strings 6 and 5.
Variations: Here are the other finger combinations for contrary motion practice: 1 3, 1 4, 2 3, 2 4, 3 4.

HELPFUL CONSIDERATIONS

- Keep the guitar and neck elevated with a foot-stool or strap.
- Begin using repeated notes, and progressively reduce the repetitions.
- Use arm movement to facilitate shifting the palm from the diagonal to the parallel positions in relation to the neck.

Exercise: Contrary Motion with Fixed Fingers

Objective: Students develop finger independence.
Process:

- Place fingers 1, 2, 3, and 4 lightly on the G string at frets 5, 6, 7, and 8.
- Leave fingers 3 and 4 fixed on the G string, and move fingers 2 and 3 in contrary motion from the B to the D string.
- Alternate other two-finger combinations such as: 1-3 or 1-4 or 2-4, while the other fingers remain fixed on the G string. Extend the distance between strings.

PARALLEL INTERVALS

Andres Segovia popularized parallel intervals when he published his edition of parallel octaves. In a class setting, it is especially important to begin playing these patterns using repeated notes. Begin with only two parallel fifths, because the interval of a fifth is well known in popular music as a *power chord*. Then, move on to three or more parallel fifths and other intervals.

Exercise: Parallel Fifths

Objective: Students develop finger strength and independence while developing an awareness of the sound of the interval.
Process:

- Place the first finger at the first fret of the sixth string. Place the third finger on the third fret of the fifth string. This is the interval of a fifth.

The chord symbols is F5. F5 is also known as the F *power chord*.
- While leaving fingers 1 and 3 in place, create an F♯5 chord by placing the second finger on the second fret of the sixth string, and placing the pinky on the fourth fret of the fifth string.
- Alternate between F5 and F♯5. Use repeated notes: F5, F5, F5, F5, F♯5, F♯5, F♯5, F♯5. Gradually reduce the repetitions.
- Add one new interval per day, until you can play a chromatic scale in parallel fifths. In other words, tomorrow add the G5 chord to the F5 and F♯5, and so forth.

PARALLEL INTERVALS: BROKEN STYLE

In the previous exercise, when shifting from F5 to F♯5, the fingers moved at the same time. This is referred to as *block style*. In the next important variation, the notes are plucked in succession, which is referred to as *broken style*. What makes it interesting is the following rule: only one finger can move at a time.

Exercise: Parallel Intervals; Broken Style

Objective: Students strengthen their power of concentration.
Process:

- Let's begin with a loop from the F5 to F♯5, and back to F5.
- Here is the order that the notes are plucked: F-C, F♯-C♯, F-C, F♯-C♯, and so forth.
- The key to this exercise is to move only one finger at a time.
  Variation: Expand the previous exercise by using the same finger pattern, but separating the fingers by an additional number of strings. For example, the fingerings for F5-F♯5 are on strings 6 and 5, so next increase the distance between the fingers by playing the same fingering on strings 6 and 4. The new interval will be an *octave*. The next expansion would be an *eleventh* (strings 6 and 3), a *thirteenth* (strings 6 and 2), and an *eighteenth* (strings 6 and 1). Use the arm to facilitate shifting intervals, and stop when you begin to feel strain.

Teaching Individual Tuning

Develop the coordination to pluck the string, turn the knob, and listen at the same time.

Some important concepts for tuning a guitar follow.

- The ability to tune the guitar is essential for students to enjoy guitar as a life-long pursuit.
- Tuning the guitar takes time to learn. Expect student proficiency by the end of the semester.
- The ability to tune the guitar involves multiple, simultaneous skills.
- The ability to tune the guitar reinforces the awareness of the open strings and unison-tuning frets. This awareness can help reveal the locations of notes on the entire neck.
- The ability to tune the guitar improves the students' aural skills.
- There are several methods for tuning a guitar. *Unison tuning* is the most common.
- Electric tuners are highly recommended.
- At the beginning of the year you and your advanced student helpers will tune the guitars.
- In a noisy classroom environment it is helpful to place the ear as close as possible to the instrument.

ELECTRIC TUNERS

I recommend the use of a clip-on electric tuner. For convenience, you may leave it permanently attached to your guitar.

THE TUNING KNOBS

To adjust the string pitch, we change the string tension using the *tuning knobs*.

- Each knob corresponds to an open string: E, A, D, G, B, and E.
- To raise the sound of a string, it should be tightened.
- To lower the sound of a string, it should be loosened.
- Most beginners do not turn the tuning knob far enough. It is common to turn the knob a third of a revolution or more.

STEPS IN UNISON TUNING

When two adjacent strings sound exactly the same, they are said to be *in unison*. *Unison tuning* is the most common way of tuning the guitar.

- Place your middle finger on the fifth fret of the sixth string. Be sure it is arched enough so it doesn't bump the next string.
- Pluck the note, and remember the sound. This is referred to as the *reference string*. Pluck the string loudly enough to hear it. Move your ear closer to the guitar if necessary.
- Pluck the fifth string, and determine if it needs to be adjusted higher or lower to match the sixth string. Since the fifth string will be adjusted, it is referred to as the *variable string*.
- Repeatedly pluck the fifth string while turning the tuning knob until it matches the sixth string. When it matches, you are in tune. When two strings are slightly out of tune, you hear a pulsing known as *beats*. When two strings are in perfect unison, there are no beats.
- Starting with the sixth string, use the following unison-tuning frets to tune the guitar: 5-5-5-4-5. Notice that the third string is fingered on the fourth fret.

TUNING PRELIMINARIES

Exercise: The Pluck Turn

Objective: Students develop the coordination to pluck the string, turn the knob, and listen at the same time.

    Process: Practice plucking a string and turning the knob at the same time: tighten, loosen, tighten, loosen, etc. This is called the *pluck turn*.

Exercise: Finding the Tuning Knobs without Looking

Objective: Students learn to find the tuning knob by feel.

    Process: Give verbal instructions to the students such as, "Place your fingers on knob 4, knob 3, etc." Have them find the tuning knobs without looking at them.

Exercise: Teach the Names of the Strings

Objective: Students memorize the string names.
    Process:

- Have the class play each string four times, reciting their names: E E E E, A A A A, etc.
- Call out random string names, and have the students play them in repeated notes.
- A popular acronym for remembering the string names is (E)lephants (A)nd (D)onkeys (G)row (B)ig (E)ars. Have students invent their own acronym.

TUNING ACTIVITIES

- Teach the definition of *unison*.
- Students recite the pattern of unison reference frets, which are: 5, 5, 5, 4, 5.
- Students silently finger the reference frets and pulse each fret four times.
- Use echo imitation to lead the class in unison tuning. For example, say "A-A, unison A," and have the students echo you on their guitars and with their voices.
- If you are unsure whether or not the strings are in unison, intentionally lower (detune) the variable string, and then raise it until it reaches unison.

Exercise: Teacher-Student Partner Tuning

Objective: The student is allowed to focus on one tuning skill at a time.

Process:

- The student and teacher cooperatively tune the same guitar.
- Detune the fifth string.
- The student fingers the reference note, which is the fifth fret of the sixth string. The teacher simultaneously adjusts the tuning knob and plucks the string.
- Variation: The student turns the tuning knob while the teacher fingers the reference note and plucks the string. Repeat the process on other strings.

Demonstration: Demonstrating Beats with an Electric Guitar or Electric Bass

Objective: Students listen for and identify beats.
    Process:

- Tune an electric bass or electric guitar.
- Purposely allow two strings to be slightly out of tune so that a beating or pulsing can be heard.
- Have students move their hands up and down in tempo to the beating.
- Demonstrate how beating changes speeds as the strings approach unison.
- If available, set a snare drum near the bass amplifier. The snare will also beat.
- When this occurs, it is called *sympathetic vibration*.

TUNING BY EAR: "THE TUNING SONG"

The guitar is tuned in fourths and thirds as follows: Starting from the low E: 4th, 4th, 4th, 3rd, 4th. Students can learn to hear the intervals of fourths and thirds by learning a tuning song based on "Amazing Grace." Sing the following words while plucking the corresponding open strings:

    A-maze: E-A
    A-maze: A-D
    A-maz-ing: D-G-B
    A-maze: B-E

Exercise: The Tuning Arpeggio

Objective: Students develop the right-hand technique to tune the guitar by ear.
    Process:

- Using the thumb, play the strings in the following order, and memorize the sound of the

open strings by humming:
6, 6 5, 6 5 4, 6 5 4 3, 6 5 4 3 2, 6 5 4 3 2 1
- Using the index or middle finger, play the strings in reverse order:
1, 1 2, 1 2 3, 1 2 3 4, 1 2 3 4 5, 1 2 3 4 5 6
- Check the octave of strings 6 and 1.

Exercise: Tuning Quiz

Objective: Students gain confidence by tuning only two strings.
   Process:

- Tune the student's guitar.
- Detune the high E string.
- Have the student independently correct the tuning.
- Remind her to:

    o play loudly,
    o memorize the sound of the reference string,
    o place her ear near the guitar,
    o pluck the string and turn the knob at the same, and
    o listen for unison.

OTHER TUNING CONCEPTS

- **Standard tuning** Standard tuning refers to tuning as we have learned consisting of the intervals 4th, 4th, 4th, 3rd, 4th; E, A, D, G, B, E.
- **Drop-D tuning** Drop D is the same as standard tuning, with the sixth string lowered to a D. This tuning is used to give a deeper bass to songs in the key of D or Dmin. It is also used to make power chords easier to play.
- **Alternate tuning** Refers to when the guitar is tuned to intervals other than standard tuning. A common example is D, A, D, G, A, D. Alternate tunings provide interesting and refreshing sounds. I have devoted a couple of chapters to the subject in my book *Mastering Fingerstyle Guitar*.
- **Open tuning** Open tuning is tuning the guitar to a chord. Two common tunings used in blues are D and G tuning.

    o **D tuning** D, A, D, F♯, A, D
    o **G tuning** D, G, D, G, B, D

⑫

Group Tuning Techniques

There are several ways to tune the entire class. Choose the method that works best for you.

PREPARATION

I highly recommend using a clip-on electric tuner. You can leave it permanently attached to your guitar, and it will save you time and effort. Suggest that your students obtain tuners or that they find friends in class who can help them tune before class starts. Students should become independent at tuning as soon as possible.

TUNING CDS

Many of the guitar method books contain CDs with tuning notes. You can set the tuning track on your CD player to loop, and play it at the beginning of class. If you tune using the tuning track, model the tuning process and give verbal cues for each note such as, "knob one, knob two, etc." Place your ear close to the guitar to hear it better. Ask students to pluck softly and hold the guitar close to their ear.

Exercise: Staccato Tuning

Objective: The guitars remain quiet enough so that everyone can hear the tuning notes.
   Process:

- Teach students the meaning of the word *staccato*.
- Demonstrate how to play a palm mute with the right hand. Gently muffle the strings by laying the palm of their right hand on the strings close to the bridge. Use the thumb to pluck the notes.
- Direct students to place their left hand on the appropriate tuning knob.
- Have them pluck the muted high E string with their thumb and adjust the pitch to match the reference pitch. Students should hold the guitar close to their ear to hear it better.
- Use verbal instructions as you move from string to string.

Exercise: Conducted Tuning

Objective: Students practice responding to a conductor and listening to those sitting around them. This is a good opportunity to teach them about conducting.
   Process:

- Teach the conducting concepts of *preparation gesture*, the *ictus* (downbeat), the *fermata*, and the *cutoff*.
- Play the reference pitch E.
- Using your baton, direct the entire class to pluck the low E once, and only once, at the precise moment that you conduct it. Make sure students have their left hand on the tuning knob before they pluck the string.
- After the students pluck and sustain the note, they should determine if they are too low or to high in comparison to the group and should then adjust the pitch using the tuning knob.
- Repeat this process for all six strings.

Exercise: Line Tuning

Objective: To achieve precise ensemble tuning by quickly checking everyone individually as they are lined up in their rows.

Process:
- Inform the students that you will point to each one of them in succession. Their goal is to listen to the reference pitch and then adjust their string in less than five seconds. Everyone needs to be alert and ready to participate.
- Point to a student, play the reference note on your guitar, and have the student adjust her tuning in as short an amount of time as possible.
- When you come to a student who is in tune, quickly move on.

III

MUSIC READING

13

The Natural-Note Scale

Scales are to the musician as running is to the athlete; that's why we refer to scale practice as *running scales*.

SCALE MOTIVATION

Motivate your students to master scales for the following reasons:

- *Finding the notes.* Practicing scales develops the awareness of the location of one's fingers. For this reason, mastery of scales improves everything—music reading, chord changing, and all aspects of playing. (The term for the awareness of the finger's location is *proprioception*.)
- *Flow.* Many students do not understand what it means to be proficient at a scale. For the student to benefit from practicing scales, you must insist on the unrestricted, smooth flow of notes. Eliminating muscular interference is an important goal of scale practice. The study of scales exposes problems of hand position that may be restricting flow. A reasonable goal is to play a one-octave scale in one second or less.
- *Music reading.* The student's success with reading is directly proportional to their skill with scales. Reading music is easiest when the student can focus on the reading contour of the notation without thinking about finding the notes on the guitar. This is only possible when scales become automatic. Driving provides a good metaphor. Notation is like a road map. The scale is like a road. Just as a smooth road facilitates driving, a smooth scale allows the fingers to move without interruption. Just as a map indicates north, south, east, and west, notation indicates pitch motion that is higher, lower, or repeated.

- *Music theory and ear training.* A scale is a measuring device much like a musical ruler. As a ruler measures distance, a scale measures pitch. Familiarity with the major scale provides students with the numerical coordinates, known as *scale degrees*, for understanding melody and harmony. Aural ability is improved by understanding scale degrees, which in turn accelerates learning.
- *Improvisations and composition.* Being skilled at playing scales enhances one's ability to improvise and compose. Students should be encouraged to use scale material to improvise melodies and to invent technical exercises as soon as possible. Next, they should write melodies and technical exercises. Have students write, and read, their own series of notes.

THE NATURAL-NOTE SCALE

In order to read music, the student must be able to identify and play the seventeen natural notes in the open position. The *open position* refers to the hand position in which each finger corresponds to a fret. Open position is also known as first position by string players. The natural notes in open position use all six of the open strings plus eleven fingered notes. From bass to treble, here is the pattern:

0 1 3, 0 2 3, 0 2 3, 0 2, 0 1 3, 0 1 3

The pattern becomes even easier to remember if you point out that the pattern 0 1 3 occurs on three strings, the pattern 0 2 3 occurs on two strings, and one string only has two notes. The learning sequence is also important. Teach the scale as follows:

- by fret number
- by alphabet letters
- by notation

The natural note scale includes all the open strings, so it would be a good idea to review them before we start:

E f g, A b c, D e f, G a, B c d, E f g

Notice that the capital letters represent the open strings and that the letters are in alphabetical order.

MINI-SCALES AND SCALE LOOPING

It is best to start with scale fragments or *mini-scales*. A *scale loop* is a number of notes that repeat themselves, such as A B A B A B A or A B C B A B C B, etc. Explain to the students that practicing scale loops using mini-scales should become routine, and remind them that they should use loops to warm up before class.

Exercise: *Scale Looping*

Objective: Students gain confidence by looping a small sequence of notes.

Process:

- Begin by playing a two-note scale consisting of E and F on the first string.
- Play each note four times, and give verbal instructions to gradually reduce the repetitions—three times, two times, one time.
- When the class reaches one repetition per note, get faster and faster, like and airplane taking off. Speed is important. Teach the word *accelerando*.
- Repeat the process with other groupings of notes, such as E F G F. As always, emphasize lightness and using a minimum of motion. There is a natural tendency to try harder as the speed increases. A strategy for simplifying the thought process is to think of a contour rather than individual notes.
- Axioms: Less motion equals greater speed. Lightness equals velocity.
- I like the idea of presenting all the natural notes within four to six weeks. This way you can go back and reinforce them in creative ways for the entire semester.

Exercise: *Ascending and Descending Scale Steps*

Students need to learn the relationship between pitch direction and guitar fingerings. The first step is to guide them using visual cues.

Objective: Students connect the guitar fingerings with ascending and descending pitch.

Process:

- Provide students with a starting note, such as the open A on the fifth string.
- Direct them to play an ascending or descending scale step by pointing your finger up or down.
- Do the reverse—you perform scale steps, and the students point either up or down.

Exercise: *The Musical Alphabet*

After the students can play the natural notes and understand ascending and descending pitch, practice the musical alphabet.

Objective: Students make a connection between the order of the alphabet letters and ascending and descending pitch.

Process:

- Have the students recite the musical alphabet forward and backward: A B C D E F G A B C . . . and A G F E D C B A G F. . . .
- Point up or down, and have them recite the alphabet based on your visual cues.
- Variation: Tell them your starting note, and then play either up or down in scale steps, and have them recite the alphabet letters. As an additional challenge have them point in the appropriate direction as they recite the letters.
- Relate the fingered scale steps to the open strings. Ask, "Since the open fifth string is the note A, on what fret is the note B?"

Exercise: *Connecting the Natural-Note Scale to Reading Melodies*

Objective: Students make a smooth transition from the scale into reading music.

Process:

- Make a transparency of a large, easy-to-read staff.
- Write the natural-note scale on the transparency.
- Have students play the scale in repeated notes with the following rules: (1) they lock their eyes on the music, concentrate, and (2) say the names of the note.
- Point to the notes in the scale that comprise a song you are working on. For example, if you are learning to read "Twinkle, Twinkle, Little Star" in the key of C, point to the notes C C G G A A G in the scale, and have the students play the notes.

OTHER SCALE POSSIBILITIES

- Omit important reference tones. For example, play the scale in repeated notes, but substitute rests whenever they reach the note C.
- Color code the skips. For example, write E in black and F in orange, and G in black and A in orange, etc.
- Play the scale in skips, without color coding. E G B . . . and F A C. . . .
- Play the scale backward.
- Play it backward in skips.
- *Embedded chords.* Color code the spelling of various chords, and have students figure them out. For example, write all seventeen notes, but color code the notes of the C chord, C E G C E.
- *Mini assessment.* Use your pointer to select a random note, and call on individual students to demonstrate where it is played.
- Write the natural-note scale in two directions, ascending and descending, starting from an important key tone, such as C, A, G, or E.
- Identify those students who are struggling, and provide them with extra worksheets that reinforce the concepts.
- For scale- and note-reading practice and worksheets with an emphasis on line reading, I recommend my book *A Modern Method for Fingerstyle Guitar.*

14

Music Reading

Teach music reading by talking less and making your students think more.

Exercise: Motivation for Reading Music

Objective: To understand why we learn to read music.

Process: Ask students why they think music reading is important, and, as a class, make a list of the reasons.

Here are fourteen possible benefits of reading music:

- *Increases their ability to learn independently.*
- *Facilitates independent life-long learning.* Students can obtain music books and learn on their own.
- *Enhances their ability to play with others.* Rehearsal time is used more efficiently when group members can read their parts from written music.
- *Provides a visual representation of pitch.* Notation provides a graphic indication of when the melody ascends or descends. This is not the case with tablature.
- *Clarifies rhythmic understanding.* The element of rhythm can be clearly represented through written notation.
- *Accelerates development of aural skills and learning music theory.* By visualizing musical structure through notation, students are prepared to hear and identify intervals.
- *Facilitates transcription from records.* Students are able to write down and analyze music from recordings.
- *Provides tools for composition.* Notation enables musicians to save musical ideas, which can later be extended, transformed, connected, and embellished.

- *Develops intelligence.* Reading music stimulates the brain.
- *Is gratifying.* It is gratifying to learn a new skill and become good at it.
- *Is fun.* Reading music can be recreational, similar to reading a book.
- *Facilitates memory.* Seeing music on the page, and being able to analyze the structure, facilitates memorization.
- *Reduces dependence on memory.* One doesn't need to memorize everything if one can read it.
- *Quantifies learning.* Students can set measurable goals in terms of a number of measures to be learned each day.
- *Allows you to talk less and the students to think more.*

HOW TO TEACH MUSIC READING

It is important to have a teaching strategy that you are confident in. A proven strategy eliminates frustration for your students and for you. The following strategies will accelerate learning and provide satisfying results for the students and for you.

Let's review. Our reading unit began, in the last chapter, with reading readiness, which included:

- developing smooth and speedy scale technique,
- understanding of the musical alphabet forward and backward, and
- understanding the connection of ascending and descending pitch with the scale fingerings on the guitar.

PLAYING, WRITING, AND READING

A powerful concept for learning reading is the sequence of playing, writing, and then reading music.

Step 1: Playing the Notes

To achieve flight, an airplane must achieve a certain speed. Similarly, the instrumentalist must be able to play scales with adequate speed in order for music to flow.

Exercise: Teach E, F, and G on the First String by Fret Number

Objective: Students are able to play three notes smoothly and quickly.
Process:

- Do a posture check.
- On the first string, review the mini-scale 0, 1, 3.
- Using repeated notes, have students echo play some various combinations of 0, 1, and 3, such as
0 0 1 1 3 3 3
0 0 3 3 1 1 3
- Progressively reduce the repeated notes until the class can play patterns such as
0 1 3 1
1 3 1 0
3 1 0 1
- Encourage speed and finger memory by looping and accelerating finger combinations.

Exercise: Converting Fret Numbers to Note Names

Objective: Students connect the alphabet letters to the fingerings they already know.
Process:

- Teach the note names using echo imitation. For example, you say and play, "E E F F G G," and the students echo play the notes while saying their names. Insist that they say the note names while playing them.
- Next, sing the note names, without playing, and have the students play them back to you.
- Go a step further by singing combinations of E F G using syllables such as doo, doo, doo, and have the students play the notes and say their names.

You know the students are successful when:

- they know the fingerings and letter names for notes on the first string
- they can play without looking at their hands
- they play quickly and with an uninterrupted flow.

Step 2: Writing Music

Once the students can play the notes on the first string, they are ready to write the notes that they have been playing.

Exercise: Writing Note Heads on the Staff

Objective: Students memorize notes by writing them.
Process:

- Have students create a reference chart. Starting in the fourth space, write the notes E, F, and G on the overhead, and have students copy it onto their staff paper.
- Explain that these are the symbols for the fingerings that they already have been practicing.
- Have them write the fret numbers just underneath the note heads (0, 1, 3).
- Have them write the string number 1 inside a circle above each note. Teach the word *nomenclature*, which means *musical symbols*.
- Have them write the alphabet letters above the notes.
- Give students your starting note, and then play various combinations of E, F, and G in quarter notes while the students listen. Have them listen and then write the examples on the staff paper. If necessary they can consult the reference chart. They should include the alphabet letters, fingerings, and string numbers. For now, use note heads only.
- Provide the answers so that the students have immediate feedback.

Step 3: Read

- After writing several examples, have the class play the examples. They should read the music from their own handwriting, if possible. An optional preliminary is to recite and sing the note names before playing.
- Students must never look at their fingers while reading music.
- Variation: Use measures from songs you are learning for melodic dictation.

Summary of Playing, Writing, and Reading

- *Playing.* Review the fingerings and the note names on an individual string. Have students create a reference chart of these notes, including fingerings, alphabet letters, and string numbers.

- *Writing.* Play short melodies using the notes, and have students write down what they hear. Students must include the nomenclature. Provide the answers.
- *Reading.* Have student read and play the music that they have just written.

LINE READING

Line reading refers to reading music by observing the musical contour of steps, skips, and leaps. Line reading allows a musician to bypass the process of decoding notation and to simply follow the melodic contour higher or lower. I learned the benefit of line reading firsthand when I was learning to play the viola. The viola is written in the C clef (alto clef), which was unfamiliar to me. Because I had practiced my scales and intervals, once I located the first note, I could read the music by following the line rather than "reading the notes." There are some excellent worksheets for line reading in my book *A Modern Method for Fingerstyle Guitar*.

Exercise: Line Reading at a Glance

Line reading is a fundamental reading concept that is essential for reading success. Decoding the names of the lines and spaces when reading is too slow. Make a comparison to English: which is easier, to individually read the letters R E A D or to, at a glance, read the word *read*?

Objective: Students learn to read groups of notes at a glance.
Process:

- Teach the meaning of *myopia* (tunnel vision) and *peripheral vision.*
- Explain the terms *steps, skips,* and *leaps.*
- Using the overhead, provide students with a starting note, such as E on space 4.
- Cover the overhead, and write a melody on the transparency consisting of three or more notes in stepwise motion.
- Flash the melody on the screen for one second, and quickly cover it again. Instruct students to read the group of notes "at a glance" based on the notes' contour.
- Direct the students to play the melody by memory.
- Repeat the procedure, and progressively get more complex.
- Use this method with excerpts of songs you are working on.

Exercise: Written Analysis of Melodic Contour

Objective: Students perceive melodic motion.
Process:

- Provide students with the music for a song or ensemble that they are working on.
- Have students analyze the example for steps, skips, and leaps.
- Use a pencil to write in arrows and the symbols S (step), SK (skip), and L (leap) to indicate the melodic contour. Later, you can define the distance of the leaps using interval numbers. For example, if there is an ascending leap of a fourth, the students write an L4 with an arrow pointing upward.
- Learn to identify intervals at a glance. As students get more advanced, have them write scales in intervals. For example, first write the C scale, leaving space between the notes. Use hollow note heads. Next, using solid note heads, have the students add the note a fourth higher than each scale tone. Write the fingerings and alphabet letters, and play the examples using repeated notes.

Summary of Line Reading

Read music as you would read words. Using peripheral vision, see groups of notes at a glance. Observe the patterns of steps, skips, and leaps. Avoid reading music one note at a time.

Axiom: Never read individual notes.

INTUITIVE READING

Intuitive reading allows students the opportunity to use their own reasoning to decode music notation. The process is used by the famous Rosetta Stone company to teach foreign languages, and it works equally well for music. It is fun, builds confidence, and can be more effective than using verbal explanations. It is a powerful tool to learn the language of music.

Exercise: Intuitive Learning

Objective: Students use their own intuition to understand notation.
Process:

- Write two short examples on the overhead such as:
  E F G (on the first string)
  G F E

- Play one of the examples, and have students use intuition to determine which one you are demonstrating.
- Use the intuitive process to teach rhythms as well. For example, write two different rhythms, play one of them, and ask the students to decide which one you are demonstrating.
- When you begin using your method book, demonstrate a random measure from a line of music, and have the students hold up their fingers to indicate which measure you played.
- Play two versions of the first measure of a piece, and have students hold up their fingers to tell you which one matched the written music.

Exercise: Intuitive Reading of Rhythms

Objective: Students enjoy the physical movement of strumming while learning to identify and perform rhythm figures.
  Process:

- Using the overhead projector, display a one-measure rhythm example. Include 1 + 2 + 3 + 4 + written under the music and the strum marks above the music.
- Using muted strumming, play two samples. Students use intuition to determine which example is the correct one.
- Using the overhead projector, display a four-measure rhythm example.
- Play one measure from the example, and ask students to use intuition to determine which measure you're playing.
- Play and vocalize the example three different ways:

1. recite the strumming pattern: down, down, down-up, down;
2. recite corresponding *words*: walk, walk, running, walk; and
3. recite the counting: 1 2 3 + 4.

- Loop each measure four times while vocalizing.
- Loop the entire phrase, as written, four times.
- When possible, use rhythms from songs you are learning.

Exercise: Intuitive Reading of Melodies

Objective: Students use intuition to decode melodic notation.
  Process:

- Display one measure of music, or use a measure from a song in your method book.
- Play two examples, one correct and one incorrect, and have students tell you which example matches the music.
- Display four measures of music or a line from a song in your method book.
- Play one of the measures, and ask students to identify which measure you are playing.
- Play the music. Have students loop each measure four times, and then loop the entire phrase four times.
- Tip: *Intermittent looping* means looping each measure four times but inserting a measure of rest between each repetition. This gives students more time to think.

PREREADING

Before jumping into a new song in your method book, it is important to preread the material. The following steps will ensure that your students have an understanding of the music before you play it as a class.

Exercises: Prereading

Objective: Prereading exercises allow students to learn the music before performing it on the instrument.
  Process:

- Using echo imitation, teach the class to sing the words, if applicable.
- Recite the note names as you conduct them in whole notes.
- Chant the rhythm. For example: walk, running, walk, rest.
- Recite steps, skips, and leaps as you conduct them.
- Express the rhythm with body percussion, such as clapping.
- Identify the key tone. For example, how many times does the key tone appear in the first line?
- Identify the highest and lowest notes.
- Identify the number of occurrences of a given reference note. For example, how many times does the note C occur in the first four measures?
- Identify points of interest, such as accidentals or large leaps.
- Perform a melodic analysis: on a separate copy of the music, have students write out the

alphabet letters and fret numbers of the notes. Make sure to always have students create a reference chart before giving this melodic analysis assignment.

• Use intuitive learning examples, or line reading exercises, as previously described.

TEACHING THE STAFF AND MUSICAL SYMBOLS

We have already mentioned that decoding the names of the notes while reading is too slow, and that is why we master the scale and read lines whenever possible. Nonetheless, students need to recognize the lines and spaces instantly, so let them know that this is their goal.

Exercise: Graphic-Arts Design

Objective: Students use visual art to reinforce concepts of the staff.
   Process:

• Open your method books to the page describing the staff and musical symbols.
• Have students imagine that they are applying for a job at a music-publishing company. Their job application requires them to create a sample page for a kid's book that teaches the staff and musical symbols.
• Provide crayons, colored pencils, and markers. Encourage students to use color coding, diagrams, and fun symbols to make the page appealing to kids.
• Use creativity and color to improve on what is presented in the method book.

REFERENCE LINES

Some students will be overwhelmed by the idea of memorizing the five lines and four spaces. To simplify matters, have students memorize one line, such as the middle line, B. They can figure out the rest by knowing the musical alphabet. Here are some ideas for reference notes that students have told me work for them:

• *Line 3.* The middle line of the staff is B.
• *Line 2.* The G line, because it is marked by the G clef.
• *Line 1.* The E line, because it is the first line and because the guitar is tuned to E.

• *Ledger line 1.* The C line is important because C is the center of our musical system.
• *Spaces 1, 2, 3, and 4.* The notes spell the word FACE.
• *Space 3.* This is middle C and, coincidentally, the center of the guitar's range.

ADDITIONAL USEFUL AND FUN READING PRACTICE

Exercise: The Hand-Bell Concept (Interlocking Parts)

Objective: Students learn to follow music and understand one note or two notes.
   Process:

• Assign students to play only one note, such as middle C.
• Review the fingering and the location on the staff of the note.
• The instructor plays the melody but remains silent whenever C occurs, at which time the class plays.
• As students gain more experience, assign more and more notes to them until the teacher doesn't play at all.

Exercise: Dropping Notes

Objective: Students learn how to keep their place even when they cannot perform all the notes.
   Process: Have students play only the first note of each measure while the teacher plays the remainder of the measure.

Exercise: Creating a Reference Chart

Objective: Students create their own chart before doing any written work. Creating the reference chart should be done as a routine, preceding all written work. When proficient, the students can create their chart for the natural-note scale in about sixty seconds.
   Process:
• Write the seventeen natural notes from low E to high G on staff paper (fifteen seconds).
• Add the fingerings 0 1 3 / 0 2 3 / 0 2 3 / 0 2 / 0 1 3 / 0 1 3 below each note head (fifteen seconds).
• Add the string numbers. String numbers are written inside small circles above the notes. For example, above the low E write a 6 inside a circle, and draw a bracket over the F and G to indicate they are also on the sixth string.
• Add the alphabet letters E, F, G, etc.

Exercise: Timing Written Worksheets

Objective: Students can monitor their progress by comparing scores from week to week. Measuring progress in this manner is called *formative assessment*.

Process:

- *Staff.* Students identify notes on a staff by writing the letter names under the notes.
    - Time the exercise. A reasonable goal would be to identify sixty notes in sixty seconds.
    - Students mark their score after sixty seconds. For example, the first week the student may only finish twenty notes in sixty seconds for a score of 20/60. The goal is to improve note recognition until it is instantaneous.
    - Once they mark their score, allow some additional time for working.
- *Fretboard diagram.* Students identify and notate fingerings on a fretboard diagram.
    - Provide a sheet of fretboards with various notes from the natural note scale.
    - Students identify the note by name and notate it on staff paper. (Special paper is provided in the appendix.)
    - Allow approximately two seconds per example.
    - Once students mark their score, allow some additional time for working.

Exercise: Short Reading Opportunities

Objective: Instructor uses short games and puzzles to engage students.

Process:

- *Name that tune.* Place the first phrase of a song on the overhead, and ask students to name the tune.
- *Embedded chords.* Write the natural-note scale on the overhead, and color code the notes of a chord such as C: C E G C E. Have students find the hidden chord.
- *Find the wrong note.* Write a melody or chord on the overhead, and have students find the wrong note.
- *Open-string finger-picking warm-ups.* Notate finger-picking patterns using open strings, and have students decode the pattern.

CHOOSING A METHOD BOOK

A good method book will provide you with sequential melodies for reading practice. The method book will not be enough on its own to hold student's interest. It must be supplemented with ensembles and popular songs. I also recommend using a rhythm method book, such as *Rhythm Vocabulary Chart, Volume 1*, by Ed Sueta (Sueta Music Publications).

A WORD OF CAUTION ABOUT TABLATURE

Tablature is a form notation for the lute that dates back to the Renaissance. In guitar tablature there are six lines, each representing a string. The lowest line represents the sixth string. Numbers are written on the lines to represent frets. Tablature is very useful for a quick start on solo guitar; however, it problematic when teaching music reading. Using the six-line tablature staff simultaneously with teaching the five-line traditional staff will cause confusion. For this reason, I avoid tablature until after students know the staff.

INTERESTING FACTS

- The notes on the bass strings E, A, and D are all written beneath the staff.
- The names of the ledger lines beneath the staff spell FAC(E).
- Middle C is written in space 3. The guitar is written an octave higher than it sounds.
- Middle C is the middle of the guitar range and as such is an important reference note. From low E to middle C is the interval of a thirteenth. From middle C to high A the top of the guitar range is also a thirteenth.

SUMMARY

- Learn to read music without looking at your hands.
- Avoid reading individual notes; rather, read melodic lines when possible.
- In order to read melodic lines, scale passages must flow smoothly and speedily.
- To fully learn the names of the lines and spaces, recite the note names while reading scales or melodies.
- If there are some advanced students who can already read music, have them play all the examples in the fifth position. (The frets for the natural notes in fifth position, starting from the sixth string, are 5 7 8 / 5 7 8 / 5 7 9 / 5 7 / 5 6 8 / 5 7 8. The note names, starting on the sixth string, fifth fret are A B C . . . etc.)

- Avoid using tablature until after students know the traditional staff.
- As students develop reading skills, communicate with them as much as possible through written music. Talk less, and make them think more.
- Practice scales and music reading daily. Precede reading with scales and pointing to notes on the overhead.
- If students can memorize one reference note, they can figure out the rest by knowing the alphabet.
- Students should create a notation reference chart before doing melodic dictation.
- Create a mini-reference chart, and use painter's tape to tape it to the guitar.
- Use staff and grid written worksheets often.
- Make transparencies of songs to give visual cues when reading. For example, use a pointer to point to the music as it progresses.
- Use intuitive learning often.
- When students get lost, have them play in rhythm on the key tone.
- Teach students how to drop notes by playing the first note of each measure.
- Circulate around the room before class starts, and give everyone the two-second assessment, such as instructing them (1) in two seconds to play the natural-note scale or (2) in two seconds to identify and play a note that you point to in the method book.
- Teach and practice *muslish*: make words out of note combinations. For example, pronounce ABCB as if it was one word: Eh-*be*-ce-be (placing the accent on the second syllable).

Exercise: Teaching the Numbers of the Lines and Spaces of the Staff

Objective: Students can locate lines and spaces based on numerical instructions.

Process:

- Explain to students that in order to understand your instructions, they need to know the numbers of the lines and spaces on the staff.
- Display an oversized staff using your overhead projector, and point out the numbers of the lines 1, 2, 3, 4, and 5 from bottom to top.
- Point out that the when the lines run through the middle of a note head, the note head is said to be *on a line*.
- Point out that when the note heads are written between the lines, the note is said to be *in the space*. The spaces are numbered 1, 2, 3, and 4 from the bottom up.

USING THE HUMAN HAND TO TEACH THE STAFF

- Simulate a staff by having the students hold their left hand in front of them so their fingers and thumb are horizontal. The fingers represent the lines, and the space between the fingers represents the spaces.
- Use the index finger of the other hand to point to different locations on the hand staff, and have the student mirror you and recite the letter names of the fingers and space between them.

⑮

Ensembles

Never forget that it's all about the music.

Every classroom may be viewed as an ensemble. Even the simplest melodies from your method book can and should be viewed as ensemble opportunities. For example, look what you can do with "Yankee Doodle":

- introduction with rhythmic string percussion emulating marching drums
- melody alone
- melody with pedal tone (single note or fifths)
- melody with chords
- chords with singing
- chords with violin or flute
- ending with string percussion

Ensembles motivate students by providing the gratification of music making. Ensembles can be played by the entire class, or in small groups. Playing in small groups provides students with the opportunity to create their own arrangements.

The focus of this chapter is developing music reading through the use of ensembles. Written ensembles provide motivation for reading music because the end result sounds great.

PRELIMINARIES

Many of the following exercises I have already mentioned in the previous chapter on reading; even so, I will mention them again here. Before jumping into an ensemble, do some prereading exercises. Effective prereading will create quicker success when you begin playing the piece as a group. In general, students will enjoy more gratification by mastering small excerpts each day than by struggling with the entire piece. You may choose all or some of the following preliminaries.

Exercise: Checklist for Learning New Music

Use this checklist rehearsing the group. These techniques may also be used for individual practice.

Objective: Students develop a methodology for individual practice.

Process:

- Review the scale of the piece. Practice scale loops for speed.
- In a designated phrase:
  o locate the key tone everywhere it occurs;
  o locate the highest note;
  o locate the lowest note;
  o identify the steps, skips, and leaps;
  o locate points of interest, including sharps or flats, leaps, repeat signs, coda, first and second endings, etc.;
  o locate and work out unusual rhythms;
  o play each note as a whole note;
  o play, and loop, measures in whole notes and as written; and
  o loop entire phrases.

Exercises: Ensemble Preliminaries in More Detail

Objective: Students study the musical road map before beginning the musical journey.

Process:

- *Scales.* Practice the scale the piece is written in. Work toward a smooth, light, speedy flow. Loop mini-scales for speed and skill building. Have students practice without looking at their hands. Play the scale ascending and descending, in skips as well as steps.
- *Overhead projector flashcards.* Use a pointer to point to notes in the scale that are used in the piece.

- *Intuition.* Make a transparency of the piece, and put it on the overhead. Cover all but four measures. Play one of the measures, and have students use intuition to identify which measure you are playing. Variation: Cover all but one measure, play two samples, and have students choose the correct one.
- *Group recitation.* Recite the note names. Recite the steps, skips, and leaps.
- *Melodic dictation.*
    o As a routine, have students create a notation reference chart of the natural-note scale with fingerings, string numbers, and note names.
    o Provide students with the first note, and then play a short excerpt from the ensemble. Have the students write the example on staff paper.
    o Provide the answers as you go so that students can have immediate feedback.
    o Have the students play the excerpts they have written. Loop the measures if you feel it is necessary.
- *Rhythm preliminaries.*
    o Using the overhead projector, write a rhythm extracted from the piece.
    o Using an open string, play two samples.
    o Have the students determine which sample is correct.
    o Write a four-measure rhythm extracted from the piece. You may write the counting under the rhythms and the down-up picking pattern above it as a cue.
    o Play one of the measures, and have the students decide which measure you are playing.
    o As a class, loop each measure four times, and then play the entire example as written four times.
    o Add vocalizations, such as "down, down, down/up, down"; "1 2 3 + 4"; or "walk, walk, run-ning, walk."

Exercise: Melodic Analysis

Objective: Students write the fingerings of an ensemble piece.
    Process:

- As a routine, have students create a reference chart of the natural-note scale that includes the note names, fingerings, and strings.

- On their own copy of the piece, have students write the fret numbers and note names for the notes.
- Time the exercise. For example, if the music has sixty notes, the goal would be to complete the work in sixty seconds. Vary the timing requirements based on your class. The goal is to improve from week to week.

LIST OF REHEARSAL TECHNIQUES

- *Measure looping.* Loop each measure four times, and then proceed to the next.
- *Intermittent looping.* Insert a measure of rests between each loop.
- *Echo imitation.* You play a measure, and then the students echo you. ("I play, you play.")
- *Whole-note conversion.* Treat each note as a whole note. To provide additional support, make a transparency of the ensemble piece, and point to each note as students sustain the note in whole notes.
- *Rotating parts.*
    o As a preliminary exercise, have all the students play part 1 while you play part 2. Have students play part 2 while you play part 3, and so forth.
    o Assign each student to a part.
    o After playing a passage, instruct them to rotate parts. For example, the student who played part 1 moves on to play part 2, the student who played part 2 moves on to play part 3, and the student who played part 3 moves on to play part 1.
    o Certain pieces, such as warm-up chorales, give students the opportunity to review the entire range of the guitar in this manner.
- *Silent practice.* When rehearsing a particular part, direct the other parts to practice their left-hand fingerings.

Exercise: Dropping Notes

Objective: Students learn to keep track of measures by playing the first note of each measure only.
    Process:

- Ask students to perform only the first note of each measure and to drop the rest.
- Variation: Have students play beat one as a whole note, and then you play the rest of the measure.

Exercise: Interlocking Parts

Objective: Students will focus and perform one or two notes that can be used later as a reference note. This process is the same as a hand-bell choir.

Process:

- Assign students to one or two notes of a passage.
- Have them follow the music but only play when their note(s) arrives.

Exercise: Reading at a glance

Objective: Students learn to read by viewing the melodic contour at a glance.

Process:

- Write a measure of the ensemble music on a transparency while keeping it out of sight of the students, using a piece of paper to block the light.
- Provide students with the first note of the measure.
- Remove the piece of paper, and flash the measure for one second, and then cover it again. This forces the students to read the contour of the melodic line rather than the notes.
- After viewing the measure for one second, students then must play the measure by memory.

SUGGESTIONS FOR STUDENT-LED GROUP REHEARSALS

Playing in small groups gives the students practice being independent and creative, especially at the high-school level. (At the middle-school level or lower, students may not be capable of independent work). Students may be encouraged to personalize arrangements by adding introductions, percussion, vocals, varying textures, and trying other ideas. Students need and enjoy the independence, but they also need guidance on how to rehearse. Here are some guidelines:

- Have enough members in the group so the group can function if someone is absent. Assigning two people to each part helps ensure success.
- Instruct students to sit in a circle so that they can all see each other.
- Teach the group how to start the song. For example, in common time, the leader counts the group in by saying, "One, two, three, four," and then the group starts together.

- Choose a conductor to start the song and to lead the rehearsal.
- When there are two people to a part, match advanced students with those of lesser experience to encourage more mentoring.
- Carefully decide which parts each student will play.
- Decide on a daily goal of a specific excerpt of the music.
- The leader should guide the group with
  - whole-note conversion,
  - measure looping, and
  - looping groups of measures.
- When necessary, the leader advises the individuals to practice an excerpt individually and then call the group back together. Individuals should learn how to use measure looping and whole-note conversion on their own.
- The instructor may work with an ensemble and ask for demonstrations as an assessment technique.
- Advanced students can be asked to lead sectional rehearsals on specific parts.

SECTIONAL REHEARSALS WITH THE INSTRUCTOR

It is useful to meet with small groups of players who are all working on the same part. Assign an excerpt, such as a four-measure phrase, as the daily goal. While you work with one group, the other students should practice individually. This method allows you to observe everyone up close and is also useful for assessment.

WRITING ENSEMBLES

If you enjoy writing ensemble pieces, I suggest writing in three parts: melody, bass, and one middle part. Since it is predictable, the melody will be the easiest part. The bass will provide practice with ledger lines. The middle part will be unpredictable and therefore require the highest reading skill. If all three parts are connected or bracketed as a system, the students will be able to easily rotate parts. Be sure to include chord symbols and suggested accompaniment ideas. You can write three-part chorales on one staff. Students can play one part at a time or can play several parts at once as a preliminary to solo guitar playing. If you use notation software, you can project the score on a screen while the students listen to the playback. Students are captivated by the technology.

ADDITIONAL IDEAS

- *Use recording or videotaping as a motivation.* Students enjoy listening to themselves and want to succeed.
- *Scrambled seating.* Scrambled seating means that students would sit in trios consisting of all three parts.
- *Sectional seating.* Sectional seating is when all the ones sit in one area, twos in another, and so forth.
- *Espirit de corps.* Teach the class the term *espirit de corps*, which means *the spirit of the group*. Strive to achieve the spirit of the group by performing in synchronicity.
- *Group assessment.* Assess progress toward this goal by mounting an abacus over your white board, and use the beads to score the group on various parameters of ensemble performance. You can obtain an abacus from a toy store. Ensemble parameters include tuning, flow, precision, bass, vocals, form, improvisation, beginning, ending, creativity, etc.
- *Anticipation.* To generate anticipation, give a demonstration of the piece and some historical background. If possible, play recordings of the song. It is especially effective to play recordings of other classes who have successfully performed the piece in the past.
- *Using double stops for successive notes.* Wherever possible, finger two successive notes as an interval (double stop) rather than individually. For example, the low C and E in a C chord can be fingered as a major third, using fingers 3 and 2.

CONCLUDING THOUGHTS

- There are some students who will be lagging behind in reading skills. Where time permits, teach them excerpts by rote, and instruct them to use the music only as a reminder.
- Instruct students to memorize their parts and to use the music only as a reminder.
- Method books alone do not provide the motivation that ensembles do.
- Students will be more gratified by mastering four-measure excerpts per day than by struggling with the entire piece.
- Recording the ensemble provides students with the motivation to perform their best.
- Meeting with sections is a useful assessment technique.
- Distribution of parts deserves careful consideration. Instead of part rotation, allow students with less experience to play the melody and the more advanced students to play the middle voice, which is unpredictable. As they gain confidence and mastery they can move on to other parts.
- If space permits and it is age appropriate, section leaders can lead small-group rehearsals.
- Convert songs in your method book into arrangements by incorporating singers, bass player, lead guitarists, and so forth.

IV

CHORDS AND ACCOMPANIMENTS

How and Why to Teach Power Chords

Power chords are the foundation for barre chords, jazz chords, and bass playing.

The most popular chord in classic rock music is the *power chord*. The power chord is actually not a chord but an interval of a fifth. Learning power chords provides the student with the foundation for learning barre chords, jazz chords, and bass playing.

BENEFITS OF LEARNING POWER CHORDS

- Power chords are relatively easy to play and allow students to experience success quickly.
- Power chords provide the instructor with an opportunity to introduce the concept of intervals.
- The power chord helps to build hand strength and hand positioning.
- E, A, and D power chords can be played by combining an open string with one fingered note and are playable by absolute beginners and remedial students. They help students to learn the names of the strings.
- Open power chords may be used to play blues progressions in the keys of E or A.
- Power chords provide the opportunity to introduce the concept of *moveable forms*. Moveable forms are *fixed fingerings* that may be transposed in a sharp or flat direction by sliding the chord from fret to fret.
- The students will learn the names and locations of the natural notes on the sixth and fifth strings.
- The moveable power chord is the same basic fingering for the root-5 bass pattern.
- The two notes of the moveable power chord are the same two notes from which barre chords are built.

- Playing the blues progression with power chords provides students with the opportunity to practice improvisation.
- Students enjoy inventing their own songs using power chords.

OPEN-POSITION POWER CHORDS

Since power chords consist of the interval of a fifth, they are written with the root name followed by a 5. For example, an A power chord is written A5. The most basic power chords are played in open position and are fingered with a combination of an open string and one finger. Here are the fingerings for E5, A5, and D5:

- E5 is fingered 0/6 and 2/5.
- A5 is fingered 0/5 and 2/4.
- D5 is fingered 0/4 and 2/3.

The remaining open strings are muted with the first finger, which lightly lies across the strings. This is referred to as *left-hand muting*.

Exercise: Playing the Blues in A Using Power Chords

Objective: Students gain immediate gratification by playing a simple progression that requires only one finger.

Process:

- Demonstrate a blues in A using the open power chords. For a good recording, you can compare versions of "Let the Good Times Roll." Versions by Louis Jordan, B. B. King, Ray Charles, Quincy Jones, and Charles Brown are available for download on iTunes. Here is the progression for the blues in A in 4/4 time:

‖ A5 | A5 | A5 | A5 | D5 | D5 | A5 | A5 | E5 |
E5 | A5 | A5 ‖

- Teach the right-hand (RH) part first. Have students practice strumming two strings at a time with their thumb or a pick. To maintain quiet and increase precision, have them mute the strings with their left hand.
- Begin by strumming strings 6 and 5. At your cue, proceed to strings 5 and 4 and finally to strings 4 and 3.
- Teach students the fingering for the A5, D5, and E5 forms. Explain that the lowest note will be the *root* or naming tone of the power chord.
- Using verbal cues, teach them the blues in A as indicated earlier.
- Add words to blues classics such as "Hound Dog Blues," "Kansas City Blues," "Route 66," "Shake, Rattle, and Roll," and "Let the Good Times Roll." Research and discuss the cultural and geographic significance of these songs.
- Encourage the advanced students to model improvisation.

Exercise: *The Interval of a Fifth*

Objective: Students learn how numbers are used to indicate the distance between two notes.
   Process:

- Have students finger the two notes of the A5 power chord, A and E. Ask the students to listen; then demonstrate, and say, "A, E, echo me."
- The students echo, "A, E."
- Sing the following scale degrees, and have the students echo you: 1, 2, 3, 4, 5 . . . 1—5.
- Play the A power chord again so that students connect the sound of the chord with the numbers 1 and 5.
- Explain that A is the main note of the chord, the root.

Exercise: *The Boogie Variation of Blues in A*

Objective: Students build strength in their third finger.
   Process:

- Have students finger an A5 chord using the open A string and first finger on 2/4 (second fret/fourth string).
- While leaving the first finger down, add the third finger on 4/4 to create the following fret pattern:

2 2 4, 2 2 4, 2 2 4, 2 2 4, etc.
- Check to be sure that the left elbow is hanging in close to the body and that the palm is parallel to the neck. The wrist will be arched and the first finger lying across the strings, muting them as already mentioned (left-hand muting).
- Use the same fingering for the D5 and E5 chords.
- Play the blues in A using the boogie pattern.

Exercise: *The Embellished Boogie of Blues in A*

Objective: Students gain strength in the pinky of their left hand.
   Process:

- Have students silently finger the A5 power chord.
- Using fingers 1, 3, and 4 on the fourth string, play the following fret pattern:
2 2 4 4 5 5 4 4, 2 2 4 4 5 5 4 4, etc.
- Use the same fingering for the D5 and E5 chords.
- Play the blues in A using the embellished boogie pattern.

MOVEABLE POWER CHORDS

Moveable power chords contain no open strings. Therefore, the guitarist can change chords by sliding them from fret to fret, or *transposing* them. The first step in learning moveable power chords is to review left-hand position.

HAND POSITION FOR POWER CHORDS

Because of the stretch involved, power chords provide a good opportunity to explore hand position. For our discussion, we will use a C5 chord with the root on the eighth fret of the sixth string. The C5 is fingered 8/6, 10/5. It is easier to begin the study of a moveable power chord higher on the neck. This is because the frets are closer together and there is less reach involved.

- Be sure the neck of the guitar is elevated. The thumb of the left hand should be near the bottom side of the neck.
- The first finger should be resting flat on the neck, tip on 8/6, and pointing toward the ceiling. This allows the third finger to drop on 10/5 without strain. Students with small hands may use fingers 1 and 4.

- Allowing the index finger to rest on the strings mutes them and enables the guitarist to strum without sounding unwanted notes.
- If the fingers don't reach, it's probably due to the position of the thumb and angle of the neck. If the fingers aren't reaching, lay the left hand flat on the neck like a pancake, with the thumb near the bottom of the neck. Then relax into the power chord.

Exercise: Descending Power Chords

Objective: Students progressively extend their stretching ability.

Process:

- Finger the C5 power chord in eight position (8/6, 10/5), and chromatically move toward the nut.
- Silently pulse four times, and then shift to the left, and repeat.
  C C C C, B B B B, B♭, etc.
- Continue descending until you reach F5 (1/3, 3/5).

Exercise: Playing Natural Notes on the Sixth and Fifth Strings

Objective: Students learn where the root notes are for power chords based on the sixth and fifth strings.

Process:

- Have students memorize the B/C E/F rule, which states that there are two frets between every note, except between B and C and between E and F. This rule is essential to many other skills on the guitar and should be memorized and applied frequently. Have the students recite and memorize the B/C E/F rule.
- Using only the first finger of the left hand, play the natural notes on the sixth string.
- Use repeated notes, and recite the note names as you play, E E E E F F F F, and remember that there are two frets between every note, except between B and C and between E and F. Introduce the terms *steps* and *half-steps* if appropriate.
- After playing the natural notes up to the twelfth fret and back down, ask students to locate notes in random locations.
- At a later date, repeat the process on the fifth string.

Exercise: The Natural-Note Scale in Power Chords

Objective: Students place power chords on natural-note root tones.

Process:

- Beginning with F5, use repeated notes to play the power chords on the natural notes up the sixth string: F5, G5, A5, B5, C5, D5. Play each chord four times.
- At a later date, repeat the process, beginning with B5 on the fifth string: B5, C5, D5, E5, F5, G5.
- Later in the semester, combine root-6 and root-5 power chords by crossing over at the fifth fret from A5 (root-6) to B5 (root-5).
- Play blues progressions using power chords.
- Invent exercises to practice crossing from root-6 to root-5.

Exercise: Composing with Power Chords

Objective: Students exercise creativity and exploration while improving their skill with power chords.

Process: Have students team up and write a short popular-style song using moveable power chords.

THE THREE-NOTE POWER CHORD

As a stepping-stone to playing barre forms it is a good idea to incorporate the three-note power chord into exercises and songs. A three-note F5 power chord is configured 1/6, 3/5, 3/4. The fingering is 1 3 4. The fingering is the same for root-5 forms.

RECORDED EXAMPLES

Use iTunes to purchase and play recordings of songs using power chords. Some examples are "Joy to the World" by Three Dog Night, "Fortunate Son" by Creedence Clearwater Revival, "Jet Airliner" by Steve Miller, "Sunshine of Your Love" by Cream, "Born to Be Wild" by Steppin Wolf, and "Wild Thing" by Jimi Hendrix.

17

Playing Bass

Playing a root-bass exercise familiarizes students with the chord progressions of songs.

THE BENEFITS OF TEACHING BASS

- Remedial students may not have the finger coordination to play chords on the guitar.
- Some students want to be bass players.
- Students learn about the construction of major and minor chords and about the interval of a fifth.
- Bass plays an important part in ensembles.
- Students learn the natural notes on the E, A, D, and G strings up to the twelfth fret.
- Strumming is improved when the student knows where the root of the chord is.
- Playing a root-bass exercise familiarizes students with the chord progressions of songs.

There are five basic bass patterns covered in this chapter. They are identified as intervals. They are:

- root-bass,
- root-5
- 1-3-5-3
- 1-♭3-5-♭3
- boogie bass

THE ROOT-BASS

The most fundamental bass line is the *root-bass*. The root-bass consists of locating and playing the roots of chords. The root-bass helps students to ingrain the location of the natural notes and is a good supplement to note reading. Students who are unable to play chords can find satisfaction playing the root-bass.

Exercise: The Root-Bass

Objective: Students perform the roots of chords.
  Process:

- Recite the chord changes for a song.
- Locate the roots of the chords on the bass strings 6, 5, and 4.
- Play the roots of a song using various rhythms.
- If you are playing with a drum machine, try to match the rhythm with the bass-drum part.

CONVERTING POWER CHORDS INTO THE ROOT-5 BASS

The power chord, which consists of a root and a fifth, may be converted into a root-5 bass pattern by alternating the notes rather than playing them at the same time. This is called the *root-5 bass*.

Exercise: Using Power Chords to Play a Root-5 Bass Part

Objective: Students play bass lines by embellishing power chords.
  Process:

- Select a song such as "Wayfarin' Stranger" or "El Condor Pasa" in which each chord lasts several measures. Blues progressions are also an excellent choice for practice.
- Review the natural notes on the sixth and fifth string up to the twelfth fret. (Review the B/C E/F rule: There are two frets between every note except between B and C and between E and F.)
- Locate the roots of the song. At first it is easiest to play all the roots on the sixth string. Add

the fifth string at a later date, and then combine the two.
- Do a posture check. Be sure the neck is elevated and thumb of the left hand is on the bottom side of the neck.
- Transform each root into a power chord (root-5). For example, the G root 3/6 will be converted to a G5 power chord: 3/6, 5/5.
- Convert the power chords into the root-5 pattern. The root-5 pattern for a measure of common time would look something like this: root-rest-5-rest.
- Play the root-5 pattern for the song progression.

Exercise: Teaching the 1-3-5-3 Arpeggio

Objective: The 1-3-5-3 finger pattern provides an excellent hand workout and helps attune students' ears to the sound of a major chord.

Process:

- Use echo imitation to sing 1-2-3-4-5, 1-3-1, 1-5-1, and 1-3-5. Reinforce the concept by using hand gestures for the steps of a ladder.
- Relate the pattern to the fingering of a G chord. Have students silently finger a standard G chord. Point out that the two lowest notes of the chord (G and B) will serve as a *fixed-finger position*. In other words, the shape of the first and second fingers will be maintained, even as the finger formation is transposed from fret to fret.
- Do a posture check. In order to reach all the notes the neck must be elevated and the left hand thumb on the underside of the neck.
- Starting from the fixed position (3/6, 2/5), have student silently pulse their pinky on the fifth fret (5/5). In other words, alternate the pinky on, off, on, off, etc. Adjust the hand and palm position until the fingers reach comfortably.
- Using repeated notes, play the arpeggio as follows: G-B-D-B. Gradually reduce the repeated notes. (Frets: 3/6, 2/5, 5/5, 2/5; fingers: 2-1-4-1.)

- Take a practice pause, and circulate through the room to assist students as necessary.
- Play a blues progression in the key of G using the 1-3-5-3 pattern. The roots are all located on the sixth string:
  G third fret
  C eighth fret
  D tenth fret
- Tip: Since the frets are closer together higher on the neck, the finger pattern (2-1-4-1) is easier to play if you start on the tenth fret. As a warm-up, play the 1-3-5-3 bass pattern by descending chromatically, starting on the tenth fret. Use repeated notes.
- If there is interest, teach the 1 ♭3 5 ♭3 for minor chords. The frets, starting on low G, are 3/6, 6/6, 5/5, 6/6. The fingering is 1-4-3-4.
- If there is interest, teach the boogie-bass pattern: 1-3-5-6-♭7-6-5-3. Here are the frets, starting with the second finger on low G: 3/6, 2/5, 5/5, 2/4, 3/4, 2/4, 5/5, 2/5. Since there are no open strings, the pattern is moveable and can be used for any chord.

CONCLUDING THOUGHTS

- Students should develop proficiency in playing these patterns based on any root.
- These five patterns can be embellished with neighboring scale tones.
- Students interested in lead guitar should transpose the patterns into the treble range of the guitar and use them as a basis for improvisation.
- Encourage students to embellish the patterns with creative rhythms.
- The heartbeat rhythm, which is a dotted quarter followed by an eighth note, is a common bass rhythm. Later, you can refer to the heartbeat rhythm when teaching the dotted-quarter/eighth-note figure.

⑱

Teaching Chords

Discover the weight of the string and the distance needed to push it.

The rhythmic energy that is used for strumming chords helps to fulfill a student's need for physical movement during the school day. Although simple chord fingerings may be introduced almost immediately, younger students will benefit from treating the guitar as a melody instrument for a significant amount of time before learning chords. Some teachers prefer teaching melodies before introducing chords. There are four reasons for doing this:

- Students have time to develop hand dexterity.
- Students learn the locations of notes, which will be combined later to form chords.
- Students can give their full attention to reading music without having to learn chords at the same time.
- Proficiency with chords can be a disincentive for learning to read music.

I personally like to start chords as soon as possible because strumming and singing provides immediate gratification. You must decide for yourself what approach works best in your situation. The purpose of this chapter is to provide you with strategies for helping students fully learn chord fingerings. I address chord-changing strategies in chapter 20 on chord progressions.

SUMMARY OF CHORD TYPES BY LEVEL

Semester 1

- open power chords
- moveable power chords
- open-position chords
- introduction of barre forms

Semester 2

- proficiency on barre forms
- passing chords, such as G/B (G with B in the bass)
- triads on the treble strings
- embellished chords, such as sus4, maj7, and add9

Second Year

- blues chords, namely 9th and 13th chords
- jazz chords, namely root-6 and root-5
- ukulele forms, namely four-string moveable forms
- chord theory
- fretboard diagrams

Fretboard diagrams, sometimes referred to as *chord grids*, are the format in which chords are presented in most method books. Your method book will contain diagrams for all the basic chords you will need. You can use your overhead projector to explain to students how to read a chord grid:

- The six vertical lines represent the six strings. The bass strings are on the left.
- The horizontal lines represent the frets.
- The top line, which is usually thicker, represents the nut.
- The dots or circles indicate where to place the fingers.
- X's placed above a string indicate that these strings are not to be strummed.
- O's placed above a string indicate an open string.
- The fingers are indicated with numbers located above the strings, or in some books on the frets.

Exercise: Drawing a Large-Scale Fretboard Diagram

Objective: Students fully absorb the concept of a fretboard diagram by creating their own drawing.
   Process:

- Pass out blank paper and crayons, colored pencils, or markers.
- Tell students they are applying for a job at a publisher. As part of the application they are to design a one-page, large-scale, color-coded drawing that explains a fretboard diagram.

IDENTIFYING STRINGS AND FINGERS BY NUMBER

In order for you to give verbal instructions, students must be able to identify the strings and fingers by their number.

- The fingers of the left hand, starting with the index, are numbered 1, 2, 3, and 4.
- The strings are numbered 6, 5, 4, 3, 2, and 1, starting with the bass.

Exercise: Reinforcing the Names of Frets, Fingers, and Strings

Objective: Students are able to understand verbal fingering instructions.
   Process:

- Have students hold up their left hand and wiggle fingers 1, 2, 3, and 4 as you give verbal instructions.
- Place the fretboard diagram for a C chord on the overhead, and guide students in placing their fingers in the appropriate place. Circulate through the room, and use a conductor's baton to point to the various fingers, frets, and strings.
- Engage the students by having them answer or follow the questions and directions below regarding a C chord:
   The third finger is on the third fret of what string? (Fifth)
   The second finger is on what fret of the fourth string? (Second)
   The first fret is being played on the second string by which finger? (First)
   Wiggle the finger that is on the third fret of the fifth string. (Third)
- Repeat the process for different chords.

FULLY ABSORBING CHORD FORMS DURING GROUP INSTRUCTION

The following exercises are some effective ways to best learn chord forms in the classroom.

Exercise: Gauging the Pressure and the Distance

Objective: Students discover the weight of the string and the distance needed to push it.
   Process:

- Students silently finger a C chord. Instruct them not to press on the strings. In other words, the fingers are at rest in the C-chord position.
- Pulse and then release one finger at a time, and pay attention to the weight and distance. The remaining fingers should remain passive, at rest on the strings.
- Repeat the process by silently pulsing each finger and then the entire chord.

Exercise: Fingers-On, Fingers-Off

Objective: Students learn to move the fingers all at the same time.
   Process:

- Place the fingers in a C-chord formation.
- Lift the fingers the smallest possible distance, and then set them back down on the chord as a unit.
- Repeat this pulsing action, progressively lifting the fingers further from the strings.
- Have students pulse the chord thirty times in thirty seconds.
- Variation: Strum a chord for four beats, and then strum the open strings for four beats. Progressively reduce the number of strums on the open strings. For example, where O means *off*: C C C C, O O O O, C C O O, C O C O
- Variation: Use this same process to practice changing between two chords. For example: C C C C, O O O O, G G G G, O O O O, C C O O, G G O O, C O G O
- Gradually reduce the number of open strums.

Exercise: Bumping the Frets

Objective: Students practice placing their fingers close to the frets.
   Process:

- Students finger the C chord.

- Have them slowly slide their fingers toward the fret until the fingers bump the fret. Make a comparison to a car tire bumping a curb.
- A good way to remember the contact point for the finger and the fret is to tell them to feel the steel.
- If the finger is too far from the fret, there will be a buzzing sound. If the finger is too close to the fret, the sound will be muted.

Exercise: Out Home, Up Home, and In Home

Objective: The students learn the chords while developing finger independence and strength.
Process:

- Students rest their fingers silently on a C chord. This is home position.
- Leave all fingers in place, except the third finger.
- Extend the third finger out and away from the palm, and then return it to home position.
- Lift the third finger up, and then return it to home position.
- Curl the third finger in toward the palm, and then return it to home position.
- When performing this exercise as a class, you may recite "Out, home, up, home, and in, home.

Exercise: Ingraining through Transposition

Objective: Students learn to maintain a chord form while sliding it higher or lower on the neck.
Process:

- Transposition may be used for any chord form, but it is especially useful with the E, A, and D chords. The E and A chords foreshadow barre forms, and the D chord foreshadows triads.
- Have students finger the E chord, which is configured 2 2 1, starting on the fifth string.
- Practice pulsing the chord in tempo. In other words, squeeze and release the chord without leaving the strings.
- Silently pulse the chord four times, and then slide up the neck (to the right) by one fret.
- Continue pulsing and shifting as you move up the neck.
- As a preliminary to barre chords and triads, repeat this process using E and E minor, A and A minor, and D and D minor.
- Variation: Repeat the transposition exercise, and recite the names of the chords. For example: E E E E, F F F F, F# F# . . . etc.

Exercise: Pin the Tail on the Donkey

Objective: Students practice visualizing chord forms.
Process:

- Students let their left hand hang by their side.
- Ask them to visualize a C chord.
- In one continuous movement, without looking, they should bring the hand to the guitar and finger the C chord.
- Then instruct them to look at the chord and make any necessary corrections.
- Repeat.

Exercise: Chords and Rhythm Reading

Objective: Students practice new chords while reading rhythms.
Process:

- Teach the students a new chord.
- Using the overhead projector, have the students strum designated rhythm figures.

Exercise: Chord Embellishment

Objective: Students find ways to add fingers and harmonic color to basic chords.
Process:

- Strum a C chord in quarter notes.
- Add the pinky on and off of the third fret of the second string (3/2) every four beats. This is the ninth scale degree, and the chord is Cadd9.
- Lift the first finger on and off of the second string every four beats. This is Cmaj7.
- Add the pinky on and off of 3/4 every four beats. This is a Csus4 chord.
- If appropriate, you may explore the idea of scale degrees by echo singing the intervals of the notes you just added (Cadd9, Cmaj7, Csus4).
- Repeat using other chords.

Written Exercise: Create a Grid Reference Sheet

Objective: Students better grasp chord forms by drawing them.
Process:

- Pass out a sheet of blank chord grids, and have the students make their own reference sheet by copying the one from your method book. Drawings must include the X's, O's, and finger numbers.

- Color code the roots.
- Have students organize the chords in an order that has meaning for them.
- Quiz Variation: Have students fill in the blank grids without using the book.

Written Exercise: Convert Grids to Notation

Objective: Students make a connection between chord fingering and notation.
   Process:

- As a routine preliminary, have students create a reference chart by notating the natural-note scale, including the fingerings, the strings, and the alphabet note names.
- Provide students with the diagram of a chord, and have them notate the chord in block (vertical) and arpeggio form. (I have provided grid and staff paper for this purpose in the appendix.)
- Play the examples after writing them.

Written Exercise: Conversion of Notation to Grids

Objective: Students learn to identify chords in their notated form.
   Process:

- Pass out a sheet of blank chord grids.
- On the overhead projector notate a written arpeggio for a chord.
- Have the students draw the diagram for the chord using the grid paper. Be sure to include the X's, O's, and finger numbers.

Exercise: Name This Chord

Objective: Students learn what chords look like in their notated form.
   Process:

- One note at a time, notate a chord on the overhead projector.
- Have students finger the notes as you add them.
- Students name the chord when enough information is provided.
- Play the examples.

Exercise: Chords Embedded in Scales

Objective: Students visualize the relationship between the scale and a chord.
   Process:

- Write a scale on the overhead projector. Use a separate color for the notes of a given chord.
- Have students identify the chord.

THE IMPORTANCE OF PRACTICE PAUSES

After you communicate the finger position for chords, it is a good idea to take a practice pause to give students time to practice the chord. Circulate through the room, and assists students with hand position and fingerings. As you find students who are proficient, assign them to teach the students around them. Practice pauses provide informal assessment opportunities for the instructor.

INSURING SUCCESS FOR ALL STUDENTS

The instructor must provide a framework for students to succeed. Since students in guitar class can vary greatly in their ability, you must encourage students to create their own variations for success.

   Axiom: Students must find some way to participate and be successful. Here are some examples of several options that are available when strumming chords:

- Play chords using only the first three strings, such as a C with only one finger, 1/2.
- Finger chords, but don't strum.
- Finger only the roots of the chords.
- Strum the muted strings for rhythm practice, but don't finger the chords.
- Follow the music as it is played, pointing to the notation.
- Sing without playing.
- Use the guitar as a percussion instrument by lightly drumming on it.

THE CAPO: ADAPTATION FOR SMALL HANDS

If students' fingers are not large enough to play chord forms, place a capo on the seventh fret, and have them finger the chords there. The strings will be closer to the neck, and the frets are closer together. Progressively, over weeks, move the capo toward the nut.

REVIEWING SCALES TO HELP WITH CHORDS

When students master scales, shifting chords becomes much easier. I have never seen a student who was proficient with scales who could not change chords. A reasonable goal for scales is sixteenth notes at 120 beats per minute. A professional goal is sixteenth notes at 160 beats per minute.

MUTING CHORDS

At the end of chord drills, students will want to continue to strum their guitars. For this reason it is im-portant, as a routine, to practice making silence by muting the instrument. At the last strum of a song or drill, instruct the students to "Stop, mute, and rest." Place the bottom of the right hand over the bridge, and slowly turn the hand counterclockwise. This helps the chord fade out in a musical way.

19

Strumming

String percussion develops precision because the rhythms are easier to hear.

Students enjoy the physical and rhythmic activity of strumming. Guitar teachers should take advantage of students' natural desire for physical activity by using unpitched strumming exercises to focus attention, teach rhythm, and improve listening skills.

BENEFITS OF STRING PERCUSSION

One of the biggest challenges to the classroom teacher is creating rhythmic precision to a large group. String percussion is useful for developing precision because the rhythms are easier to hear. To do this, have students mute their strings by gently wrapping their left hand around the neck. This enables them to strum on the muted strings, which creates what I call a *marching-band effect*. Strumming like a marching band challenges the students to strum and listen to others at the same time. Rhythm warm-ups done in this manner are an excellent way to grab the students' attention at the beginning of class. Let's first look at how to teach the physical motion of strumming.

THE STRUMMING STROKE

Exercise: Shaking Off Water Droplets

Objective: Students relate strumming to a natural motion.
> **Process:**

- Have students hold their right hand in front of them. Let the hand hang limp, like a wilted flower.

- With the hand relaxed, have them pretend that they are shaking off water. This relaxed, repetitive flicking motion is very similar to the motion of strumming.
- Next, create the flicking motion in time to a beat. Have the students recite "One, two, three, four," as they strum the air. Point out that they are now conducting the beat.
- To gain control, have them reduce the length of their strokes so that they are only a few inches. Most strumming motion results from a rotation of the forearm. Strumming downward is called a *downstroke*, and strumming upward is called an *upstroke*.
- Add a foot tapping to the strumming motion, and imagine there is a string connecting the fingers to the toes.
- Finally, add a subtle, almost imperceptible, movement of the chin. As the hand and foot go down, so will the chin. The goal is to use body movement to reinforce the momentum of the beat.

MIRROR, ECHO, AND OVERLAPPING IMITATION

Now that students are comfortable strumming, they are ready to learn through echo imitation, overlapping imitation, and mirror imitation. It may be helpful to practice the following teaching techniques with a friend before trying them with the entire class.

Exercises: Imitation-Style Warm-Ups

Objective: Students can learn rhythm patterns by listening, observing, and doing.
> **Mirror-Imitation Process:** With strings muted, play some simple rhythms, and have the students copy what you are playing.

Echo-Imitation Process:

- With strings muted, play a one-measure rhythm, and have the students respond by echoing.
- Start simply, and gradually add complexity. Maintain a steady tempo.
- Include rests, which are performed with silent strums. For example, a quarter note followed by quarter rests would be: strum, miss, strum, miss. A whole rest would be: miss, miss, miss, miss.

Overlapping-Imitation Process:

- Start a simple pattern, and have the students copy you.
- Instruct them to continue the rhythm while you overlap a contrasting rhythm.
- When you say, "Switch," have them switch to the new rhythm you just demonstrated.
- At this point, you can return to the basic beat in quarter or eight notes or to another rhythm of your choice.
- Gradually get more complex. For example, the students may be playing quarter notes on beats one and three, and you may be playing quarter notes on beats two and four, or else they might be playing downbeats while you are playing upbeats.

Exercise: *Drum-Set Composite Rhythms*

Objective: Students develop independence by playing different parts of a drumbeat.
  Process:

- Divide the class into two or three groups.
- Use mirror imitation to teach group 1 the bass-drum part (beats 1 and 3).
- Teach group 2 the snare-drum part (beats 2 and 4).
- Teach group 3 the cymbal part (1 + 2 + 3 + 4 +).
- Use songs that you are working on as a basis for this exercise.

Exercise: *Alternating the Beat and Rhythm*

Objective: Students play and understand the difference between *beat* and *rhythm*.
  Process:

- Discuss the difference between beat and rhythm. The beat is the steady pulse, like a heartbeat. The rhythm is like the words, such as *jin-gle bells, jin-gle bells*.

- Use mirror imitation to direct half the class in playing the beat.
- Use mirror imitation to direct the other half of the class in performing a rhythm pattern.
- Ask students to notice the synchronization of the beat and the rhythm.
- Switch parts.

Exercise: *Converting the Beat into Rhythm*

Objective: Students obtain the skill necessary to perform the beat and rhythm simultaneously.
  Process:

- Perform the beat in eighth notes on muted strings.
- Add a vocalization of a rhythm pattern while continuing to strum the beat. The vocalizations can be sung in different ways:
  Stroke directions. Down, down-up, down-up, down
  Counting. One, two-and, three-and, four
  Vocal percussion. Boom, chick-y, chick-y, chick
  Words. Walk, run-ning, run-ning, walk
- Students listen to where the beat and rhythm intersect.
- Add accents that match the vocalizations.
- Convert the accents into the new rhythm.

Exercise: *Selective Strumming*

Objective: Students practice small strumming strokes.
  Process:

- Perform a strumming pattern, such as "1 2 + 3 4 +" on the first string.
- When the students have achieved the ability to play the rhythm on one string, have them progressively add one string at a time until they are strumming all six strings.
- Variation: Begin the process on the sixth string instead of the first.

Exercise: *Silent Strumming*

Rhythm patterns are created not only by strumming the strings, but also by missing them.
  Axiom: The strumming hand maintains a constant up-and-down motion, regardless of the rhythm.
  Objective: Students learn to feel the rests by performing silent strokes.
  Process:

- Use echo imitation to teach rhythms containing rests.
- Have students use vocalizations, such as "Down-up, miss, down-up, miss."
- As students get comfortable with the constant motion of the hands, add more complex rhythms, such as a dotted quarter note. For example:
  down, *miss*-up, down, miss (1 [2] + 3 4)

ACCURACY WITH BASS NOTES

Frequently strum patterns include individual bass notes. There are a couple of ways to help students gain accuracy picking individual bass notes:

- Brace the right hand by allowing the ring finger of the right hand to rest on the high-E string, as the thumb plucks the bass note.
- When aiming for the A string, aim between the E and A strings. The left side of the thumb may briefly touch the E string to help sense its location.

Exercise: Combine Two Groups to Play the Root Strum Pattern

Objective: Students learn to view strumming as two distinct parts—bass and chords.
   Process:

- Practice strumming the following treble string grouping:
- E, BE, GBE, DGBE
- Practice plucking individual bass strings.
- Divide the class into two groups. Have one group play the bass note as a whole note, and have the other half play "rest, strum, strum, strum" on the treble strings. Listen carefully to the sound of the sustained bass note combined with the strumming.
- Switch parts.
- Variation: Apply the composite root strum pattern to chords and progressions.

Exercise: Seamless Transition from Downstrokes to Upstrokes

Objective: Students develop confidence switching from downstrokes to upstrokes.
   Process:

- Have the class strum together: down-up, down-up (alternate strumming).

- Recite "Down-up, down-up. . . ."
- Add accents to the upstrokes without changing the tempo.
- Gradually fade out the downstrokes until students are playing only upstrokes on the upbeats.
- Gradually fade in the downstrokes until even eighth notes are resumed.
- Fade out the upstrokes to create quarter notes with all downstrokes.
- Experiment with composite rhythms. When students play downstrokes, you play upstrokes; when students play upstrokes, you play downstrokes.

Exercise: Converting Lyrics into Strum Exercises

Objective: Students strum the rhythm of lyrics.
   Process:

- With muted strings, play muted eighth notes.
- Recite a phrase from the lyrics while continuing to strum the beat. For example, recite, "Rock my soul in the bosom of Abraham," while strumming the beat.
- Notice the synchronization of the words and the strokes.
- Add strumming accents to match the words.
- Using a combination of strokes and misses, play only the accented strokes.
- The rhythm for "Rock my soul in the bo-som of A-bra-ham" would be: down, down, down, down-up, down-up, down-up, miss-up, down.

Exercise: Reading Strum Patterns Intuitively

Objective: Students use intuition to read strumming patterns.
   Process:

- Notate two written strum patterns on the overhead projector.
- Play one example, and have students choose which notated pattern it matches.
- Variation: Notate one written example, and play two different rhythms. Students choose which rhythm matches the notated example.

Written Exercise: Adding the Downstroke and Upstroke Markings to Written Rhythms

Objective: Students synchronize downstrokes with downbeats and upstrokes with upbeats.
   Process:

- Write 1 + 2 + 3 + 4 + on a piece of paper.
- Align a rhythm pattern above the numbers.
- Have students add the symbols for downstrokes and upstrokes in the appropriate place above the numbers. Explain that strokes occurring above the numbers 1, 2, 3, and 4, will always be downstrokes, while strokes occurring above the plus signs will always be upstrokes.
- Play the examples using muted strumming.
- Variation: As students become more advanced, have them add the counting numbers underneath a rhythm and then add the strum markings.
- Variation: Have them write the numbers 1 + 2 + 3 + 4 +, and give them rhythm dictation. Have them add the rhythms above the numbers and then add the strum markings. Play the examples.

Exercise: Working with the Metronome

For group metronome work I use a drum machine amplified through a stereo system. Many inexpensive electric keyboards contain drumbeats that work well and can be plugged in to an amplifier.

Objective: Students practice keeping a steady beat.
Process:

- Have students play a strumming rhythm in time with a drumbeat.
- Fade the drum machine down to silence for two counts, and challenge the class to retain the tempo until you fade the drum back in.
- Progressively fade the drum out for longer durations. The class must strive to maintain a perfect tempo in order to match the beat when you fade the drum back in.

STYLISTIC STRUM PATTERNS

Most method books will cover the basic strum patterns. Devise strum patterns based on the beats of your drum machine. My book *Guitar Essentials* (available at www.guitarmusicman.com) contains a listing of popular strumming and finger-picking patterns. Here are some examples: the Carter strum, the Hotel California strum, the shuffle, the Susie Q, the rumba, the bolero, the wood chopper, and the We Will Rock You.

20

Chord Progressions

The goal is thirty or more silent chord transitions in thirty seconds.

We have already looked at how to thoroughly learn a single chord. This chapter addresses changing from chord to chord.

RELATIVE SHAPES: THE FIRST THREE CHORDS—F, C, AND G

The first three chords I recommend teaching are F, C, and G. These three chords are used in a large number of songs. The abbreviated forms of these chords all have relative shapes, and they are easy to finger and remember. Once the students learn the easy F, they can think of the C and G as modifications of the F fingering. The easy F is actually Fmaj7, and the easy G is actually G6. Examine the nearly identical fingerings:

Easy F x x 3 2 1 0
C x 3 2 0 1 0
Easy G 3 2 0 0 0 0

COMMON FINGER

When two chords have a finger in common, leave the common finger in place when switching chords. The common finger serves as a brace or reference finger. Good examples include changing from major to relative minor: C-Amin, G-Emin, F-Dmin.

GLIDING FINGER

There are occasions when two chords may be connected by a finger that glides up or down on a string. Some refer to this as *the common finger/common string technique*. Others refer to it as *riding the rail*. Although there are only a few of these in beginning guitar, there are more as the student progresses. A simple example would be changing from an E-minor chord to an F chord. Notice that the third finger on the fourth string glides from the second fret to the third fret. Note the underlined fingers below:

E minor 0 2 2 0 0 0
F x x 3 2 1 0

Exercise: Silent Repetition

Objective: Students learn motion through rapid, silent repetition.
   Process:

- Perform these movements with the minimum motion necessary.
- At first students may look at their hands. As soon as possible, they must practice without looking at their hands and focus their attention on the feeling of the motion.
- Have the students gauge the pressure and gauge the distance for the easy F chord by pulsing and releasing the chord thirty times. The fingers should not leave the string.
- Visualize the transition from F to C.
- Silently, make the transition from F to C as many times as possible within thirty seconds without strumming.
- When shifting from chord to chord, the fingers move laterally. In other words, the fingertips barely leave the strings.
- The goal is thirty or more silent chord transitions in thirty seconds.

Exercise: The Preparation Gesture

In order to change chords, the guitarist must begin to move the fingers slightly before the new chord occurs. This is referred to as the *preparation gesture*.

Objective: Students start the chord change a half beat before the new chord.
Process:

- Strum the C chord, and count 1 + 2 + 3 + 4 +.
- On the *and* of beat 4, relax the fingers.
- The releasing of pressure in this manner should become automatic. You may cue students by saying, "Lift, set." Fingers should not leave the strings yet.
- Now, loop two measures of C and two measures of F. Continue releasing the finger pressure on the *and* of beat 4 as before.
- When it is time to change chords, the fingers will start their motion a half beat in advance of the chord change.
- Note: This releasing gesture also reduces hand fatigue.

USING THE CIRCLE-OF-FIFTHS KEY RELATIONSHIP

The primary chords in the key of C are C, F, and G. The next key in the circle is the key of G, whose chords are G, C, and D. Notice that we can play the new key by adding only one chord, D. Since C and A minor and G and E minor are almost identical shapes, the learning order could be F, C-Amin, G-Emin, D, A, E, B7.

Taking the concept of common shapes one step further, a logical approach to the teaching order of open-position chords is F, C-Amin-E; G-Emin-easy A; D-A7; easy B7-D7; easy Dmin-Amin7-E7.

Exercise: The Blues Progression in Five Major Keys

Objective: Students absorb chords seamlessly playing through the blues in five keys.
Process:

- Review chords F, C, G, D, A, E, and B7.
- Play the blues in the key of C (new chords F, C, and G).
- Play the blues in the key of G (new chord D).
- Play the blues in the key of D (new chord A).
- Play the blues in the key of A (new chord E).
- Play the blues in the key of E (new chord B7).

Exercise: Teaching Relative Minors

Objective: Students learn new chords by relating them to ones they already know.
Process:

- Demonstrate C and A minor.
- Ask the students to observe and describe in their own words the difference between the C-major and A-minor chords. They will observe that two fingers remain the same while only one finger moves.
- Repeat the process for G and E minor and for F and D minor.
- Seamlessly loop the following progressions: G-Emin; C-Amin; F-Dmin.

Written Exercises:

- Have students describe, using their own words, how to convert the C, G, and F chords into their relative-minor chords A minor, E minor, and D minor.
- Using crayons, colored pencils, or markers, have the students design a textbook page that teaches the concept of relative-minor chords. They should use chord grids, text, and other diagrams to illustrate the concepts.

Exercise: Teaching Parallel Minor and Seventh Chords

Objective: Students learn new chords by relating them to ones they already know. The guitar provides a good visual representation of the differences between major, minor, and seventh chord qualities.
Process:

- Define *chord quality* as chords that have the same root but vary in sound, such as E major, E minor, and E7.
- Demonstrate E and E minor.
- Ask the students to describe in their own words the difference between the E-major and E-minor chords. They will observe that one note is lowered by one fret (the third of the chord moves to the flat third).
- Explain that a major chord can be converted into a minor chord by lowering one note by one fret. Repeat with A to A minor and with D to D minor.
- Demonstrate E to E7.
- Ask students to describe in their own words the difference between the E-major and E7 chord. They will observe that one note is lowered by two frets (the root is lowered by a whole step).
- Explain that a major chord can be converted to a seventh chord by lowering one note by two frets.
- Repeat the procedure for A to A7.

- Repeat the procedure for D to D7.
- Seamlessly play through the following progressions using verbal cues as needed:
  E, Emin, E, E7
  A, Amin, A, A7
  D, Dmin, D, D7

Written exercises

- Have students describe, using their own words, how to covert the E, A, and D chords into minor and seventh chords.
- Using crayons or markers, have students design a textbook page that teaches the concept of parallel chord qualities. They should use chord grids, text, and other diagrams to illustrate the concepts.

Exercise: Chord Metamorphosis

Objective: Each new chord will be based on a form the students already know. These may be practiced silently, with the left hand only.
  Process:
- Discuss the meaning of *metamorphosis*.
- Begin with the easy F chord.
- Convert F to C and C to easy G.
- Convert C to A minor.
- Convert G to E minor.
- Convert F to the Spanish D minor (x x 0 2 0 1).
- Convert E minor to the easy A (x 0 2 2 0 0).
- Convert A minor to E major.
- Convert E major into the Spanish F (by sliding one fret up the neck).

ABBREVIATED FORMS: THE EASY B MINOR, B7, G MINOR, C MINOR, F MINOR, AND A MAJOR

Being able to play easy forms increases the possibility for playing more songs. Notice the similarity between the D, A7, and easy B minor and C minor chords:

A x 0 2 2 0 0	
B7 x 2 1 2 0 x	B minor x 2 0 2 0 x
C x x x 0 1 0	C minor x 0 1 0 1 x
D x x 0 2 0 2	D minor x x 0 2 0 1
F x x 3 2 1 0	F minor x x 0 1 1 1
G 3 2 0 0 0 0	G minor 3 x 0 3 3 x

Exercise: The Bluegrass G, C, and Easy G Minor

Objective: Students learn to use common fingers to simplify chord changes.
  Process:

- The following relative shapes are commonly referred to as *bluegrass forms* because of their frequent use in bluegrass music. They are useful because two fingers are common to all the forms.
- Have students strum eight beats of the following chord forms:
  C   x 3 2 0 3 3
  F   x x 3 2 3 3
  E minor 0 2 0 0 3 3
  A7   x 0 2 0 3 3
  G minor 3 x 0 3 3 x

SLASH FORMS: G/B

Many popular songs use what is commonly referred to as *slash chords*, such as G/B. The first letter is the actual chord, and the second letter is the bass note. Therefore G/B is read as "G with B in the bass." Slash chords are commonly used to create a smooth bass motion. If a student knows the natural-note scale, they can figure out almost any slash chord. Beginning guitarists may ignore the second letter of a slash chord. Slash chords and embellished chords (Gadd9) will be a focus of study in the second semester.

Exercise: Alphabetical Chord Drill

Objective: Students develop an orderly system for daily chord review.
  Process: Play through the basic chords alphabetically: A, A minor, A7, B7, B minor, C, C7, D, D minor, D7, E, E minor, E7, F, G, and G7.

Written Exercise

Using blank grid paper, have students create their own chord reference sheet. Use colored markers and additional text to design this sheet as a textbook page.

Exercise: Spontaneous/Mirror Imitation

Objective: Students learn to change chords by following a leader and without looking at their hands.
  Process:

- *Without strumming.* Instruct the students to observe your hands and to mirror your chord changes without looking at their hands.
- *With strumming.* Strum simple progressions, and have students mirror your progression. Be sure to exaggerate the preparation gesture.

In other words, lift your fingers a little higher than usual on the preparation beat so that the students can see it.

- Use mirror imitation to play campfire-type songs, such as "Kumbaya," "Michael, Row the Boat Ashore," "He's Got the Whole World in His Hands," "Rock My Soul," "Amazing Grace," "On Top of Spaghetti," "You Are My Sunshine," "Home on the Range," "This Little Light of Mine," "This Land Is Your Land," "Found a Peanut," "Old MacDonald," "Down by the Riverside," "Swing Low, Sweet Chariot," "'Tis a Gift to Be Simple," "Twist and Shout," "O Susanna," "Where Have All the Flowers Gone," "If I Had a Hammer," "She'll Be Coming 'Round the Mountain," and "Down in the Valley." Be prepared to teach the singing part using echo imitation.

Exercise: Aural Imitation

Objective: Students learn to identify and change chords by ear.

Process:

- Hide your hands behind a music stand.
- Play two different chords, and have the students identify them by name.
- With your hands hidden, play different chords, and have students play along with you.

SUMMARY OF CHORD-TEACHING STRATEGIES

- *By keys, progressing in the circle of fifths.* C, G, D, A, E
- *By relative or common shapes.* C-F-G; Amin-E; Emin-easy A
- *Relative minor.* C, Amin; G, Emin; F, Dmin
- *Parallel-chord qualities.* A, Amin, A7; C, C7; D, Dmin, D7; E-Emin-E7; G, G7
- *Gliding finger/common string.* When one finger glides on a string during a chord change, such as D7-G.
- *Common finger.* Two chords that have a finger in common
- *Abbreviated forms.* For example, the easy F, which is x x 3 2 1 x

CONCLUDING THOUGHT

In a classroom with many different skill levels, different students may play different versions of the same chord if necessary. For example, different students may play easy forms, standard forms, barre forms, and triads all at the same time. The simplest way to find an easy form is to imagine that the bass strings (E A D) have been removed. In certain instances, you can create an abbreviated form by omitting one finger, as you will see next.

21

Finger Picking

Finger picking is the gateway to solo guitar. Solo guitar is the gateway to independence.

I was ten years old when I first learned finger picking. I heard someone play "Puff the Magic Dragon" and was captivated by the sound. For the fifth-grade talent show I finger-picked the accompaniment for "This Land Is Your Land" without singing it. Who needs singing if you can pick? The audience agreed, because they asked for an encore.

The point I would like to emphasize is that finger picking can open up a whole new set of experiences and be very exciting for students. It is also a good time for you to talk about the pinnacle of the guitar experience, which is solo guitar playing. I like to say, "Finger picking is the gateway to solo guitar, and solo guitar is the gateway to independence."

FINGERS OF THE RIGHT HAND: *PIMA*

We use letters to indicate the fingers of the right hand. They are easy to remember as a short word—*pima*. The letters come from the Spanish words for these fingers. Here is the translation:

Pulgar thumb
Indice index
Medio middle
Anular ring finger

Exercise: *Graphic Design*

Objective: Students memorize the letters of the right hand by drawing and labeling them.
   Process:

- Pass out paper and either crayons or colored pencils.

- Students imagine that they are applying for a job at a book publisher. The publisher has instructed them to design a page for a book that will teach the fingers of the right hand (pima) and left hand (4 3 2 1 T).

Exercise: *Identifying the Fingers of the Right Hand*

Objective: Students demonstrate knowledge of the Spanish names of the fingers of the right hand.
   Process:

- Students hold up their right hand as if to say an oath.
- The teacher says, "Pulgar" and wiggles the thumb.
- The students echo the teacher by saying "Pulgar" and wiggling the thumb.
- Repeat for all the fingers.

Exercise: *The Raindrop*

Objective: The students learn the plucking stroke, which consists of the stroke and the return.
   Process:

- Hold out the right arm with the right hand resting on top of it like a wilted flower.
- Have students pretend they are flicking a drop of water off of the tip of each finger. The flicking motion allows the finger to return to its neutral position by following the principal of reversibility or spring action.
- Repeat for each finger.
- After plucking a string, allow reversibility to carry the finger back to home position.

HOME POSITION: PLACING THE FINGERS ON THE STRINGS

General Concepts

- For the simplicity of teaching purposes, rest the thumb on string 4 and the fingers on strings 3, 2, and 1 (photo 21.1).
- The angle at which the fingers stroke the string is important in reducing friction or scraping.
- The contact point of the finger and the string is toward the left side of the fingernail.
- The first finger has the most slant and points toward the bridge.
- The ring finger has the least slant and is nearly perpendicular to the soundboard.
- The thumb lies almost parallel to the bass strings.
- When viewed from above, there is a triangular space between the thumb and the index finger.
- The angle of the stroke will vary, depending on the music being played. For example, the strokes for a finger-picking accompaniment will be at a different angle than the strokes for playing the melody in a classical guitar solo. (Consult your method book for information on various strokes of the right hand.)

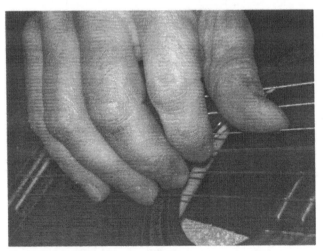

Photo 21.1: Home position

Exercise: The Spider and the Scratch

Objective: Students learn to move fingers of the right hand independently.
  Process:

- Have the class place their right hand on their leg.
- Position the hand and fingers to make the shape of a spider.

- On your cue, have students scratch their leg with one finger at a time. For example, with all the fingers anchored, scratch the leg with the index finger, then the middle, and then the ring finger.
- The fingers move in this natural manner when plucking the strings.

Exercise: Home Position

Objective: Students develop a starting position for the right hand.
  Process:

- Do a quick posture check to be sure the neck of the guitar is elevated.
- Have the students lay the palm of the right hand flat across the strings, between the sound hole and the bridge.
- Check to make sure that fingers are slightly apart.
- Slowly raise the palm, and allow the fingers to slide naturally toward the hand.
- Place the fingers i, m, and a on strings 3, 2, and 1 and the thumb on string 4. This is home position.
- Take a practice pause, and check the students' hands.
- Manually rotate the forearm if necessary so that the fingers are slanted as described earlier.
- Position check: the fingers should be able to fan in toward the palm without bumping the thumb.

Exercise: Home Position from Another Angle

Objective: Students gain an awareness of gravity as it relates to the hand's position.
  Process:

- Hang the right forearm over the edge (*bout*) of the guitar so that the hand is dangling freely like a wilted flower.
- Gently shake the imaginary water droplets off of the flower by jiggling to the left and to the right.
- Allow the jiggling to subside as you become aware that the hand is hanging naturally due to the effect of gravity.
- Lower the hand to the strings. First let the thumb catch on the sixth string, and then let the fingers i, m, and a fall onto strings 3, 2, and 1, respectively.
- Be sure the thumb is protruding to the left of the fingers and that the fingers are pointing toward your right foot.

- Allow the weight of your index finger to sink into the G string like your head sinks into a pillow. Let the finger sink into the string until if falls off the string and lands on the D string. No wonder this is called the *rest stroke*. The rest stroke is used primarily for melodies rather than accompaniments.

Exercise: *The Finger Glide and Thumb Glide*

Objective: Students discover the relationship between forearm rotation and finger angle.
Process:

- *The finger glide.*
    - o Place the thumb and fingers in home position.
    - o With the thumb remaining planted on the fourth string, slowly rotate the forearm so that the fingers slide slightly to the left and then the right while remaining on the strings. Notice the relationship between the forearm rotation and the position of the fingertips.
- *The thumb glide.*
    - o This is the reverse of the finger glide.
    - o Place the thumb and fingers in home position.
    - o Leave the fingers anchored, and slide the thumb along the fourth string, slightly to the right and then to the left.
    - o Look for a triangular space to form between the thumb and the first finger. This ensures the fingers won't bump into the thumb.

Exercise: *The Muted Arpeggio*

Objective: The students learn to move the fingers independently and to spring back to home position.
Process:

- Students place their right hand in home position.
- Leave all the fingers resting in home position. Have the thumb pluck the fourth string, and quickly spring back to home position. The resulting sound should be an extremely short, staccato sound.
- Leaving the passive fingers resting in home position, repeat this muted stroke four times for each finger. Always spring back to home position before plucking the next note.
- Progressively reduce the repetitions.
- Reminder: The passive fingers remain resting on the strings, and the active finger springs

back to home position before the next finger moves.

Exercise: *Alternating the Muted Strokes with the Sustained Stokes*

Objective: Students transfer the spring-back motion of the muted stroke to the sustained stroke.
Process: Play the ascending arpeggio, and alternate using the muted stroke with normal sustained strokes. For example: muted-pima, sustained-pima.

Exercise: *Out/Home, Up/Home, In/Home*

This is a variation of an exercise we used to learn chord forms.
Objective: Students gain finger strength and independence and a sense of where the strings are located.
Process:

- Begin with the right hand in home position.
- Leave all fingers planted except the index finger.
- Extend the finger straight out from the middle joint so that it is parallel to the guitar. Return the finger to home position.
- Lift the index finger up from the joint closest to the palm of the hand (metacarpal joint). Return the finger to home position.
- Curl the finger in toward the palm from the metacarpal joint, and then return home.
- Repeat several times for each finger while the others remain planted on the strings.

USE NOTATION TO COMMUNICATE RIGHT-HAND PATTERNS

Students should get used to the idea that new skills will be communicated through written music. Offering students frequent, short-reading opportunities prepares them for life-long learning. Since the reading opportunities are short, the students are less likely to become fatigued.

The fundamental accompaniment patterns follow:

Ascending arpeggio p i m a D-G-B-E
Circular arpeggio p i m a m i (3/4 time) D-G-B-E-B-G

As students advance, notate chords using the ascending and circular arpeggios.

Exercise: *Teaching Arpeggios on Open Strings*

Objective: Students concentrate on the right hand only.

Process:

- Place the fingers of the right hand in home position.
- Play the ascending arpeggio (D-G-B-E) in half notes, with attention to:
     o spring-back motion (reversibility)—each finger must spring back to neutral position before the next finger begins,
     o finger independence,
     o minimal movement, and
     o tone quality.
- On your cue, shift to quarter notes.
- On your cue, shift to eighth notes.
- Variation: Begin the arpeggio in half notes, and do a gradual accelerando.

Exercise: Shifting Accents

Objective: Finger independence and control.
  Process:

- Play the ascending arpeggio several times, and accent the thumb on beat one.
- After four repetitions, shift the accent to the index, then the middle, and then the ring fingers.

Exercise: Shifting Meter

Objective: Finger independence and control.
  Process:

- Loop the ascending arpeggio *pima*. Count out loud "One, two, three, four."
- Continue to loop | p i m | and a, but shift into 3/4 time. Count out loud "One, two, three," and place the accents on beat 1. The resulting groupings follow:
  | p i m | a p i | m a p | i m a |
- The pattern returns to the beginning every four measures.
- Variation: shift meter on the descending arpeggio—a m i p.

Exercise: Shifting Bass Notes

Objective: To play different chord roots, student practice shifting the thumb to different strings
  Process:

- Start in home position.
- Play p, i, m, and a on strings 4, 3, 2, and 1.
- Shift the thumb to string 5, and play 5 3 2 1.
- Shift the thumb to string 6, and play 6 3 2 1.

- Quiz the students on specific chords. For example, "Place thumb on the appropriate string for the C chord" (string 5).

Exercise: Shifting the Fingers i, m, and a to Different String Sets

- Begin with p i m a on the following strings: E G B E.
- With the thumb remaining constant on the sixth string, loop the ascending arpeggio.
- On your cue, have students move their fingers to the following strings: E/D G B, E/A D G.

Exercise: Combine Arpeggios with Chords Drills

Objective: Students learn to play chords as arpeggios.
  Process: Apply ascending and circular arpeggios to chord progressions.

- Give verbal cues for the chords of a song, and then seamlessly move into the song.
- The alphabetical-chord drill: A, Amin, A7, B7, C, C7, D, Dmin, D7, etc.
- The blues progressions in major and minor keys.

FINGERNAILS AND TONE PRODUCTION

The guitar has the potential to create a smooth singing tone, which is sometimes referred to as *bel canto*, which means *beautiful singing*. Beautiful tone is the result of several factors, including:

- type and quality of the guitar
- strings
- right-hand technique
- location of the right hand relative to the sound hole
     o near the bridge: bright sound, *ponticello*
     o over the sound hole: darker sound, *sul tasto*, *dolce*

I recommend listening to recordings of classical guitar players, such as Christopher Parkening, to hear the guitar's tone potential.

COMMON ARPEGGIO PATTERNS

Here is a list of the most common accompaniment arpeggios. We will begin in home position on strings D/G B E.

- **Ascending arpeggio p, i, m, a** D G B E
- **Circular arpeggio p, i, m, a, m, i** D G B E B G
- **Alberti pattern p, i, m, i, a, i, m, i** D G B G E G B G
- **Banjo pattern p, m, p, i** D E G B
- **M pattern** p, i, a/m, i   D G E/B G
- **Travis pattern** p – i m- a i –

The Travis rhythm is 1 2 + + 4. Use the words *I just-love to-pick* to communicate the rhythm. There are several variations of the Travis picking pattern. A good source for guitar accompaniment patterns is my book *A Modern Method for Fingerstyle Guitar*.

SCALES AND FINGER PICKING

Scales played on one string provide an excellent way to practice using the fingers of the right hand.

Exercise: The Natural Notes for One Octave on One String

Objective: Students gain experience with finger alternation.

Process:

- Preliminary: Rest the thumb on your leg as a brace, and alternate fingers *m* and *i* in a walking motion. Some teachers refer to this as finger walking.
- Rest the thumb on the low E string as a brace. Pluck the A string using the alternation of *m* and *i*.
- Take a practice pause, and check students' hand position.
- Review the B/C E/F rule, which states that there are two frets between every note except between B and C and between E and F.
- Once the class is comfortable with finger alternation, play the natural notes on the A string for one octave using repeated notes. For example: A A A A, B B B B, etc.
- The Pinch Variation: Pinch the low-E string with the thumb simultaneously as you pluck the A string with the middle finger. This is called a *pinch pattern*. Use the pinch pattern to play the natural notes on the A string combined with the low E string.
- The Hook Variation: Play the scale again with the low E drone. This time alternate the thumb and middle finger, p, m, p, m, etc. This is called the *hook pattern*.
- For variation, use different strings and different fingers.

CARE OF THE FINGERNAILS AND SKIN

The skin and fingernails are very important to tone quality and ease of play.

Shape. The shape of the nails will vary from player to player, based on the characteristics of their nails and personal preference. To determine the shape, the student should have a nail file available during practice to make experiments. The fingernail shape should contribute to minimizing friction, maximizing glide, and creating a pure sound. A *pure sound* can be defined as *having a minimum of or no noise on the initial attack*. Avoid a raspy, brittle, or thin tone, and seek a full, singing, bel canto tone. Listen to guitar players with beautiful tone to create a sonic image to imitate.

Edge. *Edge* refers to the microscopic curvature of the top edge of the nail. Although this is hard to see, the edge should be rounded, with no sharpness, and smooth to the touch. Use a fine sandpaper for crafting the edge. Six hundred– and 1500-grit sandpaper are recommended.

Finish. After shaping the nails with a nail file and crafting the edge with sandpaper, you may buff the nail with either cheesecloth or shamy skin (sheepskin). With the exception of the fingernail file, all the materials are available at your local hardware store. Once you have experienced the pure tone and effortless glide, you will appreciate the extra effort.

Nutrition. Strong nails and a sharp mind are related to excellent nutrition. This is a good opportunity for you to talk about the advantages of wellness and healthy living.

Skin. As you get older, your skin tends to get rougher. When you file your nails, file off any rough skin that may be contacting the string.

MORE FINGER-MOTION EXPLORATIONS

The following exercises provide your students with a framework for exploring the motions involved with right- or left-hand finger movement.

Finger Lifts

- On the back of the guitar, place the fingers in the spider position.
- Cue the students to lift specific fingers and finger combinations.
- Repeat lifting and releasing ten times for each finger. For example, lift *i* ten times while the other fingers and thumb remain planted; next lift *i* and *a*, etc.

- Place the fingers of the right hand in playing position on the strings, and repeat the finger lifts.

Finger Presses

- On the back of the guitar, place the fingers in the spider position.
- Cue your students to press selected fingers and finger combinations into the guitar.
- Repeat the process, starting from home position on the guitar strings.

The Wilted Flower: Relaxing the Wrist

- Students position their right forearm in front of them so that it is pointing toward the ceiling.
- Let the right hand hang from the wrist like a wilted flower.
- Use the fingers of the left hand to pull downward on the back of the wrist so that the right hand rises as a result of the pulling on the skin. In order for the hand to rise, the muscles must remain completely relaxed. Once the hand has become elevated, release the skin, and let it drop. Repeat several times. Check the wrist for looseness when in home position.

The Lateral Shift

- Begin in the spider position on the back of the guitar.
- Slide the index finger to the right and left while the other fingers remain stationery.
- Repeat this for each finger and thumb.
- Try this with groups of two adjacent fingers. For example, in the spider position place fingers 1 and 2 next to each other, and have them move as a group to the left and right while the other fingers remain stationery.
- Beginning in the spider position, and have each finger slowly draw a circle on the surface of the guitar.
- Draw circles as before, but this time let the finger gradually leave the surface to draw circles in the air, and then gradually return to home position.

Metacarpal Lifts

- Begin with the palm flat on the back of the guitar.
- Leave the palm resting on the guitar, and lift individual fingers from the joint that connects the palm to the finger (metacarpal joint). Do this for various finger combinations.

22

Teaching Songs

Cowboy wisdom dictates that you always ride a horse in the direction it is going.

Nearly all aspects of technique can be addressed by playing songs. Songs are fun and provide motivation to learn techniques. One goal of guitar class is to expose students to new songs that reflect historic, cultural, geographical, and musical value. You are the song carrier, passing on songs to the next generation.

HARNESS NATURAL STUDENT ENERGY

The movement involved in playing and singing songs stimulates breathing and blood circulation, body and mind. Songs are a good way to start the class.

USE RECORDED EXAMPLES

With the use of iTunes you can obtain recorded examples of nearly any song you are working on for a nominal fee. They will be stored on your computer and are easy to access. Connect your computer to your stereo system by obtaining the appropriate cords from your local electronics store. When you play examples for students, have them silently finger the chords or sing along. Recorded performances familiarize beginner students with the melody, harmony, and style of the music. For higher-level classes, you can study the details of the arrangements, such as the vocal harmonies, the bass line, and the exact guitar parts.

DEMONSTRATING A SONG

It is very useful to demonstrate a song before playing it as a group. If possible, memorize the song so that your eyes can be on the students instead of the music. Here are some tips for keeping students engaged during your demonstration. Have the students:

- observe and analyze your fingerings while keeping their strings muted,
- follow the printed music with their finger,
- silently finger the chords as they follow your demonstration, and
- sing the song, without playing it.

MINIMIZE STOPPING AND STARTING

By keeping your class activities moving, students will stay more engaged. Look for creative ways to seamlessly blend exercises into playing songs. Here are some preliminaries that lead seamlessly into a song:

- Synchronize the class by strumming the beat on muted strings.
- Clarify the measures by strumming beat 1 on the bass strings and the other beats on the treble strings.
- Solidify the tempo: Play the muted beat with a drum machine. As students become synchronized, fade the drum machine out for progressively longer periods of time.
- Pick two chords from the song you are leading into, and alternate between those chords. Start with two measures per chord, and progress to one measure, and then two beats per chord. Repeat the process until you have practiced all the chords in the song.
- Recite the chord changes to the song while playing the muted strings.
- Define the measures by playing the chords in all whole notes.

- Define the beat by playing the chords in quarter notes and accenting beat 1.
- Play the chord roots. Before playing the song, locate the roots: Next, play the roots of the song in tempo.
- Learn note names by playing the roots on the treble strings.
- Play the root on beat 1, and strum on beats 2, 3, and 4. This is called the *root-strum*.

SCAFFOLDING

Scaffolding means to provide the students with cues and then gradually remove them. Here are some steps to follow:

- Play along with the students, offering verbal chord cues. Give verbal cues in advance and, when possible, in groups of two chords at a time. For example, if the progression is C to G, say, "C to G."
- Instruct the students to get louder as you fade out.
- Use a laser pointer to point to the chords on an overhead projector if you have one.
- Eliminate the chord cues, and just sing out the words while the class strums independently.
- If you are using a drum machine, turn it off.
- Silently conduct without playing or singing. Use left-hand cues to indicate chord changes.
- Eliminate all cues.

LAYERING SKILL LEVELS IN THE SAME SONG

Empower students to succeed at their varying skill levels. Fortunately there are multiple options for students when playing songs in guitar class. Remind students that it is okay to participate in different ways. Following is a list of some possibilities:

- Strum and sing the song as written.
- Strum without singing.
- Strum in whole notes without a rhythm pattern.
- Strum in quarter notes without a rhythm pattern.
- Finger the chords without strumming.
- Play the roots only.
- Play the bass.
- Play string percussion on the muted strings (no chords).
- Point to the chord changes in the music without playing.

- Play percussion instruments, body percussion, or vocal percussion.
- Sing without playing.
- Hum without playing.

ENDING SONGS

Having a routine for ending a song is an essential part of classroom management. As the end of the song approaches, announce, "One, two, ready, stop, mute, and rest." Show students how to mute the strings with the right hand, and then take the rest position with the left hand. Model this as a routine.

Exercise: *Formal Right-Hand Muting for Ending Songs*

Objective: Students respect the artistic importance of a good ending.
   Process:

- Students enjoy the musicality and motion of formal right-hand muting.
- As the last chord of a song sustains, the students should place the bottom (palm) of their right hand just to the right of the bridge.
- Then as a group, slowly fold the hand over onto the strings, creating a synchronized fade-out. This sounds great and helps to prevent ragged endings.

MAKING A CLASSROOM SONGBOOK

When students help choose the songs that the class plays, they take more of an ownership in the class. Here is one way to do it:

- Place a three-ring binder or folder on each music stand.
- Place sheet protectors inside each binder.
- At the beginning of each binder, place a song list of material with which you are familiar.
- Encourage students to request songs from the list. Place song sheets of the requested songs into each binder.
- As the semester progresses, include supplemental songs that reflect the skills and techniques you are working on.
- Have extra copies of the song sheets available near your exit door for students to take home and practice. Encourage students to save copies for their song portfolio. (See chapter 2 on assessment for more ideas on the portfolio.)

CREATING EFFECTIVE SING-AND-STRUM SHEETS

Creating your own lyric sheets is a good way to prepare yourself in advance for presenting songs. Here are some suggestions for creating song sheets that maximize the learning experience on every song:

- Each song must fit on one page.
- The lyrics should be double-spaced.
- Use large and easy-to-read font.
- Write the chord symbols above the lyrics.
- Place chord grids at the bottom of the page to provide chord fingerings. (I have provided special paper for this purpose in the appendix.)
- Provide more than one option for chords where appropriate. This will keep more advanced students interested. For example:
  o basic, open-position chords
  o chords with color tones, such as added 9ths
  o triads
  o jazz voicings
- Pencil in a small staff near the top of the page, and write the first several notes of the melody as a guide for singing. This provides a *note-reading* opportunity.
- Draw a strumming rhythm figure wherever you can find room. This provides a *rhythm-reading* opportunity.
- If the song has a riff, draw a small staff, and notate it.
- In addition to lyric sheets, include lead sheets with melodies.

SONGS AND IMPROVISATION

Some songs lend themselves to lead-guitar improvisations. When this is the case, take advantage of the song to teach improvisation. Use a seamless transition from *preparation* to *playing* the song. (See chapter 25 on improvisation for full details.) Here are some steps to help you get started:

- Establish the beat for the song using your drum machine.
- Teach a five-note pentatonic scale using four repeated notes. The easiest versions of the pentatonic scales are:
  o *On one string.* E-minor pentatonic on the high E string is 0 3 5 7 10 12
  o *On two strings using only two fingers.* Starting on the second string, the E-minor pentatonic scale is on string 2, frets 3 and 5; on string 1, frets 3, 5, and 7. The fingering is 1-3, 1-3 slide. Slide from fret 5 to fret 7.
- Play short riffs in echo imitation. Begin with one note, then two, and gradually use all five.
- Have students improvise as a group while you play the chord progression. By practicing collectively and anonymously, the students can experiment without being judged.
- Tips for musical improvisations follow:
  o Improvise short phrases ranging from two to eight notes.
  o Try to play each idea twice; the second time can be a little different from the first.
  o When students find a musical idea they like, they should try to remember it.
  o Once the class is oriented to the improvisation, make a seamless transition into the song.

FORM AND ARRANGING

Students enjoy participating in arranging song forms. Here are the most common parts to think about:

- *Prelude/chorale.* Sustained chords strummed out of tempo.
- *Riff.* Repeated ostinato used for introduction, interludes, and ending.
- *Introduction/groove.* Chords strummed in tempo.
- *Verses with singing.*
- *Instrumental melody.*
- *Chorus with vocal harmony.* For advanced students you may demonstrate how to write the harmony part and have students play the melody and harmony as well as sing it.
- *Improvisation.*
- *Rhythm episodes.* During an improvisation the accompaniment may start with whole notes and progress to a steady beat and then double time. Episodes may conclude with a tutti rhythm figure and ending riff.
- *Ending.* Special riff or repetition to create a sense of closure.
- *Cadenza.* Instrumental improvisational fills used to showcase instrumentalist.

LEARNING HISTORY, GEOGRAPHY, AND CULTURAL INFORMATION FROM SONGS

Carefully selected songs provide rich learning opportunities if you aware of the social and cultural context from which they came. For example, "The Worried Man Blues" provides an opportunity to talk about the Great Depression and hobo culture. With the use of iTunes, you can find engaging performances of songs that would otherwise be considered corny. Here are some questions and ideas to help you generate discussion:

- When did you first hear this song?
- Why did you choose this song for the class to play?
- What groups recorded the song and when?
- Who wrote the song and why?

- What are the geographic considerations?
- What are the cultural considerations?
- What are the historical considerations?
- Recite the lyrics, and discuss the meaning.
- Are there any special vocabulary terms in the lyrics?
- Write the lyrics for additional verse.
- Write a new melody and chords for the existing lyrics.
- Write new words for the existing melody.
- Modify the melody and chords for the new words.

㉓

Teaching Singing and Playing

Learning how to practice is the most important goal of either guitar or vocal study.

Since guitar is frequently used as an accompaniment instrument, the ability to sing and play is important for guitar teachers and students. In this chapter I will share with you the following:

- the benefits and motivation for singing
- how the voice works
- similarities between the guitar and the voice
- a basic vocal warm-up
- how to play and sing at the same time
- resources for further study

BENEFITS AND MOTIVATION FOR SINGING

For most people, singing must be learned and practiced. Guitar class is a good place to introduce the singing technique to students who may not be the in choir. It is also a good class for recruiting students for the choir. Stress the benefits of learning to sing by discussing the following points:

- Singing is a fun social activity.
- Strumming the guitar without singing is incomplete.
- Singing improves the aural skills (the musical ear).
- Singing helps improve solo-guitar playing by improving phrasing and expression.
- Singing improves circulation and alertness.

PLAYING GUITAR AND SINGING AT THE SAME TIME: A QUICK START

Exercise: Vocalizations with String Percussion

Objective: To allow students to gradually combine singing and playing.

Process: Here are some vocal activities that can be performed while the class is simultaneously keeping the beat using string percussion:

- Mouth the words without adding pitch.
- Speak the words in rhythm.
- Hum the melody.
- Sing the melody on the syllable *ah*, then *ee* and *oo*.
- Sing the melody on consonants such as *ya ya*, *ta ta*, or *pa pa*. (Variation: use ee or oo.)
- Sing the words in echo imitation.
- Sing the words as written.
- Sing the words using eighth notes or triplet impulses or swells.

HOW THE VOICE WORKS

Before you lead your class in vocal exercises it is a good idea to understand the basics of how the voice works. There are different approaches to teaching singing. One approach is metaphoric, and the other is mechanistic. As an instrumentalist, I am biased toward the mechanistic approach. That means that I like to know what the parts of the instrument are, their function, how they combine, and how to practice. I hope that the following explanations provide you with the best understanding in the shortest amount of time.

Parts of the Vocal Instrument

- **air pump** abdominal muscles
- **vibrator** vocal bands
- **resonators** throat, mouth, skull
- **articulators** tongue, lips, and jaw

A Comparison of the Voice and the Guitar

- **air pump** stroke of the finger or pick

- **vibrator** strings
- **resonator** body of the guitar
- **articulator** fingernails and fingertips of the right hand

More Comparisons

- **sound hole** mouth opening; lips and teeth
- **body of guitar** mouth cavity; space inside mouth
- **strings and frets** vocal folds
- **soundboard (top of guitar)** back of the throat; front of the skull

AWAKENING AND CONTROLLING THE AIR PUMP

Controlling airflow for the singer is like controlling the bow for the violinist. By opening and closing the hand, you can provide a visual image of how the lungs produce a managed flow of air. Observe the following comparisons, and then perform the related exercise:

- **neutral hand position** hand at rest
- **neutral lung position** breathing muscles at rest, neither an inhale or exhale

- **extended hand position** muscles pull the hand into the open position
- **extended lung position/inhale** abdominal muscles hold the lungs open

- **flexed hand position** flexor muscles squeeze the hand into a fist
- **flexed lung position/exhale** abdominal muscles squeeze the air out

- **recovered hand position** hand muscles relax, and the hand naturally and automatically springs back to home position
- **recovered lung position** abdominal muscles relax, and lungs automatically return to neutral position, bringing in air with it

Exercise: The Four-Part Breath with Corresponding Hand Motions

Objective: Students use their hand as a visual representation of how breathing muscles work.
Process:

- Hold the right hand in front of you in neutral home position.

- Slowly open the hand, and simultaneously take a slow inhale of the breath.
- Open the hand completely as you simultaneously inhale.
- Take another sip of air, and then hold the breath for a moment, as you hold the hand completely open. (This is the set position of the throat. Touch your voice box. Notice that the voice box—the larynx—is low, and the throat is open. The goal will be to keep the larynx low during the exhale.)
- Slowly, and in a controlled manner, allow the fingers to move toward neutral position as you simultaneously exhale.
- Synchronize the hand motion, and exhale so they both arrive at the neutral position at the same time.
- Continue the hand motion toward a flexed fist. Simultaneously continue to squeeze air from the lungs.
- As the hand makes a tight fist, force any remaining air out of your lungs.
- Relax the fist, and allow it to return to neutral position while simultaneously allowing the lungs to automatically inhale air.
- If you wish to strengthen your abdominals in a shorter period of time, hold the lungs tightly open for twenty seconds and then tightly closed for twenty seconds. Repeat for five minutes a day.

AWAKENING THE PARTS OF THE VOICE

Preliminaries

- *To open the bellows of the air pump*
  - stretch the spine and elevate sternum;
  - keep the sternum high throughout the exercises.
- *To open the throat*
  - yawn and sigh;
  - stretch and lower the jaw;
  - say, *ya ya ya* . . . or *ga ga ga.* . . .
- *To activate abdominals*, after a deep inhale, and taking an extra sip of air,
  - sustain a long hiss with volume swells;
  - perform a long, intermittent hiss with volume swells;
  - pant like a dog: *ha ha ha.* . . .
- *To develop independence of the vocal folds and mouth*
  - perform a lip or tongue trill (motor boat) on a sustained siren with swells.

- *To brighten the sound*
  - perform the child's teasing chant: *nya nya nya . . .* and then transition into a song.

Apply the following vocalizations to phrases of songs.

- *To create a resonating chamber in the mouth*
  - hum with teeth apart and jaw dropped. Feel a tingle or tickle, which I call the kazoo effect.
- *To create resonance*
  - sing *nah nee nu.* Feel a buzz in the nose and cheeks. Let your tongue do the work, and avoid chewing or opening and closing the jaw, which restricts tone.
- *To improve vowel tone*
  - sing *ee ay ah oh oo* and *oo oh ah ay ee.* This is known as the *vowel circle,* which transitions from the brightest *ee* to the darkest *oo.* Make the vowel transitions inside the mouth as much as possible. Place your hands on your larynx. Notice that on *oo* the larynx is down. *Oo* is considered the *medicine of the voice.* See if you can leave the larynx low as you progress through the other vowels.
- *To awaken the tip of the tongue* sing *ta da.*
- *To awaken the root of the tongue* sing *ya ga* to help keep the throat open.
- *To awaken lips* sing *pa ba.*
- *To awaken the abdominals* sing *cha ka ha.*
- *To increase range*
  - sing octaves. Sing some scales in octaves. Place your finger at the top of your larynx. Notice that it stretches forward, pressing on your hand. Singing octaves helps to train this muscle.
- *To awaken the abdominal muscles*
  - sing phrases using *ah* in pulsed eighth notes. Sing a siren on *ah* in pulsed eighth notes.
- *To increase strength around the vocal bands*

- sing scales and trills. Just like any instrument, scales, arpeggios, and trills are useful skill builders.
- *To improve breath management (sostenuto)*
  - sustain notes for long durations, adding swells.

TONE QUALITY OF THE GUITAR AND VOICE COMPARED

Vowels are like a river of tone, which are briefly interrupted by the "noise" of consonants. Good singers strive for vowel tones that are interrupted with as brief a consonant as necessary. Similarly, guitarist guitar tone should consist of more vowel and less consonant—in other words, less noise (scratch, click, scrape, or roughness) at the start of a stroke. Once the guitarist has the ability to produce a pure tone, then the attack may be modified, accented, or colored for expressive purposes.

Finally, in singing, blending the consonants allows for a more sustained vowel tone. For example, when you sustain the words *which connect,* it becomes: wi-*chca*-ne-*ctah.* I refer to this as *compound consonants.* Use compound consonants to increase the purity of your vowels.

The following books are recommended for classroom or individual use:

- *The Perfect Blend,* Timothy Seelig, available in both book and DVD form, including warmups and explanations of how the voice works
- *Building Beautiful Voices,* by Paul Nesheim and Weston Noble, including chapters on how the voice works and written warm-ups
- *Singing, the Mechanism and Technique,* by William Vennard, featuring extensive explanations of the physiology of the voice, concluding with excellent practice exercises; considered by some to be the best book ever written on the voice
- *I'm Not Crazy, I'm Vocalizing* by Karen Oleson, featuring a sing-along recording for class warm-ups; an easy and effective way to get started singing in the guitar classroom

24

Barre Forms and Transposition

By hinting at barre forms from the beginning, students will figure them out for themselves.

Barre chords are useful because they are:

- a way to play sharp and flat chords
- a harmonic framework for improvisation
- a fingering reference for triads (figure 24.2)

APPROACHES TO TEACHING BARRE FORMS

- as transpositions of the open-position E and A chords
- as extensions of power chords
- as an open chord with a capo
- as addition exercises

BARRE PRELIMINARIES

By introducing barre concepts and preliminaries from the first day of class, students will use their own intuition to figure them out for themselves. Here are some ways to hint at barre chords before formally introducing the unit on barre chords.

- Give an overview of all the chords they will be learning, which includes open-position chords, power chords, and barre forms. This creates anticipation and helps students to see the connection of open chords and power chords to barre forms.
- Ingrain new chords by transposing them up the neck.
- Teach surf-style lead guitar.

Exercise: Surf-Style Guitar

Objective: Students experience a two-note barre form at the beginning of the year. The most simple barre form consists of covering the first two strings. Playing two strings at a time is called a *double-stop*.

Process: For blues and rock-and-roll songs, have students play lead guitar in double-stops on the first two strings.

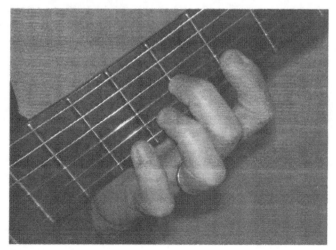

Photo 24.1 The G triad

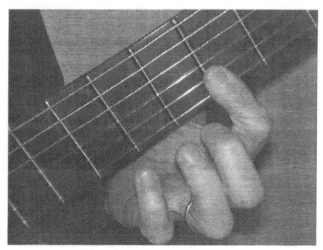

Photo 24.2 The G double stop

- Off of the guitar: With your left hand, press your thumb against the tip of your index finger until the knuckle at the tip of the finger arches inward. Use the arched fingertip to play double-stops.
- For a blues in G the frets would be G-3, C-8, and D-10. This is one way to hint at barre forms from an early stage.
- Variation: Expand the double-stop into a triad by adding the second finger.

Preliminary Exercise: Transposing Open Chords with Standard Fingerings

Objective: Students learn new chord forms by sliding them up and down the neck.

Process:

- Teach the meaning of the word *transposition*, to move from one position to another.
- Silently pulse the easy F on frets 3, 2, and 1.
- On your cue, slide the F toward the sound hole by one fret, and continue pulsing. This creates an F# triad.
- Continue sliding the chord to the right (in a sharp direction) every four beats.
- Challenge students to feel the frets and use them as tactile reference points.
- Use transposition frequently to ingrain new chord forms, especially the E, A, and D forms.
- When you teach the E and A forms, present the challenge question: "In addition to the fretted notes, how could you transpose the open strings?"

Preliminary Exercise: Transposing Open Chords with Barre Fingerings

Objective: Students learn the barre fingerings for transposing the E and A chords. Note that this exercise should wait until later in the semester. Students who already know the open chords may be encouraged to use barre fingerings from day one.

Process:

- Place the index finger to the left of the nut, and lay it flat across the strings. The fingertip should rest on the E string for E chords and on the A string for A chords.
- The thumb should be placed near the bottom of the neck, and the wrist arched.
- The neck itself must be elevated and approximately twelve inches from your eyes.
- With the remaining fingers, form an E-major chord. The frets are 0 2 2 1 0 0. The barre fin-

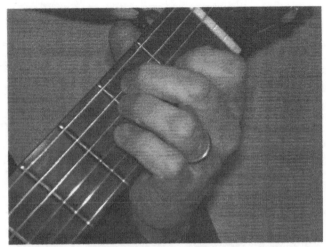

Photo 24.3 Open position E chord

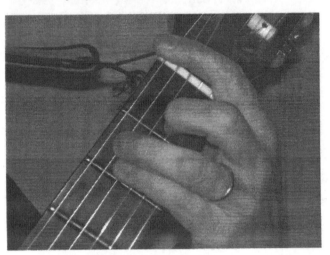

Photo 24.4 E chord using Barre fingering

gering for the E-major chord is 3 4 2. The index finger remains flat, to the left of the nut.
- Silently pulse the barre fingerings for the E chord for one or two measures, and then shift/transpose the fingering up the neck in half steps on your verbal cue. Be sure the tip of the index finger rests on the sixth string, which is the root.
- Note that we are not concerned at this time with strumming or applying pressure. That comes later.

THE CAPO AS A BARRE DEMONSTRATION

Singers frequently use the capo to transpose chords into keys that match their vocal range. Classical guitarists use the capo to achieve a sound resembling a lute. Young or remedial students can use the capo to make the guitar easier to play:

- The capo brings the strings closer to the fingerboard.

Photo 24.7 G chord, E Barre fingering

Photo 24.6 E chord with Capo on third fret

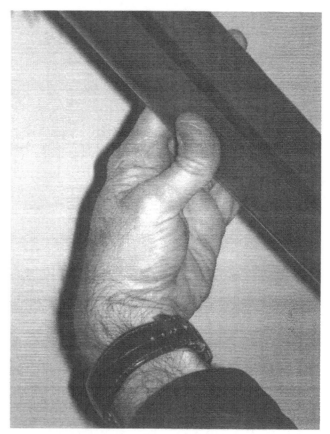

Photo 24.5 Thumb position for Barre chord

Process: Provide the fret numbers for an open E or A chord. For example, A is x 0 2 2 2 0. Write it on a fretboard diagram.

- Ask students, "If the A chord is transposed up three frets, what are the new fret numbers?" (Answer: Add three to each of the fret numbers of the A form. If the open A is x 0 2 2 2 0 and you add three to each of the frets, the answer is x 3 5 5 5 3.)
- Name the new chord. (Answer: The root of the A chord is on the A string. The new chord root is on the third fret of the A string. The third fret of the A string is C. Hence, the new chord is C.)
- Finger the new chord as a barre form. Write it on a fretboard diagram.

Exercise: Expanding the Root-6 Power Chord into a Barre Form

Objective: Students view power chords as the foundation of barre chords. Note that when viewed as an extension of power chords it becomes apparent that the barre finger does not actually need to clamp all the strings. In fact, a better word for barre is *bridge.*

- By playing in higher positions, the frets are closer together.
- There is less reach involved.

The guitar teacher can use the capo to demonstrate the principle of transposing chords. Demonstrate an E chord. Point out that the root of the chord is the open E string. Next, place the capo on the first fret, and play the E chord again. The E chord has been transposed. Where is the new root? (Answer: The first fret of the E string.) What is the name of the new root? (Answer: F.) What is the name of the resulting chord? (Answer: F.) How can we create the new F chord without using a capo? (Answer: Using a finger instead of a capo—a barre.)

Written Exercise: Transposition by Fret Addition

Objective: Students calculate the fingering for barre forms using addition. The exercise may be done with or without twelve-fret grid paper.

For example, on the G barre 3 5 5 4 3 3, the first finger only needs to press strings 6, 2, and 1.

Process:

- Demonstrate how the first two notes of the power chord are the first two notes of a barre form.
- Play the natural notes on the sixth string. Use the first finger exclusively, and allow it to lie flat across the strings.
- Play the natural-note scale again using root-6 power chords. For example, start with the G5 power chord, which is configured as 3 5 x x x x.
- Play the natural note scale again using three-note power chords. For example, the G5 three-note power chord is configured 3 5 5 x x x. The fingering is 1 3 4.
- Add one more finger. Configure G as 3 5 5 4 x x. Allow the first finger to lay flat across the strings. Congratulations, you have constructed the fingering for a G barre chord.
- Play the natural-note scale in repeated notes using the G barre form. Do not be concerned yet about a clear sound. That can wait until later.
- Variation: Silently pulse the chord four times in each position.

SUMMARY FOR ROOT-6, G-BARRE FORM

G root	3 x x x x x
G power chord	3 5 x x x x
G three-note power chord	3 5 5 x x x
G major	3 5 5 4 x x
G-major barre	3 5 5 4 3 3

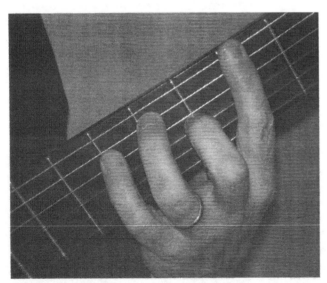

Photo 24.8 G power chord

Repeat the process for G minor with 3 5 5 3 3 3.

Exercise: Expanding the Root-5 Power Chord into a Barre Form

Objective: Students view power chords as the foundation of barre chords.

Process: The process for the root-5 barre forms may be played using the easy fingering. To play the easy fingering, start with a power chord, fingered 1-3, then flatten the third finger to cover three strings. The new fingering is 1 3 3 3.

- Using repeated notes, practice the natural notes on the fifth string using exclusively the first finger. Allow it to lay flat across the strings.
- Power-chord scale: Play the natural-note scale on the fifth string using root-5 power chords. For example, the C5 power chord is configured on frets 3 and 5 (C, G).

Photo 24.9 C power chord

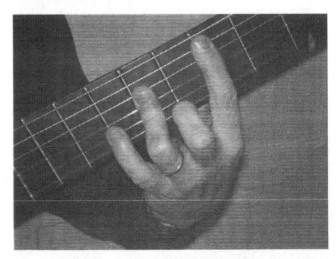

Photo 24.10 C Barre chord, easy fingering, C root 5

- Play the natural-note scale again using three-note power chords. For example, the C5 power chord is configured 3, 5, 5. The fingering is 1 3 4.
- Play the natural-note scale again in repeated notes using the easy fingering for the C barre form, x 3 5 5 5 x. Do not be concerned yet about clarity on the treble strings. Be sure that the tip of the index finger is on the A string.

SUMMARY FOR ROOT-5, C-BARRE FORM

C root x 3 x x x x
C power chord x 3 5 x x x
C three-note power chord x 3 5 5 x x
C major x 3 5 5 5 x
C-major barre x 3 5 5 5 3
C major (easy fingering*) x 3 5 5 5 x
- * Note that some students will prefer to finger C major using the fingerings 1 2 3 4. The easy fingering of 1 3 3 3 may not be possible if the third finger is not flexible.

Written Exercise: Transposing Barre Forms on Fretboard Diagrams

Objective: Students gain understanding of movable barre forms through the diagramming process.
   Process:

- Pass out a sheet of blank, twelve-fret chord grids. (I have provided you with a template in the appendix.)
- Make a reference chart by labeling the natural notes on the sixth string. (Frets: 0, 1, 3, 5, 7, 8, 10, 12; E F G A B C D E.)
- On a separate grid, have students draw an open-position E chord.
- Write the fret configuration of the E chord below the grid: 0 2 2 1 0 0.
- Circle the root tone on the sixth string (0).
- Using simple addition, ask students to transpose all six notes of the E chord up by one fret. To do this they use addition. For example, by adding one to each fret, the new chord is 1 3 3 2 1 1.
- Circle the new root (1), and indicate the barre by drawing a line across the first fret.
- Identify the new root (F). Use the reference chart if necessary.
- Ask the students to transpose the E chord to other frets. "Transpose the E chord up 5 frets, and name the chord." Identify the root tone on the fifth fret. The new chord is A, 5 7 7 6 5 5.
- Repeat the procedure using the E-minor form.

- Practice transposing the A and A-minor chords to different root locations on the A string using a similar process.

Exercise: Using the Boney Side of the Finger

Objective: Students learn the mechanics of successful barre technique.
   Process:

- Place the first finger directly on top of the third fret.
- Then, bring the elbow in close to the body, and slightly rotate the wrist counterclockwise until the boney side of the finger makes contact with the strings.
- Be sure that the finger is straight, wrist arched, thumb low, elbow close to the body, and the neck of the guitar elevated.
- The flesh of the finger will protrude over the fret.
- To reinforce the concept of using the boney side of the finger, push against the side of the finger, and resist. Then, push against the bottom, fleshy side of the finger and resist. The finger should exhibit more strength and resistance when pushed from the boney side than from the fleshy side.

Exercises: Developing Strength and Independence

Objective: Students gain the strength necessary to play barre forms.
   Process:

- *Isometric exercise.* Off of the guitar, have the students squeeze their thumb into the base of the first finger on the left hand. Hold for ten seconds, then repeat.
- *Stretching exercise for easy C barre, root-5.* Off of the guitar, with the left hand have students press the tip of the third finger against the thumb. Press until the third joint bends in toward the palm.
- *Digital pattern.* Have the students lay the first finger of their left hand across all six strings, in barre position. Do a series of digital patterns on each string, while the first finger remains at rest, lying across the strings. Here are some examples of finger patterns to play on each string. Use repeated notes:
  2 2 3 3 2 2 3 3
  2 2 4 4 2 2 4 4
  3 3 4 4 3 3 4 4
  1 1 4 4 1 1 4 4
  1 1 3 3 1 1 3 3
  1 1 2 2 1 1 2 2

Exercise: The Progressive Barre

Objective: Students build confidence by barring only two strings and then expanding from there.
  Process:
  • Barre the first and second string, and play the chromatic scale in repeated notes. Use pulsing to avoid fatigue.
  • Progressively increase the number of strings that are covered from two to three to four, etc.
  • When you reach the fifth and sixth strings, recite the names of the roots, which are being played with the first finger.

Exercise: The Fret Is Like a Curb

Objective: Students learn to place the barre finger close to the fret.
  Process:

  • Do a posture check.
  • Have students lay the first finger of their left hand across the neck in barre position with the tip of the index finger touching the E string.
  • Silently, pulse four times, and then, without looking, slide the finger from the first fret to the second fret. The finger should glide into the second fret like a car tire bumps into a curb.

AFTER THE PRELIMINARIES

Now that you understand barre theory, have developed hand strength, and know where the finger contact point is, you can concentrate on integrating barre forms into songs. Remember that one of the advantages of barre forms is the ability to play sharp and flat chords, such as F# and B♭. Two other commonly used barre forms are F minor, B minor, and G minor. The most obvious place to start is simple songs in the key of C that use the F chord. Encourage students to use the barre form (1 3 3 2 1 1) instead of the easy F (x x 3 2 1 x).

Exercises: Find Songs That Use One or Two Barre Forms

Objective: Students build confidence by performing songs with only one barre form.
  Process:

  • Find a song that uses one or two barre chords. A good example is "Hotel California" by the Eagles, which uses a B minor and an F#. Both chords use the same fingering but on different root strings.

• One trick is to aim for the power chords, B5 and F#5, and let the other fingers follow. For some students grabbing the power chord may be a meaningful milestone, and there will be others who can play the entire F♯ barre form.

Exercise: Progressions for Barre Practice

Objective: Students learn practice routines for individual practice.

• *Chromatic sequence.* Move barre forms chromatically up the neck. For example, start with the open E chord, using barre fingering, and then move to F, F♯. Use pulsing to avoid fatigue.
• *Barre-chord scales.* Use repeated notes and chord pulsing to play barre chords based on the natural notes. E types include F, G, A, B, C, and D, and A types include B, C, D, E, F, and G.
• *Barre-chord scales with crossover from E to A type.* Play barre forms, with roots crossing from root-6 to root-5, as follows:
root-6 F G A
root-5 B C D E F
• *Blues progressions with E- and A-type barres.*
    ○ root-6: for the blues in C, the roots are at the following frets on the E string:
    C = 8
    F = 1
    G = 3
    ○ root-5: for the blues in C, the roots are at the following frets of the A string:
    C = 3
    F = 8
    G = 10
    ○ combined E and A types: In the key of C the roots are at the following frets:
    C = 3 (root-5)
    F = 1 (root-6)
    G = 3 (root-6)
• *Diatonic chord families.* This intermediate exercise also teaches music theory. Here is the progression:
I, ii, iii, IV, V, iv, V, I
For example, starting on root-6, play F, Gmin, Amin. Starting on root-5, play B♭, C, Dmin, etc., F. Play this progression in as many keys as possible.

SPECIAL STRENGTH-SAVING TECHNIQUES

• *Pulsing.* When strumming quarter notes, release the muscles on the *and* of beats 2 and 4. This is sometimes referred to as *pulsing*.

- *The double barre.* On some barre forms, such as the root-6 F minor, you may be able to place the second finger on top of the first finger to obtain more pressure.
- *Ukulele-style four-string movable forms.* There are some students whose hands will not allow them to play barre forms. In that case, they can refinger the barre forms to play ukulele-style moveable forms, which utilize only strings 4, 3, 2, and 1:

G barre	3 5 5 4 3 3
G movable ukulele form	x x 5 4 3 3
G minor	3 5 5 3 3 3
G-minor moveable ukulele form	x x 5 3 3 3
C barre	x 3 5 5 5 3
C moveable ukulele form	x x 5 5 5 3
C-minor barre	x 3 5 5 4 3
C-minor moveable ukulele form	x x 4 5 5 4 3

Photo 24.11 G ukulele chord

IMPROVING STUDENT ACTION: QUICK FIX

- Action means the distance of the strings from the neck.
- If a student's strings are too high off the neck for successful playing, place a capo on the first or second fret.
- Tune the guitar down the appropriate amount.

REVIEW OF BARRE TECHNIQUE

- Arch the wrist, which naturally elongates the fingers.
- The thumb will be near the bottom of the neck.
- Keep the elbow close the body.
- Keep the neck of the guitar elevated.
- Use the boney side of the index finger to pinch the strings into the fret.
- Light-gauge strings make barre forms easier to play.
- A properly adjusted action makes barre forms easier to play.

A FINAL WORD: THE RAILROAD-TRAIN ANALOGY

I like to compare the barre chords to passenger trains on railroad tracks. For example, the A Train rides on the A string and stops at roots on the A string. The A Train carries A chords as passengers. The E Train rides on the E string and stops at roots on the E string. The E Train carries E chords as passengers.

Train Schedule

Train	Passengers	Track	Stops
E Train	E chords	E string	roots on the E string
A Train	A chords	A string	roots on the A string

For kids you may use the analogy of the three bears.

The Three Bears

Papa Bear:	
Full G Barre Form	3 5 5 4 3 3
Mamma Bear:	
G Ukulele Form	x x 5 4 3 3
Baby Bear:	
G Triad	x x x 4 3 3

V

INTERMEDIATE SKILLS

25

Improvisation

The improviser's attitude is one of exploration and discovery.

Guitar is well suited for improvisation. Although improvisation is most often associated with lead guitar, it is also used in composing music and in creating original practice exercises. Improvisation involves scrambling the notes of an existing riff or scale and putting them back together in a new order. It also involves learning predetermined patterns that are specific to a certain culture or style.

GETTING STARTED

Your class can begin improvising the first day of class. We have already learned "Flaming Ice Cube" in chapter 3. Since "Flaming Ice Cube" consists of constant eighth notes, the whole song can be taught using verbal cues: 0-0-12-12-0-0-10-10-0-0-7-7-5-5-3-3. The notes to "Flaming Ice Cube" outline the minor pentatonic scale, which is frequently used in popular rock music. Student can be encouraged by the procedure of having the entire class improvise at the same time—collectively and anonymously. In this manner, no individual has to be self-conscious about standing out or being judged.

Exercise: Scrambling "Flaming Ice Cube"

Objectives:

- Make a connection between the fingerboard distance and pitch.
- Create spontaneous melody on a single string.
- Become familiar with the higher frets.

Process:

- Play "Flaming Ice Cube" on the first string: 0-0-12-12-0-0-10-10-0-0-7-7-5-5-3-3.
- *Exploration #1.* Keep the same rhythm, but change the order of the pitches.
- *Exploration #2.* Keep the same order of the pitches, but change the rhythm.
- *Exploration #3.* Improvise by freely changing the order of pitches and the rhythm.
- *Accompaniment.* Add a drum machine, and play an E5 open power chord: 0 2 x x x x.

RIFFS

A *riff* is a short musical idea that is repeated over and over. The riff provides not only scale material but also, more importantly, the stylistic sound. Some teachers refer to this stylistic sound as the musical *vernacular*. The training riff presented here uses only two fingers, the first and third fingers of the left hand.

Exercise: Training Riff 1

Objective: Students attune their ear to the vernacular (style) of rock and blues improvisation.
   Process:

- Training riff 1 is played entirely in quarter notes, is two measures long, and outlines the E-minor pentatonic scale. It is played on strings 2 and 1. The notes on the first string are underlined:
  The frets are 5, 3, 5, 3, 5, 7, 5, 3.
  The fingering is 3, 1, 3, 1, 3, 3, 3, 1.
- Teach the riff, using echo imitation and repeated notes.
- Use a play-along recording, and have students improvise collectively and anonymously in the key of E minor.

• Optional Accompaniment: For accompaniment have half of the class play a blues in E using open power chords: E5—0 2 x x x x, A5—x 0 2 x x x, and D5—x x 0 2 0 0. Here is the E blues progression using all open power chords (notice there is no B7chord): ||E5| | |A5| |E5| |D5| |E5||

Exercise: Riff Rondo

Objective: Students practice varying a musical idea by alternating the training riff with free improvisation.
  Process:

• Demonstrate how to alternate the two-measure training riff with two measures of improvisation.
• Use an accompaniment recording, and have students alternate the riff with two measures of improvisation.
• Reassure students that there is no right answer. The object is to use the riff as a starting point for musical exploration.

THE BLUE NOTE AND STRING BENDING

To achieve a blues sound, we will expand the pentatonic scale by:

• raising the minor third a quartertone (this is called the *neutral third*), and
• stretching the fourth scale degree upward, approximately a half step, producing the flatted fifth. This is achieved by stretching the string, which is referred to as *string bending*. The neutral third is produced by stretching the flatted-third scale degree about a quartertone.

How to Bend a String

• On the first and second strings, use the third finger to stretch the string upward, away from your palm.
• On all other strings, stretch the string downward toward your palm.
• The finger usually used to bend the string is the third finger. For sufficient strength when bending a string, we frequently use fingers 1, 2, and 3 at the same time.
• To bend the appropriate distance, and raise the pitch the desired amount, you usually need to touch the adjacent string or even slide beneath the adjacent string. In most instances the fin-

gers will touch and also stretch the adjacent strings.

Exercise: Training Riff 1 With String with Flatted Fifth and Neutral Third

Objective: Students attune their ear to the blue note and practice string bending.
  Process:

• This riff is a variation on training riff 1.
  The notes on the first string are underlined:
  B = bend, N = neutral third.
  The frets are 5, 3, 5, 3, 5, B, 5, N3.
  The fingering is 3, 1, 3, 1, 3, 3B, 3, 1B.
• Teach the riff, using echo imitation. As you play, recite the fret numbers.
• Put on your play-along recording, and have students improvise in a blues in E.

Exercise: The Blues in E Using Roots Only

Improvisations are improved when the improviser is aware of the chord changes. One way to practice this is by playing blues solos using roots only. Later you can extend this exercise by playing chord-tone solos, using triads.
  Objective: Students learn to use chord roots as a basis for improvisation.
  Process:

• Teach the root locations for the blues in E. Use the third finger of the left hand to have the students locate the following:
  E 5/2
  A 5/1
  B 7/1
• Turn on the play-along recording of blues in E.
• Have the students play the chord roots in quarter notes.
• Lead the students with interesting rhythms using echo imitation.

Exercise: Embellishing the Roots

Objective: Students learn to improvise by embellishing chord roots.
  Process:

• Review the chord roots for blues in E.
• Have the students embellish the roots by playing the note a whole step (two frets) beneath them.
• Variation: Have the students embellish the roots by playing the note a whole step above them.
• Improvise freely.

Exercise: A Minor Pentatonic in Three Octaves; Diagonal Form

Extending the range of an improvisation is easier than you think. This is because you can play pentatonic scales in three octaves, using the same fingering for each octave. The fingering is 1-3-1-3-slide. The entire scale is played using only two fingers, 1 and 3!

Objective: Students extend their range by using symmetrical fingerings for three octaves. Note that the fingering pattern does not begin on the root. Instead, it begins on the ♭7. The scale degrees are as follows: ♭7, root, ♭3, 4, 5.

Process:

- Use your overhead projector and a full neck grid to color code each octave.
- Each octave uses only two strings.
- Use four repeated notes to give verbal cues for the A-minor pentatonic scale. The underlined frets are the roots. The / represents a string crossing.
  Octave one, strings 6 and 5. 3 3 3 3 5 5 5 5 / 3 3 3 3 5 5 5 5 7 7 7 7
  Octave two, strings 4 and 3. 5 5 5 5 7 7 7 7 / 5 5 5 5 7 7 7 7 9 9 9 9
  Octave three, strings 2 and 1. 8 8 8 8 10 10 10 10 8 8 8 8 10 10 10 10 12 12 12 12
- Perform echo imitation in each octave.
- Have students build a solo by starting with the low octave and moving up the neck at your cue.
- Point out the common tones between the A-minor barre chord (parent chord) and the scale.

Exercise: Finding the Relative Major Key Using Interchangeable Fingerings

Objective: Students will learn to find the relative major of the minor pentatonic scale.
Process:
- Teach the A-minor pentatonic scale across the neck at the fifth position. With the underlined notes signifying the roots, the frets are 5 8 / 5 7 / 5 7 / 5 7 / 5 8 / 5 8.

Exercise: Finding the Relative Major Pentatonic Scale

- Locate the minor-key tone on the sixth string (5/6).
- Count three frets in a sharp direction from the key tone. For example, the root of the A-minor pentatonic is 5/6, so add three frets and identify the note: 5 + 3 = 8. It is note C on fret 8.
- Play the C-major pentatonic scale. The notes are interchangeable with A minor, but the new key tone is C, on fret 8.

- Use the following major-chord progression to demonstrate that the pentatonic fingerings for C major and A minor are interchangeable: IIC I IAminI IDminI IG I II

THE EDUCATIONAL VALUE OF CLASSIC RIFFS

The popular-guitar tradition includes songs that are famous for riffs. The guitar instructor can use these riffs for educational purposes by suggesting a few variations. My favorite training riff is "Sunshine of Your Love" by Cream, because it outlines the minor blues scale. I also like "I Shot the Sheriff" by Bob Marley for the same reason. Once the students know a riff, they can improvise by scrambling the order of the notes and changing the rhythms without having to learn a scale.

WHEN STUDENTS BRING RIFFS TO CLASS

Here are some suggestions as to how you can vary a riff for educational and improvisational value.

- Gradually increase the speed of the riff, and play it as fast as possible.
- Change the rhythm.
- Scramble the order of the pitches.
- Change the rhythm and the order of the pitches.
- Refinger the riff so that it contains no open strings.

And once a riff is refingered with no open strings, try the following suggestions:

- Play the riff in different keys by moving up the neck. Say the names of the key while you are playing. For example: G, G#, A, etc.
- For advanced students, have them play the riff in one key, but start on each of the six strings. For example, play "Sunshine of Your Love" starting on strings 6, 5, 4, 3, and 2.

ACCOMPANIMENT OVERVIEW AND SUMMARY

Play-along recordings. Check with your favorite music store for their suggestions for play-along recordings.

Class accompaniment. Half the class can play a blues-chord progression or bass line, while the other half plays the improvisation.

Written-ensemble accompaniments. Write a three-part guitar ensemble that outlines the blues progression. While the class plays the ensemble, selected students may improvise.

Write your own blues riffs. Write a bass line in the keys of E, A, D, G, and C. Use it for reading practice as well as an accompaniment for improvisation.

Keyboard accompaniment. Electric keyboards can provide accompaniments consisting of an entire rhythm section. These accompaniments can be transposed higher or lower and made faster or slower.

Sing-and-strum songs. As you build your collection of sing-and-strum songs, you will find that many present opportunities for improvisation. Some students will want to play lead guitar, while others strum or play bass.

Some additional practice suggestions follow:

- Play along with recording of master improvisers.
- Perform bass lines in the treble register.
- Improvise using triad chord forms.
- Play along with popular recordings.
- In free rhythm, improvise over a drone tone or a single chord. This technique is very useful because you can experiment without having to play in tempo. This technique is called *fermata practice.*
- Listen to and copy short excerpts from master improvisers. Play them in twelve keys.
- Limit your rhythm by improvising in whole notes. Move on to half notes, quarter notes, and eighth notes. When using eighth notes, accent the first one of each group as a guide tone.
- Have a riff conversation where the teacher and student talk to each other by alternating phrases.
- Practice slide guitar using a bottleneck.
- Use echo imitation. Echo phrases with the class. Include vibrato, bends, slides, slurs, muting, staccato, and so forth, if possible.

Exercise: Walking, Standing, and Running Tones

Objective: Students determine how notes of the chromatic scale relate to a chord.
Process:

- The instructor plays a chord, such as E minor or E7, in repeated whole notes.
- The students play a chromatic scale, on the high E string, over the chord in whole notes. As they play, they respond to the notes by expressing the following classifications:

  o *Standing tone.* Tone that you can sustain and it sounds good (chord tones: 1, 3, 5).
  o *Walking tone.* Tone that sounds good but is less settled (color tones: b5, 6, b7, 9).
  o *Running tone.* Dissonant tone that you should quickly slide off of.
  o Another metaphor is the traffic signal: green tones, yellow tones, and red tones.

IMPROVISATION MAXIMS

- Try lots of ideas, remembering the ones you like.
- Have an attitude of curiosity, exploration, and nonjudgment.
- Make the most from the least.
- A good idea should be repeated.
- Listen to, and copy, the experts.

A Later Step

After students have become proficient with the A-minor/C-major pentatonic scales, with the root based on the 6th string, they are ready to learn the root-5 forms.

Exercise: Teach the D-Minor Pentatonic Root-5, Using the Repeated Notes and Verbal Cues

Objective: Students learn pentatonic scales based off of root-5 chords.
Process:

- The frets for the three octave diagonal form are:
  Octave 1. Strings 5 and 4: 3 3 3 3 5 5 5 / 3 3 3 5 5 5 5 7 7 7 7
  Octave 2. Strings 3 and 2: 5 5 5 5 7 7 7 7 / 6 6 6 6 8 8 8 8 10 10 10 10
  Octave 3. String 1: 8 8 8 8 10 10 10 10 13 13 13 13 15 15 15 17 17 17 17
- The frets for root-5 D-minor in fifth position are: 5 8 / 5 7 / 5 7 / 6 8 / 5 8
- The corresponding chord progression for F-major pentatonic is:
  ||F | |Dmin| |Gmin| |C | || (F-major/D-minor pentatonic)

26

Student Combos

Guitar students can benefit from the procedures used in an art class.

In art class, the students are provided with techniques and guidelines and then go to work on their projects. Like the art teacher, the guitar teacher may assist students by providing materials, encouragement, challenges, ideas, aesthetic criteria, and demonstrations.

WHEN TO ASSIGN COMBOS

When students have achieved proficiency with reading music, chords, and improvisation, they can benefit by applying their skills in an artistic way. You will have to carefully decide if your class is mature enough to work independently and if you have the space necessary for them to work.

OBJECTIVES OF COMBOS

- reinforce and apply written ensemble music or sing-and-strum pieces
- change of pace from weekly routine
- collaboration among other students
- performance opportunities
- exploration of form and arranging
- creative application of skills and techniques
- experience arranging accompaniments including bass, chords, melody, improvisation, and other instruments and vocals
- experience with rehearsal techniques
- written summaries provide critical thinking and writing opportunities
- independence
- provides the instructor with time to interact with individual students
- enjoyment and self-expression

REPERTOIRE

The instructor should provide a number of song options that reflect the appropriate skill level of the class. The students choose which song they prefer from the options that you provide. If students want to choose their own song, insist that they locate their own materials in advance for your approval.

PLANNING AND REHEARSAL CONSIDERATIONS

- The success of combos is dependent on proper orientation before students begin rehearsing.
- I recommend two people to a part. This allows students to assist each other, and if there is an absence, the parts will still be covered.
- Students should sit in a circle so that they can see each other during rehearsal.
- Discuss the criteria of a successful performance in advance.
- Discuss the importance of having a leader or conductor who will manage the rehearsal and start and end the song.
- Electric instruments usually provide a distraction from the learning goals. On the other hand, there may be special situations in which to incorporate them. This would depend on the maturity of the students and the practice space available.
- Having bongo drums and percussion available adds interest to combo performances.

REHEARSAL STRATEGY

- Suggest parts such as bass, strumming, finger picking, singing, percussion, improvising, etc.
- Decide on the daily goal.

161

COMBO PROFICIENCY SLIPS

Name:_____

Date: _____Class Period:_____

Song Performed:_____

Tuning	4	3	2	I
Group Precision	4	3	2	I
Individual Accuracy	4	3	2	I
Flow	4	3	2	I
Creativity	4	3	2	I
Vocals	4	3	2	I
Bass	4	3	2	I
Dynamics	4	3	2	I
Improvisation	4	3	2	I
Beginning	4	3	2	I
Ending	4	3	2	I
Musical Spirit	4	3	2	I

Comments:

Name:_____

Date: _____Class Period:_____

Song Performed:_____

Tuning	4	3	2	I
Group Precision	4	3	2	I
Individual Accuracy	4	3	2	I
Flow	4	3	2	I
Creativity	4	3	2	I
Vocals	4	3	2	I
Bass	4	3	2	I
Dynamics	4	3	2	I
Improvisation	4	3	2	I
Beginning	4	3	2	I
Ending	4	3	2	I
Musical Spirit	4	3	2	I

Comments:

Name:_____

Date: _____Class Period:_____

Song Performed:_____

Tuning	4	3	2	I
Group Precision	4	3	2	I
Individual Accuracy	4	3	2	I
Flow	4	3	2	I
Creativity	4	3	2	I
Vocals	4	3	2	I
Bass	4	3	2	I
Dynamics	4	3	2	I
Improvisation	4	3	2	I
Beginning	4	3	2	I
Ending	4	3	2	I
Musical Spirit	4	3	2	I

Comments:

Name:_____

Date: _____Class Period:_____

Song Performed:_____

Tuning	4	3	2	I
Group Precision	4	3	2	I
Individual Accuracy	4	3	2	I
Flow	4	3	2	I
Creativity	4	3	2	I
Vocals	4	3	2	I
Bass	4	3	2	I
Dynamics	4	3	2	I
Improvisation	4	3	2	I
Beginning	4	3	2	I
Ending	4	3	2	I
Musical Spirit	4	3	2	I

Comments:

Figure 26.1: This sheet may be photocopied for class or other groups within purchaser's institution only. This provision does not confer any other rights to the purchaser or his or her institution.

- At the end of the period, reflect on the goal and what might be the next step.
- The leader should call practice pauses during which each person should practice their individual part.
- The leader will call the group back together after practice pauses.
- The leader directs practice loops on small sections of music.
- The leader directs practice loops on large sections of music.

INSTRUCTOR INVOLVEMENT

Be sure the students are clear on rehearsal methods by reviewing them daily. Assign combos to their practice locations. If space is limited, or students are too young, you may not be able to have independent combos. When the students perform for the class, introduce the individuals in the group. This is an opportunity to create connections among students. Offer the incentive of taking the groups "on tour" to play for other classes if their music is sufficiently prepared. Record the groups, and listen to the playback.

COMBO ASSESSMENT

In-class performance. Make a list of criteria for a successful performance. This list would include: tuning, precision, flow, creativity, form, vocals and vocal arranging, bass, dynamics, improvisation, beginning, ending, and spirit. Provide students with proficiency slips (figure 26.1), and have them fill out their name and song performed and circle the appropriate entries. An abacus may be used for combo assessment. In my room the abacus is mounted over the white board using double-sided tape. The success criteria are written next to each set of beads. Slide the number of beads to the right, which reflect the success on a scale of one to ten.

Reflective writing. Have students write a summary of the experience. Provide them with a guide for their writing that would include the following:

- a list of the names of the group members and what part each played
- song title and some background on the song
- reflection of the most and least successful parts of the performance
- reflection of the most and least successful parts of the rehearsals
- a comment on the criteria for success listed on the proficiency slip
- a comment on assessment of how useful the experience was and whether the student would like to do it again

School or public performances. The music developed during combo projects may be used as part of a public guitar-night performance. Additionally, successful combos may perform for other classes or the office staff. Incorporating observers from outside of the classroom creates a motivation to produce quality results.

Teaching Music Theory

The guitar is a superb tool for teaching music theory because the chromatic scale is clearly laid out with each string.

Theory concepts can be taught as you feel the class is ready and you feel comfortable with them yourself. Remember, most guitar classes are general music classes, so this is a golden opportunity to teach music theory.

CONCEPTS COVERED

- half steps and whole steps
- scales and modes on a single string
- chord construction
- diatonic chord families
- relative major and minor chords
- parallel major and minor chords
- triads and inversions
- transposition
- intervals
- sharps, flats, and enharmonic notes

THE CHROMATIC SCALE ON ONE STRING

The twelve frets of an octave on a single string provide a clear illustration of the chromatic scale. Teach the students the word *chromatic* and its definition, a scale containing twelve half steps that comprises an octave.

Exercise: *The Chromatic Scale*

Objective: Students review the location of frets by number.
Process:

- Point out the purpose of the dots on the guitar neck. The dots allow you to locate frets 5, 7, 9, and 12 without counting each fret.

- Using repeated notes, play the chromatic scale with the first finger of the left hand. For example:
0 0 0 0 1 1 1 1 2 2 2 2
- Variation: Finger the notes with fingers 2, 3, or 4, but remind students that the first finger will always remain resting on the string. Advanced students may alternate fingers with the repetition of each note.
- Quiz the students by asking them to locate frets by fret number.

Exercise: *The Chromatic Scale by Note Name*

Objective: Students use the B/C E/F rule to name the notes of the chromatic scale.
Process:

- Teach or review the B/C E/F rule: there are two frets between every note except between B and C and between E and F.
- Have students recite the note names as they play the chromatic scale on the low-E string using repeated notes.
- Ascending the chromatic scale recite sharps, and descending the scale recite flats.
- Quiz the class on the location of sharp and flat notes.
- Teach the concept of enharmonic notes, such as A# and B♭.

Exercise: *The Natural Minor Scale*

Objective: Students visualize the half steps and whole steps in the natural minor scale.
Process:

- Using repeated notes and the B/C E/F rule, play the natural notes on the A string:

A B C D E F G A
The frets are 0, 2, 3, 5, 7, 8, 10, 12.

- Play the natural notes on the A string again, and have some of the students strum the A-minor chord. Notice how the chord and scale fit together.
- Play the natural notes on the A string again, and have some students strum an A-major chord. Identify the wrong notes.
- Explain that the natural notes on the A string form a scale called the A natural minor scale.
- Determine the formula of whole steps and half steps for the A natural minor scale by observing how many frets there are between each note. Play the scale again, and recite "whole" and "half" to indicate the natural minor scale formula: W H W W H W W
- Write the formula on the board.

Exercise: The Natural Notes Create Modes on Each String

Objective: Students Learn to Locate the Natural Notes on All Six Strings
Process:

- Using the B/C E/F rule, play the natural notes on all six strings.
- Point out that by starting and ending on different notes, each string represents a mode.
  E string Phrygian
  A string Aeolian
  D string Dorian
  G string Mixolydian
  B string Locrian
- The only modes not demonstrated are the major (Ionian) and the Lydian mode.
- Determine the whole steps and half steps for each mode, and write them on the board.

Exercise: Relative Major and Minor Scales Demonstrated on One String

Objective: Students hear and see the relationship between A minor and C major.
Process:

- Review the natural notes on the A string, which create the A natural minor scale.
- Play the natural notes on the A string again, but start on note C, on fret 3.
- Continue playing the natural notes up to high C at the fifteenth fret.
- Explain that this is the C-major scale and that it uses the same notes as the A natural minor

scale. In other words, the notes of the A-minor and C-major scales are interchangeable. The C-major scale is also referred to as the C Ionian mode.

- Because both scales use the same notes, they are referred to as relatives. In other words, C is the relative major of A minor. Conversely, A minor is the relative minor of C major.

Exercise: Building the A-Major Scale on the A String

Objective: Students use half and whole steps to build the A-major scale.
Process:

- Review the B/C E/F rule.
- Using repeated notes, play the C-major scale on the A string. Remember to play the natural notes beginning on the third fret, and playing up to the high C at the fifteenth fret.
- Determine the pattern of whole and half steps in the C-major scale.
- Write the pattern on the board: W W H W W W H.
- Explain that this is the pattern for major scales and that it should be memorized. The major scale is like a ruler: it provides reference points for understanding music theory.
- Use the pattern of W W H W W W H to build the A-major scale on the A string.
- Determine the note names and number of sharps that occur in the A-major scale on the A string: A B C# D E F# G# A.
- Repeat the procedure for the other strings:
  E string four sharps
  A string three sharps
  D string two sharps
  B string five sharps

Written Exercise

Use staff paper to write out the notes of the major scales on each string. Indicate the fret number and note name for each note.

SCALE DEGREES IN THE KEY OF C

In order to measure the distances between notes, each note in the major scale is assigned a number, which is referred to as a *scale degree*.

Exercise: Scale Degrees and Intervals in the Key of C

Objective: Students learn to hear and understand the concept of scale degrees and intervals.

Process:

- Review the C-major scale for one octave in open position. Here are the frets, starting from the A string: 3 / 0 2 3 / 0 2 / 0 1
- Play the scale again in repeated notes, and recite the scale-degree numbers for each note. For example, first degree, second degree, etc.
- Use echo imitation to reinforce student understanding. For example, sing "One, two, one," and have students echo by playing C D C.
- Progressively extend the scale degrees further from the root.

Exercise: Playing and Labeling Intervals

Objective: Students learn to play and identify the sound of intervals.

Process:

- Demonstrate the intervals in the key of C by plucking the root C and the corresponding scale degree at the same time. For example:
  C2 C and D
  C3 C and E
  C4 C and F
- Using repeated notes, have the students play intervals up to the interval of C13. C13 is C and A. For example:
  C2, C2, C2, C2, C3, C3, C3, C3, etc.
  Use the thumb and middle finger to pinch the intervals.
- Do an ear-training quiz by playing intervals in C, and have students play them back and say their names.
- Provide students with the interval number, such as C4, and have them determine the notes and the fingering.

Written Exercises

- *Notate intervals.* Have students create a reference chart for the key of C, and label the scale degrees. Ask them to notate various intervals of C. Play the examples.
- *Identify intervals (interval dictation).* Play intervals, and have students write them down on staff paper.
- *Intuition.* Notate two intervals on the overhead. Play one of them. Have students choose the correct interval and name it.

Exercise: Color-Coded Intervals in the Natural-Note Scale

Objective: Students learn to identify intervals when reading music.

Process:

- Using your overhead projector, write out the seventeen natural notes. Use a different color to indicate notes that are a third apart.
- Have students play all seventeen notes.
- Have students play only the colored notes.
- Explain that they are playing the intervals of diatonic thirds.
- Use the same technique to teach diatonic fourths and fifths.

RELATIVE MINOR AND MAJOR PENTATONIC SCALES

Students begin practicing guitar improvisation using the minor pentatonic scale. Blues and rock music generally use the minor pentatonic, but country and pop music use the major pentatonic.

Exercise: The G-Major and E-Minor Pentatonic Scale

Objective: Students learn to use the interchangeable fingering for improvisations in the key of E minor or G major.

Process:

- Play the E-minor pentatonic scale across the neck. The frets, starting on the low E string, are 0 3 / 0 2 / 0 2 / 0 2 / 0 3 / 0 3.
- Play the same notes, but start on the note G, three frets higher:
  3 / 0 2 / 0 2 / 0 2 / 0 3 / 0 3
- Inform students that by starting on G, they are playing the major pentatonic scale.
- Teach them how to find the major and minor pentatonic fingerings:
  - To find the relative major scale, count up three frets from the minor-key tone.
  - To find the relative minor scale, count down three frets from the major-key tone.

Quiz: Relative Major and Minor

- What is the relative minor of C major? (Answer: Count down three frets to A minor.)
- What is the relative major of A minor? (Answer: Count up three frets to C major.)

TRIADS

Scales, intervals, and triads are the building blocks for music and are an important part of music education. Guitarists use triads for several purposes:

- accompaniment
- reference tones for improvisation
- harmonizing melodies

Exercise: Demonstrating the Triad Inversions of a C Chord

Objective: Students understand that major chords are comprised of only three scale degrees: 1, 3, and 5.

Process:

- Review the fingerings, scale degrees, and intervals for the C scale in open position starting on the A string: 3 / 0 2 3 / 0 2 / 0 1.
- Demonstrate a triad by fingering a C chord and plucking the notes C, E, and G on strings 5, 4, and 3. Determine the scale degrees (1, 3, and 5).
- Explain that since the triad starts on the note C, it is called *root position*.
- Pluck strings 4, 3, and 2 to demonstrate the first inversion. Determine the scale degrees (3, 5, and 1).
- Pluck strings 3, 2, and 1 to demonstrate the second inversion. Determine the scale degrees (5, 1, and 3).
- Loop each inversion using a variety of fingerpicking patterns:
  p , i, m
  m, i, p
  p, i, m, i

REMEMBERING TRIAD FORMS

Triad fingerings are easily remembered if they are related to forms the students already know. The underlined frets represent the triad. The bold frets represent the roots.

- root-5, C barre chord, x 3 5 **5** 5 3 triad = **5** 5 3
- root-6, F barre chord, 1 3 3 **2** 1 1 triad = 2 1 **1**
- open-position D chord, x x x **2** 3 2 triad = 2 **3** 2

Exercise: Moveable Triad Forms; Triad Scales

Objectives: Students relate triad fingering to barre forms and the open position D and transpose these forms up and down the neck.

Process:

- *Triad scale, chromatic.* Finger the triads indicated above. Locate their roots. Transpose them up and down the neck chromatically.
- *Triad scale, natural notes.* Transpose the triad up and down the neck based on the natural

notes. For example, start with F major, x x x 2 1 1, and then in repeated notes play triads G, A, B, C, etc., by sliding the first form up the neck.

- Use a variety of arpeggio patterns to add interest to the triad scales.

Exercise: Converting Barre Forms into Triads

Objective: Students relate triads to barre forms.

Process: Convert the following minor barre chords into minor triads, and transpose them up and down the neck.

- The root-5 C minor, x 3 5 **5** 4 **3** triad = **5** 4 3 (root is underlined)
- The root-6 F minor, 1 3 3 **1** 1 1 triad = 1 1 **1**
- The open-position D minor, x x x **2** 3 1 triad = 2 **3** 1
- Repeat the process for major forms.

QUICK DEMONSTRATIONS

Chord construction and diatonic chord families. Divide the class into three groups. Assign each group a starting note of a C chord: C, E, G. Play the natural notes ascending, in repeated notes. Listen to the resulting diatonic triads: C, D minor, E minor, F, G, A minor, and B diminished.

Relative major and minor chords. Play a chord drill alternating between C and A minor, G and E minor, and F and D minor. Have students notice the notes that are common to each chord. Have them take advantage of the common fingers.

Parallel major and minor chords. Learn chord fingerings by alternating between D major and D minor, E major and E minor, and A major and A minor. Instruct the students to focus on which notes change and which stay the same. For ear training, hide your hand behind a music stand, and demonstrate either the minor or major chord, having students identify which is which.

28

Teaching Jazz Chords

Learning jazz chords improves a student's ability to hear intervals.

Jazz chords are chords that contain color tones, such as the 6th, 7th, 9th, and 13th. The best way to introduce them is gradually by incorporating one or two of them in a blues or pop song. Therefore, when you are constructing lyric sheets for beginning songs, it is a good idea to include the option of some jazz chords for more advanced students. In addition to applying them in musical situations, learning and playing these chords improves aural skills. Proficiency with jazz chords is an important milestone for second-year guitar.

Like barre forms, jazz chords can be built off a sixth-string root or fifth-string root. By learning the G root-6 and C root-5 major scales in second position, it is possible to build chords using simple arithmetic. As an overview we will look at the C and G chords and their intervallic formulas. Because there are no open strings in these chords, they are moveable, like barre forms, and can be transposed to any root that is needed. Most jazz standards can be played with twelve forms or less.

CHORD FORMULAS

The major chord types can usually be substituted for one another or even for a basic major chord. The same holds true for the minor- and seventh-chord types. The following formulas are not chord voicings or fingerings; rather, they are formulas that apply to any root. The voicings will be discussed later.

Major-Chord Types

| major | 1-3-5 |
| C6 | 1-3-6-8 |

Cmaj7	1 3 5 7
Cmaj9	1 3 5 7 9
C69	1 3 5 7 9

Minor Chord Types

minor	1 ♭b 5
Cmin7	1 ♭3 5 ♭7
Cmin6	1 ♭3 5 6
Cmin9	1 ♭b 5 ♭7 9
Cmin7b5	1 ♭3 ♭5 ♭7

Seventh Chord Types

C7	1 3 5 ♭7
C7 (9)	1 3 5 ♭7 9
C7 (♭9)	1 3 5 ♭7 ♭9
C7 (♯9)	1 3 5 ♭7 ♯9
C7 (13)	1 3 5 ♭7 9 13
C7(sus)	1 4 5 ♭7

Other

| C diminished | 1 ♭3 ♭5 6 |
| C augmented | 1 3 ♯5 |

Exercise: Learning the C-Major Scale in Second Position

Objective: Students build movable chords from scale degrees in second position.

Process Part 1: Teach the scale.

- Demonstrate the scale, and ask the students to analyze your fingering. Here are the frets: x / 3 5 / 2 3 5 / 2 4 5 / 3 5 6 / 3 5
- Using repeated notes and verbal instructions, play the scale by fret number with the class.
- Use a fretboard diagram if you feel it is helpful.

- Write the second position C-major scale on the overhead projector. Add the symbols for string numbers and finger numbers. Add a Roman numeral (II) to indicate the position. Here are the notes up to the thirteenth degree:
  C D E F G A B C D E F G A
- Although they can play the scale by fret number, take a practice pause, and encourage students to connect the written music with the fingerings that they have learned.
- Using repeated notes, play the scale while reading the notation and reciting the note names.
- It is important that, once the students are familiar with the fingering, they play the scale again and recite the scale degrees:
  1-2, 3-4-5, 6-7-8, 9-10-11, 12-13
- Point out that the first and eighth degrees are an octave and that degree 9 is the same as degree 2, etc.
- C root-5 scale, to the 13th degree, summary:
  fret numbers 3 5 / 2 3 5 / 2 4 5 / 3 5 6 / 3 5
  notes names C D E F G A B C D E F G A
  scale degrees 1 2 3 4 5 6 7 8 9 10 11 12 13

Process Part 2: Play the scale in block intervals.

- Review the second position C scale, reciting the scale degrees.
- Using repeated notes, have the students use their thumb to pluck the root while plucking the scale tones using the middle finger.
- The block intervals look like this:
  C, C D, C E, C F, etc.
- Recite the interval names while playing the scale:
  C2, C3, C4, etc. (For CD, use open string.)
- Variation: Play the scale in broken intervals:
  C D C D, C E C E, etc.
- Quiz the students:
  - Play various intervals and have them identify them.
  - Ask students to play various intervals.
  - Play one example (C3), and offer two choices for the correct identification of the chord (C3 or C4?).
  - Play two examples (C3 and C4), and ask which one is C3.
  - Sing intervals using *doo, doo,* and have students play back and name the interval.

CHORD VOICINGS

If you try to construct a jazz chord based on the chord formula, you will discover that they are impossible to play because of the way the guitar is tuned. There-fore, to build chords we rearrange the intervals to fit on the guitar. This arrangement of intervals is called a chord voicing.

ROOT-5 JAZZ-CHORD VOICINGS

The following are the voicings for contemporary moveable forms based on the C scale with the root on the fifth string. Using a sheet of grid paper, have the students construct the following chords. The X indicates a skipped string.

Exercise: Construct Jazz Voicings from Intervals

Use the worksheet provided in figure 28.1 to complete this exercise.

Objective: Students use the second-position C scales to construct root-5 jazz voicings.

Process:

- Use an interval reference chart (below) to construct jazz voicings in notation and on chord grids.

Interval Reference Chart for C Root-5 Jazz-Chord Voicings

The major types follow:

C major	1-5-8-10
C6	1-3-6-8
Cmaj7	1-5-7-10
Cmaj9	1-3-7-9
C69	1-3-6-9

The minor types follow:

C minor	1-5-8-b10
Cmin7	1-b7-b10
Cmin6	1-6-b10
Cmin9	1-b3-b7-9
Cmin7b5	1-b5-b7-b10

The seventh types follow:

C7	1-5-b7-10
C7 (9)	1-3-b7-9
C7 (b9)	1-3-b7-b9
C7 (#9)	1-3-b7-#9
C7 (13)	1-3-b7-9-13
C7sus	1-4-b7-9

The diminished and augmented types follow:

C diminished	1-b5-6-b10
C augmented	1-3-#5-8

A Later Step: Root-6 Jazz Voicings

After a month or so of working with the C root-5 scale, use the same process to teach the G root-6 scale. Here are the fingerings to the 13th degree:

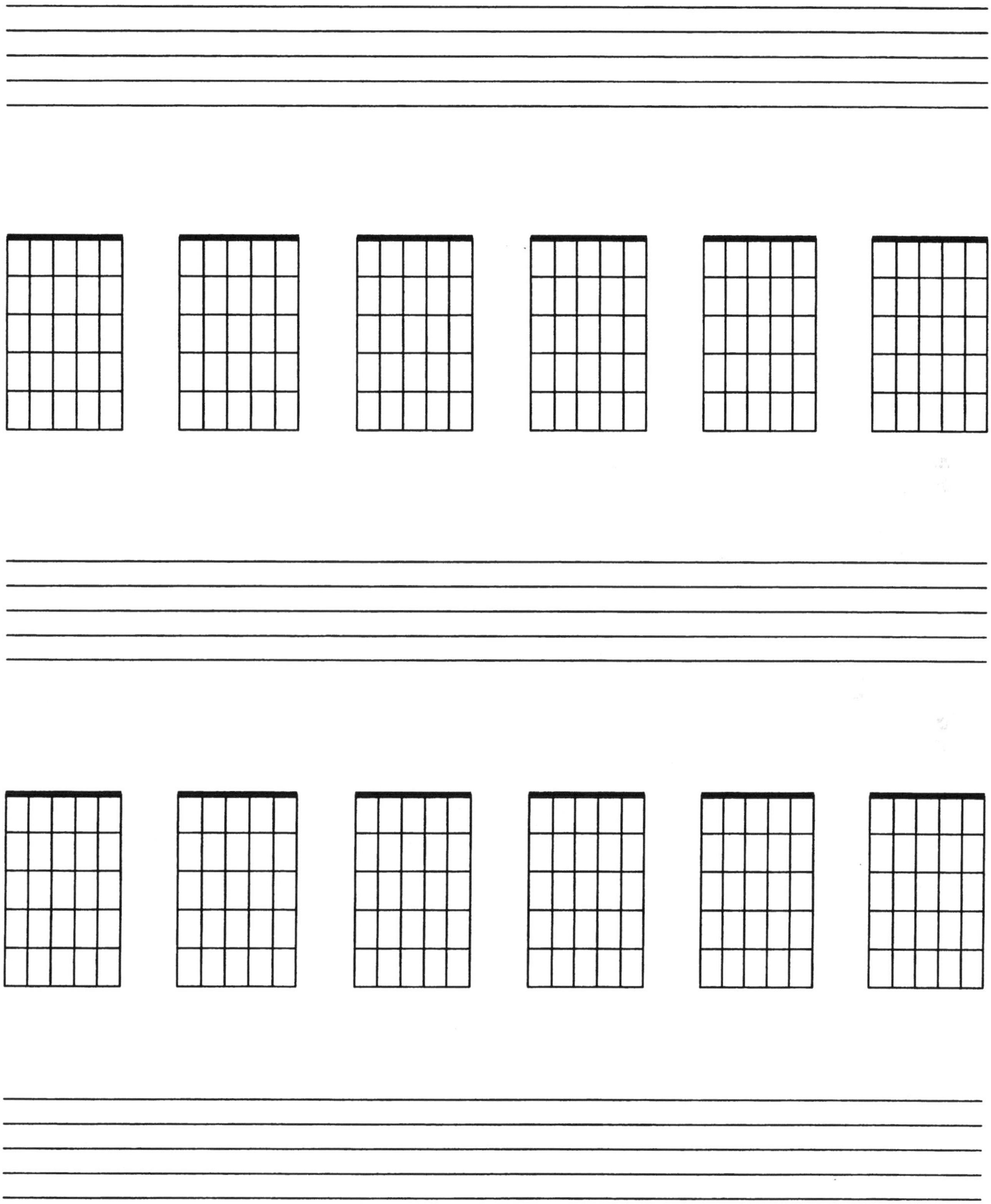

Figure 28.1: This sheet may be photocopied for class or other groups within purchaser's institution only. This provision does not confer any other rights to the purchaser or his or her institution.

fret numbers 3 5 / 2 3 5 / 2 4 5 / 2 4 5 / 3 5
note names G A / B C D / E F# G / A B C / D E
scale degrees 1 2 / 3 4 5 / 6 7 8 / 9 10 11 / 12 13

Interval Reference Chart for G Root-6 Jazz-Chord Voicings

The major types follow:
G major 1-5-8-10
G6 1-6-10-12
Gmaj7 1-7-10-12
Gmaj9 1-7-9-12
G69 1-6-9-12
The minor types follow:
G minor 1-5-8♭10-12
Gmin7 1♭7♭10-12
Gmin6 1-6♭10-12
Gmin9 1♭7♭10-12-9
Gmin7♭5 1♭7♭10♭5 (♭12)
The seventh types follow:
G7 1♭7-10-12
G7 (9) x-3♭7-9-12
G7 (♭9) x-3♭7♭9-12
G7 (#9) x-3♭7-#9-12
G7 (13) 1♭7-10-13
G7sus 1♭7-9-11
The diminished and augmented types follow:
G diminished 1-6♭10♭12
G augmented 1♭7-10-#12

Exercise: Ingraining Chord Forms

Objective: Students memorize fingerings by playing chord forms in various sequences.
  Process:

- Use jazz voicings to strum the following sequences for one or two measures each.

Chromatic sequence C, C#, D, etc.
Cycle of fifths C, G, D, A, etc.
Natural-note roots C, D, E, F, etc.
- Quiz: Ask students to finger various jazz-chord forms. For example, ask them to finger: Cmaj7, Fmaj7, Dmaj7, B♭maj7, etc.

Written Exercises: Build Chord Voicings from Intervals/Chord Formulas

Objective: Students build, understand, and memorize chords by using their numerical formula.
  Process:

- Use the chord building grid/staff worksheet provided in figure 28.1.
- Refer to the interval reference chart provided in this chapter to build C and G jazz chords.
- On the top staff, notate a reference chart of the parent scale. Include the finger numbers, string numbers, and position numbers (e.g., ll with a bracket for second position). Most important is to number the scale degrees from 1 to 13.
- On the second and third staves, provide students with the reference intervals, and have them write the fingering on the grids provided For example: Cmaj7 is 1-5-7-10.
- Variation: On the second and third staves, provide students with a written arpeggio, and have them determine the reference intervals and write the chord on a grid. For example: Cmaj7 (C G B E) reference intervals are 1, 5, 7, 10.
- Variation: Provide students with a grid diagram, and have them notate the chord arpeggio on the staff and determine the reference intervals. For example, Cmaj7 reference intervals are 1, 5, 7, 10; the arpeggio is C G B E.

29

Teaching Solo and Classical Guitar

Solo guitar is the gateway to musical independence.

CHAPTER OVERVIEW

- introduction
- hinting at solo technique from the beginning
- classroom-teaching strategies
- review of right-hand position and patterns
- types of pieces

INTRODUCTION

One of the very special qualities of the guitar is its ability to be played as a solo instrument. In some sense, everything we have done so far has been leading us to this point. As pointed out earlier, finger picking is the gateway to solo guitar, and solo guitar is the gateway to independence. Solo guitar represents the pinnacle of guitar skill and opens the door to a wealth of beautiful music that can be enjoyed for a lifetime. Depending on your school and students, solo guitar could be emphasized from the very beginning. If this is the case, you may benefit from joining the Guitar Foundation of America (GFA), which is the professional organization that specializes in classical-guitar education. Their website is www.guitarfoundation.org/.

Solo guitar refers to any song that is arranged for guitar in such a way that the guitar can stand alone. Examples could include pop songs, hymns, the blues, Celtic music, and folk songs. Virtually any song can be arranged for solo guitar. *Classical guitar* refers to a body of accepted works, mostly from Europe. Classical-guitar arrangements cover all the periods of music history, ranging from the Renaissance to the Baroque, Classical, Romanic, and Modern periods. They range from elegant recreational pieces to the most demanding concert pieces. By teaching European classical music we have a unique opportunity to teach European history and culture. Classical music comes to life for students when they visualize European destinations and exotic times and places. In my view, all history classes should include music history. What better way to get a feel for history than to hear it? Conversely, all guitar classes should include history. (Note that *Spanish guitar* refers to classical guitar music originating in Spain. *Flamenco guitar* is specialized music influenced by the folk culture in Spain and stands in a category by itself.)

I like to think of the guitar as a choir. Hold your right hand in front of you to view the choir. The two primary voices are the thumb, which is the bass, and the ring finger, which is the soprano. The index and middle fingers are the tenor and alto. As we begin, the general thing to remember is that the thumb plays the bass, and the fingers play the treble. As an encouragement, reflect on how much the left hand has been able to accomplish with notes and chords. Since most people are right handed, imagine what the right hand should be able to do.

I have written a book specifically for learning solo-guitar technique and pieces, *A Modern Method for Fingerstyle Guitar*. It is based on my experience in the classroom and with school-age students and therefore is a good match for studying solo guitar in the classroom.

One of the challenges of learning solo guitar pieces is reading the music. Some teachers feel that the use of tablature can expedite the learning process. Others feel that tablature is a crutch. Because I originally learned solo guitar using tablature, I feel that it is a legitimate form of scaffolding—that is, the student gets a quick start with the tablature and eventually leaves tablature for the advantages of note reading. Another positive aspect to tablature is its easy conversion into excellent right-hand exercises. To do this, convert all the numbers in a tablature arrangement into zeros. Use the zeros as a guide to practice right-hand patterns on all open strings. (To assist you and your students in finding the notes, I have included a note-location reference chart below in figure 29.1.)

In my opinion, solo guitar should be approached like we approached barre forms—as early as possible. We hint at barre forms and hint some more until students figure them out by themselves. Similarly, if the instructor hints at solo playing from day one, the students will start playing solo guitar before it is time to formally teach it. Dr. Michael Quantz, associate professor of music at the University of Texas at Brownsville and a leading advocate for music education through classical guitar, suggests aiming toward classical guitar playing from the beginning, and I agree. Here are some suggestions as to how you might hint at solo guitar, which may lead your students to learn independently.

HINTING AT SOLO GUITAR FROM THE BEGINNING

Hint #1: Play song melodies with the middle or ring finger. Using beginning songs in your method book, such as "Ode to Joy" (key of C), "Amazing Grace" (key of C), or "Frere Jacques" (key of G), have students play the song entirely with their middle or ring finger, while the thumb rests on the fifth string as a brace. The thumb will be used later to add the root bass part.

Hint #2: Play song roots with the thumb. For the same songs, have the student play the roots in the bass using the thumb. This time the fingers remain resting on the treble strings as a brace. They will be combined with the thumb later to create a solo.

Hint #3: Combine the bass and melody parts of a song. Play the melody of "Ode to Joy"—E E F G G F E D—and combine it with the bass roots—C C C C F F F F. Do this by pinching the thumb and the finger at the same time. Do the same with "Amazing Grace" and "Frere Jacques." In a diverse classroom, if the melody is too simple for some students, suggest they pinch the bass and melody at the same time. By demonstrating the combination of melodies with bass notes, students will begin to experiment on their own.

Hint #4: Play accompaniments in block chords and broken chords. Play the chords for "Ode to Joy" in the block style. This means that the thumb plays the chord root while the fingers play the treble

strings simultaneously. The next step is to play the song progression using broken chords, using the fingering p, i, m, a.

Hint #5: Play scales on a single treble string while plucking an open-string bass. Pluck the A bass note with the thumb while playing the natural notes on first string for one octave. In other words, using the ring finger, play E E E E F F F F F G G G G, etc., on the first string, while using the thumb to pluck the A bass note. For a variation, alternate the thumb and ring finger instead of pinching them.

Hint #6: Play scales on a single bass string while plucking one, two, or three open treble strings. Play the natural-note scale on a bass string using the thumb of the right hand. Simultaneously pluck the open high E string. Repeat using treble strings B and E and finally G, B, and E. Vary the picking patterns. Use repeated note scales in a group environment. As a variation, play the natural bass notes across the neck: E F G / A B C / D E.

Hint #7: Superimpose scales over an open-string bass. Start with a mini-scale. For example, pinch the open-A bass note while playing E E F F G G F F, etc., on the first string. This can be done as a skill builder early in the year for variety. As students progress, increase the range of the scales. The next step would be to play the A-natural minor scale superimposed over the A bass note: A B C D E F G A. As always, begin with repeated notes and then progressively reduce the repetitions.

Hint #8: Superimpose scales over a fingered bass note. Start with a mini-scale. For example, pinch the C bass note while playing E E F F G G F F, etc., on the first string. Notice that the melody is now played with the left-hand fingers 0, 1, and 4. As students progress, increase the range of the scales. The next step would be to play the C-major scale over a C bass note: C D E F G A B C. (Note that on the low C it is possible to play the bass note only. On the second note, D, play D and C together, continuing up the scale from there.)

Hint #9: Embellish open chords by adding fingers. Encourage students to experiment adding notes to chords. For example, on a C chord, experiment adding the fourth finger of the left hand to different frets, such as the third fret of the second string. This is a good preliminary for playing melody and bass parts of guitar solos.

Hint #10: Teach commonly used finger-picking patterns. Learn and master finger-picking accompaniment patterns. My feeling is that finger picking is the gateway to solo guitar.

Hint #11: Play scales using varied right-hand patterns. By practicing scales without the pick, students will improve their right-hand finger skills,

Solo Guitar: Note Location Reference Chart

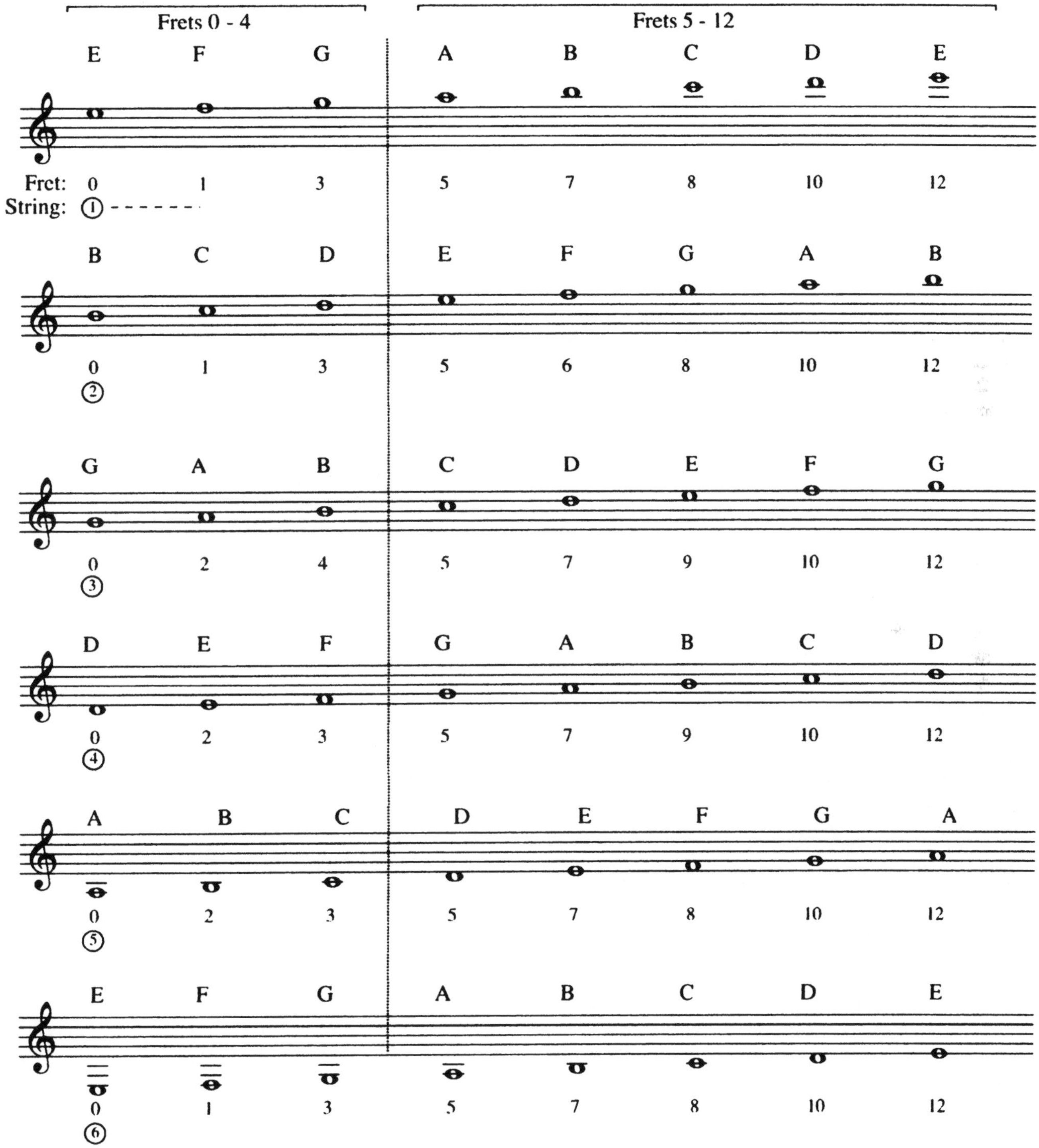

Figure 29.1: This sheet may be photocopied for class or other groups within purchaser's institution only. This provision does not confer any other rights to the purchaser or his or her institution.

which are essential to playing solo guitar. Alternating fingers *i* and *m* is so common that some teachers refer to this as *finger walking*. Using the thumb as a brace on the low E string, play the C-major scale for one octave using the following patterns:

i m, m i, i a, a i, m a, a m, i m a m, p m, p i, p a
m i, p i m a, p i m a m i, etc.

Hint #12: Melodize accompaniment patterns. Embellish accompaniment patterns by adding notes to the melody string. For example, on a C chord play the following picking pattern: p a m i, p a m i, etc. With the left hand, experiment adding the pinky on the note G (3/1) and then lifting it off. The resulting melody will be G E G E. Find ways to add notes to the highest string of accompaniment patterns.

Hint #13: Practice reading double stops. As part of your music-reading sequence, create simple exercises that combine two notes. One example could be limited to the treble strings, another to the bass strings, and yet another combining the bass and treble. First have the students play the top line with their fingers, and then have them play the bottom line with their thumb. Finally, have them play the combined notes as written.

Hint #14: Convert notated chords into chord grids. Provide students with a blank sheet of chord grids. On the overhead write a C chord on the staff: C E G C E. Have the students convert your staff notation of the C chord onto the chord grid. Use different arpeggio patterns. The ability to identify arpeggios in written music is an important skill in playing solo guitar. As always, begin by creating a reference chart and end by playing the examples.

Hint #15: Notate chords in block and broken form. For reading practice, have students convert chord grids into written notation in both block and broken form. For example, provide the grid for a C chord, and then have the students write the notes on staff paper. (Always have the students make a reference chart first.) In the block form, the notes are written one above the other. In the arpeggio form, they are written from left to right: C E G C E. Seeing chords notated as blocks and arpeggios is excellent preparation for reading solo guitar music.

Hint #16: Talk about finger picking and solo guitar in the same breath. Finger-picking accompaniments are the gateway to solo guitar. As students develop their ability to play accompaniments to songs such as "The House of the Rising Sun," make them aware that these same skills can be used to play beautiful classical solo pieces.

Hint #17: Show video recordings of accomplished classical guitar players. A picture truly is worth a thousand words. Seeing classical guitar being played removes some of its mystery and brings it down to Earth. Mel Bay Publications has some excellent videos available. You could also contact Guitar Solo Publications (gsp.com) to ask for recommendations.

Hint #18: Precede solo pieces with ensemble arrangements of the same piece. Familiarize students with the sound of a solo piece by first presenting it as a two- or three-part ensemble. Once students are familiar with the melody and harmony, present them with the solo arrangement, and they will be able to learn the piece much faster. You can prepare the ensemble yourself by making the melody part 1, the roots and bass line part 3, and adding a harmony line to serve as part 2.

CLASSROOM TEACHING STRATEGIES

Finding a Good Method Book

When I first ventured into the study of classical guitar as boy, I obtained Mel Bay's *Complete Method for Classical Guitar*. It was sequenced in a way that I was able to learn from independently. The musical examples were attractive and inspiring. I still feel it is one of the best methods available because the presentation is friendly rather than pedantic and because there is a wealth of excellent song material. *The Modern Classical Guitar Method* (Mel Bay) by Stanley Yates is a good choice for absolute beginners because of its simplicity. Later in my career I used *The Christopher Parkening Classical Guitar Method* (Hal Leonard Publications), which provides detailed text and an excellent repertoire at both the recreational and concert levels. There are other methods available, including methods that are of historic interest to serious students. Guitar Solo Publications (gspguitar.com) is an excellent source for these methods.

Exercise: Analyze and Learn Two Measures Per Day

Objective: Students focus on an excerpt a day.
Process:

- On the overhead projector, display two measures of a solo piece.
- Add the left-hand fingerings in detail, and discuss any points of interest.
- Have the students add the fingerings on their music.
- Add the right-hand fingerings in detail, and discuss any points of interest.
- Students should memorize the excerpt.
- Have the entire class play, and loop excerpts in unison. Use intermittent, then continuous, looping.

- Progressively learn the entire piece. Use the music only as a reminder.
- As students become more advanced, as an assessment, have them add the right- and left-hand fingerings in detail.

Exercise: The Relay

Objective: Students are able to hear the entire piece played repeatedly and learn from their peers.

Process:

- Assign each student one or two measures to learn (and memorize) during the class period. Student 1 learns measure 1, student 2 learns measure 2, and so forth.
- During a practice pause, check each student's fingering and understanding.
- After a reasonable amount of time, have the students play their measures in succession without a pause. Some verbal cues on your part may be necessary.

Memorization

Memorization allows the student to concentrate on technical requirements rather than reading music. It is my recommendation that students memorize excerpts as they proceed and use the music only as a reminder. This concept—using music as a reminder of what you have set into finger memory—is very important in solo guitar as well as ensemble work.

Use Practice Pauses

Solo guitar requires individual practice. Allow the students to work individually as you circulate through the room to assist them.

The Master-Class Format

The entire class can benefit from observing instruction that is given to an individual student. Have one student come to the front of the class and sit next to you, facing the class. Give a short lesson on an excerpt of music. Take a practice pause, and have the entire class work on the music.

Exercises Derived from the Selected Piece

Right hand. Analyze the right-hand fingering patterns that are used in an excerpt of music, and practice the right-hand part entirely on the open strings. Mute the strings to create classroom precision. Use intermittent looping and looping to facilitate finger memory.

Left hand. Superimpose the scale of the song over the appropriate root tones. For example, in the key of C, the students would play the C root with the thumb and the ascending scale degrees with the middle finger. Do the same for intervals or triads of interest. If there is a melodic passage that needs work, transpose it chromatically, and then play it in as many positions as possible. Where broken intervals or chords are concerned, simplify the music by viewing and practicing the parts as a series of left-hand block forms. Identify intervals that can be fingered as double stops, and mark them with a bracket.

Listening

You can inspire students by providing them with opportunities to listen to accomplished performers. All guitarists should be familiar with Andres Segovia, the father of modern classical guitar. He has a vast number of recordings available. Julian Bream has produced a video entitled *Guitarra*, which is an outstanding documentary on Spanish guitar—both the history and repertoire. A very good source for solo guitar music and recordings is Guitar Solo Publications, found online at gspguitar.com.

Provide Inspiring Music

You can help motivate students by showing enthusiasm for the solo guitar repertoire. Christmas songs are very good entry-level guitar solos. Here are four books that I have written that make good choices for school-age students, all by Mel Bay Publications:

Christmas Encyclopedia
Fingerstyle Blues Method
Fingerstyle Classics Made Easy
A Modern Method for Fingerstyle Guitar

Exercise: Convert Two-Part Solos into Duets

Objective: Students play the treble and bass parts separately and then together.

Process:

- Find, or arrange, solo pieces that are written in two parts—the melody and the bass. The melody is written with the stems up and the bass with the stems down. You and your students could create your own based on simple songs from your method book.
- Have the entire class play the melody (stems up) using only the ring finger. Let the thumb serve as a brace on one of the bass strings.

- Have the entire class play the bass part. They should rest their fingers (i, m, and a) on treble strings 1, 2, and 3.
- Divide the class into two groups. One group will play the bass part, the other the melody. Switch parts.
- After the students are familiar with both parts, instruct them to put the parts together.
- Remedial students may play the chords in arpeggios or with strumming.
- Variation: Write out a simple chorale in three voices (melody, bass, and middle). Have students play the individual parts, and then combine the parts in different ways.

Preparing Published Music

- Have the students write the string and fret numbers for the notes in a given arrangement.
- Assist the students in identifying and labeling chords symbols and intervals.
- Compose right-hand exercises based on the right-hand patterns in the piece.
- Compose scale and fingering exercises based on the melody.
- Add finger-style accompaniments using the chords of the classical piece.
- Identify intervals that can be fingered as double stops, marking them with brackets.

Diverse Classes

Find solo pieces that include chord symbols. Beginners can strum or finger pick the chords, while more advanced students can play the solo part. Some students may play the melody only.

A REVIEW OF RIGHT-HAND PATTERNS

For a review of hand positions, refer back to chapter 21 on finger picking.

Lets look at some finger-picking patterns that are particularly applicable to solo guitar.

The Pinch and Hook

The *pinch* is a folk term for playing a bass and treble note at the same time. The classical term is *block interval*. A block interval is played by plucking the thumb on a bass note while plucking a finger on a treble note at the same time.

The *hook* is a variation of the pinch. The classical term is *broken interval*. The notes of a broken interval are played in succession. All of the follow-ing exercises should be practiced as both hooks and pinches.

Exercise: Pinch and Hook on Open Strings

Objective: Learn to use the thumb and fingers of the right hand.
   Process:

- *Variable thumb.* Place the thumb on the second string and the ring finger on the first string. Play repeated pinches, and have the thumb move from string to string every four beats. The ring finger continues to play the high E string.
- *Variable fingers.* Start with the thumb on the sixth string and the ring finger on the fifth string. Play repeated pinches, and have the ring finger move from string to string. The thumb continues to play the low E string.
- *The pinch with alternation.* The pinch with alternation is used frequently in solo-guitar pieces. The pinch provides the melody and bass, and an alternating fill tone provides additional rhythm and harmony. Pinch the thumb and middle finger on strings 3 and 1. Next, play the index finger on the B string alternately between each pinch. Create variations by shifting to different sets of strings.

TYPES OF PIECES

Two-Part Solos: The Skeleton Arrangement

A skeleton arrangement consists of a melody played by the fingers and the bass played by the thumb. The melody notes are written with the stems up. The bass notes, played by the thumb, are written with the stems down. Students can create their own skeleton arrangements by adding roots to the melodies in their method book. (Note that these work best if the melodies are limited to the first three strings.)

Arpeggio Solos

Arpeggio solos consist of interesting chord progression played in arpeggios. Arpeggio solos have a distinct look when appearing in notation. As a preliminary exercise, have students convert the arpeggios into block chords. For solo guitar playing, it is important that students learn to view an arpeggio as a single chord—with a single left-hand fingering. Learning to see arpeggios as chords simplifies the reading process.

Bass Melody with a Treble Drone

The most famous example of this type of solo is the Spanish traditional piece *Malagueña*. Here is the most famous excerpt:

- Learn the melody: starting on the fourth string and ascending:
  E G# B, E G# B, A C B, A G F, repeat.
  Play it with the thumb.
- Between every melody note, play a repeated note with the middle finger on the open high E.

Melody and Accompaniment

Identify the melody. Identify the bass. Identify the fill tones. Emphasize the melody by playing it a little louder than the accompaniment.

Recreational Pieces

There is a wealth of recreational guitar music that was written for the express purpose of being played in the home. A good method book will contain many examples of this type of piece.

Concert Pieces

Concert pieces are pieces that were composed for concert performance and require a great deal of time and skill to play. High-school students can perform music on this level. A good compendium of examples in this category can be found on my recording *Sparks from the Seven Worlds* (guitarmusicman.com).

30

Tablature

Because of the potential confusion between the traditional staff and tablature staff, it is recommended that tablature be taught only after the students have a firm understanding of the traditional staff.

Tablature is a graphic system of notation that dates back to the Middle Ages. The simplicity of the system makes it an attractive alternative to standard notation for learning things quickly—especially solo-guitar pieces. Many of your students will have already learned tablature from friends or private instructors. Students who are unfamiliar with tablature can learn it in a few minutes.

EXPLANATION OF TABLATURE

- The tablature staff consists of six lines.
- Each line represents a string.
- The lowest line represents the lowest sounding string. In other words the bottom line is the low E string.
- Numbers represent the frets and are written on the lines. For example, if the number 1 is placed on the bottom line, it means to play the first fret on the sixth string.

TABLATURE DEMONSTRATION

- Have the class place their guitars in their lap, with the sound hole facing up.
- Lay a piece of tablature-staff paper on top of the strings. In this position, students can make a visual connection between the bottom line of the tab paper and the low E string.

LIMITATIONS AND PROBLEMS WITH TABLATURE

- Beginning students will confuse tablature lines with staff lines. This can make note reading difficult or impossible. For this reason, I delay the introduction of tablature until students are proficient with the staff.
- It is difficult to indicate rhythms in tab.
- It is difficult to indicate the left-hand finger numbers.
- It is impossible to visualize rising and falling pitch on the tablature staff.

THE NOTATION-TABLATURE CONVERSION CHART

In appendix B have provided you with a chart for converting notation into tablature. I have had one elementary school teacher tell me that this chart was the key to the students' early success.

Exercise: Locating the Notes

Objective: Students use a reference chart to convert notation into tablature.

Process: On the notation-tablature conversion paper, have students write the melody to a song they are learning. The melody will be on the standard staff. Have students use the chart and add the tablature fret numbers.

Exercise: Create Your Own Notation-Tablature Conversion Chart

Objective: Students fully understand the relationship between notation and the location of the notes on the guitar fretboard.

Process:

- Use paper that consists of a standard and tablature staff. (I have provided you with a template in the appendix.)
- Write note heads for the seventeen natural notes on the standard staff: E F G A B C . . . etc.

- Write the alphabet letters underneath the note heads.
- Use a ruler to place the corresponding numbers on the tablature staff:
013 / 023 / 023 / 02 / 013 / 013

31

Hammering-On, Pulling-Off, and Two-Hand Tapping Techniques

Useful visualizations include trigger action, a fly swatter, or a golf stroke.

DEFINITIONS

Ascending slurs hammering-on
Descending slurs pulling-off

DESCRIPTION OF MOTION

The motion of the hammer-on is very similar to using a hammer. There is a backswing, a downswing, and a point of impact. It is important that the fingers are arched, which allows the tip of the finger to produce the hammer effect. Other useful visualizations include trigger action, a fly swatter, or a golf stroke.

Exercise: The Hammer-On

Objective: Students discover the motion of a hammer-on.
   Process:

- Mute the strings with the right hand.
- Place the fingers so they are over frets 5, 6, 7, and 8 of the sixth string. The palm will be touching the side of the neck unless you have very large hands.
- In slow motion, stretch the first finger backward, away from the string, as far as it will go. Reverse the motion, and move very slowly down to the string until reaching the point of impact on the tip of the finger.
- Repeat the motion moving quickly in a trigger-like action. Use enough speed and force to create a drumming sound on the fretboard. (This drumming sound is actually an exaggeration

for teaching purposes. As the student develops, she will only use the force necessary.)

- Now drum on the muted string in half notes. The backswing or trigger action should begin the moment before the beat.
- Repeat the motion without muting the string. Be sure to leave the finger down. The note that is hammered should ring out and sustain as a result of the impact of the finger.
- Using repeated notes, practice hammering with each finger.
- Repeat on the first string, and observe the difference in your palm position. The palm has moved away from the neck. You will also notice that the string will not sound as loudly because it is thinner.

Exercise: Left-Hand Plucking; Pull-Offs

Objective: Students make a connection between a pull-off and string plucking.
   Process:

- Have the students mute the strings of their guitars with their right hand.
- Place the fingers of the left hand an eighth of and inch above the fingerboard with the fingers well arched. Do this over frets 5, 6, 7, and 8.
- Use the first finger of the left hand to strum the strings. The finger motions should be toward the palm of the left hand. After each strum, the finger needs to spring back to its starting position. Repeat left-hand strumming with each finger.
- Now reduce the motion and pluck only the high-E string using the fingers of the left hand.
- On your cue, have the students pluck the string with each finger four times.

- Repeat on the second string. As you switch to the second string, the plucking motion should be in the direction of the first string. On classical guitars the finger may actually bump into the adjacent string. On guitars with narrower necks, the finger will glide over the adjacent string.
- Continue from string to string.

Exercise: Hammer-On Etude

Objective: Students use hammering-on to improvise using the pentatonic scale.
   Process:

- Review the E-minor pentatonic scale, using repeated notes, on the first string. The frets are 0, 3, 5, 7, 10, and 12 .
- Using hammer-ons, play the following fret pattern:
0 3, 0 3, 0 3, 0 3, 0 5, 0 5, 0 5, 0 5, etc.
Seek equal volume between the plucked open string and hammered notes.
- Using hammer-ons improvise on the first string, using the E-minor pentatonic scale. Provide a background of E-minor blues.

Exercise: Pull-Off Etude

Objective: Students use pull-offs to improvise using the pentatonic scale.
   Process:

- Play pull-offs on the high E string using the E-minor pentatonic scale. Here are the frets:
3 0, 3 0, 3 0, 3 0, 5 0, 5 0, 5 0, 5 0, 7, 10, 12, etc. Try to achieve equal volume between all notes.
- Have students improvise on the high E string as before. Provide an E-minor accompaniment for support.
- Experiment: Combine pull-off and hammer-ons for the improvisation in E minor.
- Avoid playing sharp. When pulling-off to a fretted note, such as 7-5, students will frequently stretch the string in the sharp direction before releasing it. To avoid sounding sharp, the string must not be stretched. The first finger in this case must remain absolutely stationery on the fifth fret.

The following exercises help build strength and prevent this unintentional string bending.

Strength Exercise: String Bending in Contrary Motion

Objective: To avoid sounding sharp on pull-offs.

   Process:

- Place the third finger on the seventh fret of the third string.
- Place the first finger on the fifth fret of the fourth string.
- Pull the third finger toward the palm, and simultaneously push the first finger away from the palm, in contrary motion.
- Repeat this with different finger and string combinations.

Strength Exercise: The Push-Off

Obective: To play pull-offs without stretching the string.
   Process:

- On the third string, place the third finger on seventh fret. The third finger will not move during this exercise.
- Place the first finger on the fifth fret; it will *push* the string.
- Leaving the third finger in place, push the first finger away from the palm until the string is released.
- Try again, but this time pull the first finger toward the palm until the string is released. The third finger remains still throughout.

Exercise: Speed Patterns

Objective: Students use hammering-on and pulling-off to play fast. The following are some speed patterns that combine ascending and descending slurs.
   Process:

- Pluck only the first note of each group; slur the rest.
- Loop each group at least four times.
0 3 0, 0 3 0, 0 3 0, etc.
3 0 0, 3 0 0, 3 0 0, etc.
3 0 3, 3 0 3, 3 0 3, etc.
- Incorporate slurs with other skills:
    o Combine slurs with scale practice.
    o Combine slurs with digital finger patterns.

Exercise: Digital (Numerical) Slur Patterns

Objective: Students develop the ability to play ascending and descending slurs using all finger combinations. In a classroom setting, use repeated notes on each string.

Process:

- Move from string to string slurring the following triplets:
1 2 1, 2 1 2, 1 2 1, 2 1 2, etc.
Remember to pluck only the first note of each group and to switch strings at each comma.
- Repeat using all finger combinations:
1 3 1, 1 4 1, 2 3 2, 3 4 3, 2 4 2
- Try compound fingerings:
1 3 1 2 4, 1 3 1 2 4, etc.
- Barre variation: When preparing to play barre forms, use the preceding digital slur patterns but with the first finger lying in barre position.

RIGHT-HAND TAPPING

Tapping is a speed concept that has been popularized by many rock-guitar virtuosos. Guitar teachers need to be familiar with this technique. *Right-hand tapping* refers to using the tip of the index finger of the right hand to hammer notes on the fretboard. For our purposes, right-hand tapping will be indicated with a capital T. For example, T5 means to tap the fifth fret. P means to pull-off with either the right or left hand.

Exercise: *Tapping and Pull-Offs with the Right Hand*

Objective: Students practice tapping technique with the E-minor pentatonic scale.
   Right-Hand Process:

- Place your thumb on the side of the neck near the eighth fret to serve as a brace.
- Place your middle finger behind your index finger so that they nest together. This provides

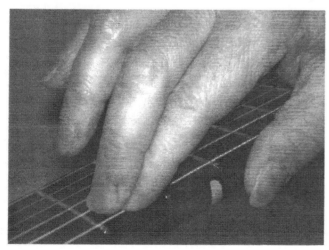

Photo 31.1: Right-handed tapping finger position

additional weight for the tap (figure 31.1).
- Tap (hammer-on) the fifth fret of the low E string in quarter notes: T5, T5, T5, T5.
- Next, after tapping the fifth fret, pull the finger away from the A string until the string releases and produces an open E. The effect is T5, P0, T5, P0, etc. Experiment tapping and pulling all of the notes of the E-minor pentatonic scale on the low E string: 0, 3, 5, 7, 1 0, 1 2.
- Variation: Repeat the procedure on the high E string.

Exercise: *Combining Right Hand and Left Hand*

Objective: Students combine tapping and pulling off with both hands to create speed patterns. LH means *left hand*, while RH means *right hand*. LP means left-hand pull.
   Process:

- LH: Preplant your third finger on the third fret of the first string.
- Tap your RH first finger on the fifth fret. Follow the RH tap by an RH pull-off. The effect is T5, P3, T5, P3, etc.
- Expand the preceding pattern by pulling with the left hand off the third fret with this effect: T5, P3, LP0, T5, P3, P0. A quick triplet sound will result: A G E, A G E, etc.
- Repeat this pattern using creative combinations of the E-minor pentatonic scale.

Exercise: *Sixteenth-Note Tapping Pattern*

Objective: Students will invent patterns using combinations of four notes. T means *right-hand tap*, P means *pull-off*, and H means *left-hand hammer-on*.
   Process:

- On the first string: T5, P0, H3, LP0, etc.
- Movable patterns: T7, P3, H5, LP3, etc.
- Compose a two-hand tapping etude using the previous patterns. Incorporate the E-minor pentatonic scale and arpeggios from the key of E minor.

32

Reference Frets and the Entire Fretboard

The open strings, the unison tuning frets, the octave, and their neighbors reveal the location of nearly all the notes on the neck.

THE OPEN STRINGS AND THE OCTAVE

Knowing the names of the open strings can reveal the notes of the entire neck. For this reason it is essential to teach and reteach them. From low to high, they are E A D G B E. The twelfth fret represents the *octave* of the open strings, so the note order is the same: E A D G B E.

THE OPEN STRINGS AND OCTAVE AND THEIR NEIGHBORING TONES

When the students understand that there is a whole step between every note except B and C and between E and F, they can use logic to figure out the notes adjacent to the open strings and octave.

Exercise: Locating Neighboring Tones of the Open Strings and Octave

Objective: Students practice applying the B/C E/F rule to locate the natural-note neighbors of the open strings and the octave.

Process: Using your knowledge of whole steps and half steps, locate and name the following:

- the upper neighbors of the open strings E A D G B E
  Answer: F B E A C F
  Frets: 1 2 2 2 1 1
- The lower neighbors of the twelve-fret octave E A D G B E

Answer: D G C F A D
Frets: 10, 10, 10, 10, 10, 10

THREE REGIONS OF THE FINGERBOARD

There are twelve frets in the octave. There are four fingers on the left hand. Considering the fingers of the left hand as a unit, we can view the fingerboard as three regions: Low region is 1, 2, 3, 4. Middle region is 5, 6, 7, 8. And high region is 9, 10, 11, 12.

THE FIFTH FRET IS A REFERENCE FOR THE MIDDLE REGISTER OF THE NECK

We have shown that the notes in low region and high region can be viewed as neighbors of the open strings and the octave. The fifth fret provides a reference for the middle register of the neck. When we learn unison tuning we learn the names of the notes at the fifth fret. Therefore, one of the hidden benefits of unison tuning is learning the names of the notes at the fifth fret. They are A, D, G, C, E, and A. Notice the similarity of the tuning reference notes A, D, G, C, and E to the open strings (E) A, D, G, B, and E. The note C on the fifth fret of the G string should be memorized because it is middle C.

MIDDLE C

The guitar is written an octave above where it sounds. Therefore, middle C on guitar is written on the third space of the treble clef. Middle C is also an important reference note at the fifth fret of the G string.

In my view, middle C is the middle of the guitar as well as the piano. This is a most interesting coincidence. Observe the following:

- From low E to middle C is the interval of a thirteenth.
- From middle C to high A, at the seventeenth fret, is also a thirteenth.

Exercise: Locate the Upper and Lower Neighboring Tones for the Notes at the Fifth Fret

Objective: Students use their knowledge of whole steps and half steps (the B/C E/F rule) to identify the natural notes adjacent to the fifth fret.

Process:

- Identify the notes at the fifth fret using your knowledge of unison tuning.
- Use the B/C E/F rule to identify and locate the upper and lower neighboring tones
  Answers:
  Notes at the fifth fret A D G C E A
  Lower neighbors G C F B D G
  Upper neighbors B E A D F B

WHAT WE HAVE LEARNED SO FAR

Once the student knows the open strings, the unison tuning frets, and the octave, they can view all the notes of the neck as neighbors of these three reference positions: 0, V, XII. The only fret that is not adjacent to a reference fret is the eighth fret. When appropriate, have students memorize the notes across the eighth fret: C, F, B♭, E♭, G, C.

POSITIONS

It is helpful for the teacher to refer to different regions of the neck by the term *position*. Here's how it works: When first finger of the left hand is on fret 1, we are said to be in *first position*, which is also referred to as *open position*, since it includes the open strings. When the first finger is located at the second fret, we are said to be in *second position*. The symbol used to designate a particular position is a Roman numeral. For example, the symbol for fifth position is Roman numeral V. The symbol for a barre at the fifth position is CV. A half barre at the fifth position is indicated as 1/2 CV.

THE FIRST FINGER

It must also be mentioned that the first finger holds a special significance since at any given moment it has the ability to barre any number of strings. I view the first finger as a floating capo that is always close to the strings and always ready to act as a brace, a barre, a mute, or to play a note.

OCTAVE PATHS AND SYMMETRICAL FINGERINGS

On the piano, the layout of the notes moves clearly from octave to octave. On the piano there is only one key per note. On the guitar there are five different places you can play the high E: 0/1, 5/2, 10/3, 14/4, 19/5. The multiple locations of the same note can add complexity and confusion to learning the instrument.

The navigation of the guitar is simplified when the student is aware of a logical sequence of octaves. Therefore, the student should take note of the angle of octaves as they progress across and up the neck. In the case of the low G, the octave path is 3/6, 5/4, 8/2, and 15/1. When improvisers build melodic motifs around these octave paths, the fingering patterns are similar from octave to octave. In other words, the fingerings are nearly symmetrical from octave to octave. This is hard to understand written in a book, but if you finger the G octave path I have mentioned, and experiment with some embellishments around each G, you will see for yourself.

Exercise: A Fun Game Using Octaves and Unisons

Objective: Students learn the neck by playing one note on all six strings.

Process:

- Have the class play the note E on all six strings. Repeat each note four or more times.
  Answer: 0/6, 12/6, 7/5, 2/4, 9/3, 5/2, 0/1, 12/1
- Repeat the process for every natural note.

VI

REMEDIAL TECHNIQUES

33

Remedial and Artistic Uses of the Capo

Although this chapter on the capo is included under remedial techniques, the capo is a legitimate artistic tool for serious guitarists. For example, in the classical field it can be used to make the guitar sound more like a Renaissance lute. The second section of this chapter addresses the more theoretical and artistic aspects of the capo.

INTRODUCTION TO THE CAPO

The capo is a clamp-on, barre-like device that is used to transpose open chords. Vocalists often use a capo to raise the key of a song to accommodate their vocal range. The capo has important additional uses in guitar instruction.

Lowering the action. In some instances students will come to class with guitars that are almost impossible to play because the strings are too high above the frets. This is referred to as *high action*. The capo lowers action on whichever fret it is placed, making the guitar much easier to play. The first or second fret will work for this purpose. For class work, the guitar can be tuned down a half or whole step so that the student will have the same pitch as the class.

Shortening the reach for the left hand. The frets on the guitar get closer together as their positions on the neck become higher. Young students or students with small hands will find it much easier to play with the capo positioned on the fifth fret. They do not have to reach as far to play, and the strings are closer to the neck. Over time, you may progressively move the capo toward the nut.

FURTHER USES FOR THE CAPO

Transposition. The capo is an excellent aid for teaching transposition. It is a good idea to preface your introduction of barre forms with a demonstration of the capo.

Exercise: Use the Capo for Transposition

Objective: Students gain practice transposing open chords.
   Process:

- Review the natural notes on the sixth string and fifth string.
- Ask, "If I transpose the E chord up one fret with the capo, what would the new chord be?" Hint: The root of the E chord is on the sixth string—when it moves up one fret, it becomes an F.
- Place the capo on the first fret, and play an E chord. Ask the students to name the chord based on the capo position. Answer: F.
- Variations: Continue this process using Emin A, and Amin.

Understanding and using the five major chord forms. There are five basic major chord fingerings on the guitar. They are C, A, G, E, and D. They spell the word *caged.* Using a capo, two guitarists can use different chord forms to create a richer sound. For example, one guitarist can play in the key of D, and the other in the key of A with the capo at the fifth fret. An understanding of this concept helps you and your intermediate students understand how the guitar is laid out. Let's examine the thinking behind this.

Exercise: Capo Quiz

Objective: Students gain practice transposing the five basic chord forms.

Process:

- Ask students to transpose the five basic chord forms by counting the chromatic half steps.
- For example, using the A chord form, on what fret would the capo need to be in order to play in the key of C? Think chromatically:
A open position
A# first position
B second position
C third position
Answer: C.
- Repeat for the other chord forms.

Exercise: Two Students Play a Song with the Capo on Different Frets

Playing a song with the capo in two different positions creates a colorful blend of tones.

Objective: Two students play the same song with the capo in different positions.

Process:

- Choose a song in the key of G.
- Have one student place a capo on the third fret and play an E-major chord. Note: This is actually a G chord.
- Ask the next student, "In order to use a D-chord form to play in the key of G, on what fret would you position the capo?"
Process: Using the capo, slide the D form (x x 0 2 3 2) chromatically up the neck, and recite the chord names, D, D#, E, etc. When you reach the G, place the capo there. In other words, the D form played with a capo on the fifth fret equals a G chord (x x 5 7 8 7).

Capo Puzzles

Ask the student, "To play in the key of G with the capo on the fifth fret, what chord form would you use—C, A, G, E, or D?"

Process: Use the process of elimination to determine the right chord form.

- For example, let's test the C chord with the capo on the fifth fret. We know that the root of the C is on the fifth string. With the capo on the fifth fret, the root of the C chord would be on the eighth fret of the fifth string, which would be an F. Since we are looking for a G chord in fifth position, the C would be incorrect.
- Test each chord using this thought process to determine the right answer.
- Answer: D form with the capo on 5 = G.

Exercise: Playing the C Chord in Five Capo Positions

Objective: Students play the C chord in five different positions using a capo.

Process:

- When the C chord is placed throughout the neck, the order of major chord forms spells the word *caged.* Here is a demonstration.
- Have the students silently finger the C chord.
- Ask the student, "Moving up the neck, what chord form comes after C?" Since the order of chords spells *caged,* the chord following C is A. Then ask, "What chord form comes after A?" Answer: G. Etc.
- Use the acronym CAGED to place the capo on the correct frets moving up the neck. Use your ear and intuition to determine accuracy.
- Here are the chord formations and capo positions for the C chord in five locations:
open position C form
third fret A form
fifth fret G form
eighth fret E form
tenth fret D form
Note: All of the above are different versions of the C chord.
- For further understanding, locate the root tones for each of the C-chord positions listed above.

34

The Benefits of Teaching Melodies on One String

The benefits of playing on one string apply to all string players.

Melodies on one string are particularly useful for remedial students. Consider the following:

- visual relationship between pitch and distance
- opportunity to think about, and adjust, hand position
- clear view of an octave
- learning the numbers of the frets
- shifting from position to position
- gratification of making music immediately
- string-crossing skill in not required
- easy to teach a large group by using echo imitation and fret numbers

Exercise: Teaching "Amazing Grace" on One String

Objective: Students learn their first song by echoing the teacher.
Preliminary Process:

- Review the numbers of the frets. Remind students that the dots on the neck represent certain frets.
- Play the chromatic scale on the third string using four repeated notes per fret. Have the students recite the fret numbers as they play.
- Then quiz students by saying, "Play 7" or "Play 5," etc.
- Now you're ready to teach the song.
  Process: Teach your class "Amazing Grace" in the key of C.
- Sing and strum the entire song. Then demonstrate the melody on the G string. Playing this song on the G string puts the song in the key of C. Think about vocal range and chord ac-

companiment as you decide on which string to teach a melody.
- Without the guitar, have the students sing or hum the melody in echo imitation.
- Using fret numbers, sing one-measure phrases, and have the students echo you by playing on the G string. Here are the phrases:
0, 5, 9, 9--7, 5, 2, 0--0, 5, 9, 9--7, 12--9, 12, 9, 5--2, 5, 2, 0--0, 5, 9, 9--7, 5
- Have the class play the whole song. Give verbal cues if necessary.

Exercise: Construct an Arrangement of "Amazing Grace"

Objective: Students combine contrasting sections to create a musical arrangement.
Process:

- *Introduction.* Strum the C chord for two measures.
- *Part 1.* Sing the words with chord accompaniment.
- *Part 3.* Have the class play the melody while you play the chords.
- *Part 4.* Sing the second verse with chord accompaniment.
- *Ending.* Conduct C-F-C.

Exercise: Playing Songs by Ear

Objective: Students use their ear to play music independently.
Process:

- Pass out paper.
- Have students figure out the melody to "Happy Birthday," "Twinkle, Twinkle, Little Star," and "Jingle Bells" on the first string by ear.

- Have them write out the fret numbers. "Happy Birthday" starts on 0, "Twinkle" on 0, and "Jingle Bells" on 4.
- Play the song.
- Encourage students to figure out other popular melodies, such as the theme from *Star Wars*, and write the numbers on paper.

Exercise: *Compose a Rock Riff on One String*

Objective: Students experiment creating and remembering an original riff.
   Process:

- Pass out paper.
- Review the minor pentatonic scale on the high E string:
   0, 3, 5, 7, 10, 12.
- Use "Flaming Ice Cube" as an example of an original riff that uses one string (see chapter 6).
- Allow students time to compose their own riffs. Have them write down the numbers.
- Have students perform riffs for the class.

- Provide power-chord accompaniment where applicable.

Exercise: *Blues Improvisation on One String*

Objective: Students explore the sound of the E-minor pentatonic scale on the first string.
   Process:

- Review the E-minor pentatonic scale on the high E string:
   0, 3, 5, 7, 10, 12.
- Use echo imitation to explore short riff ideas.
- Allow students to improvise while you play an E-minor chord for accompaniment.
- Encourage students to remember the musical ideas they like. Maxim: A good idea should be repeated.
- A final thought: The Greek philosopher Pythagoras used a single string instrument called a monochord to experiment with music. Have students research Pythagoras and the monochord.

35

Using Riffs for Educational Purposes

Think of a riff as an improvisation construction kit.

A *riff* is a short repeated phrase. The classical term for a riff is *ostinato*, which means *a repeating motif*. The most famous guitar riffs originated in the 1960s and include songs such as "Sunshine of Your Love" by Eric Clapton's group Cream, "Day Tripper" by the Beatles, "Jumping Jack Flash" by the Rolling Stones, and "Smoke on the Water" by Deep Purple, among many, many others. Riffs are popular with students because they sound good, are short, and are easy to play. The guitar is fortunate to have a *canon* (accepted collection of repertoire) of riffs that can be used as skill builders. Most of the classic riffs are built on the blues scale and can be rearranged to create improvisations. When I was a kid we all had to learn the riffs to "Secret Agent Man," "Green Onions," and "What I Say." Classical music pedagogy used riffs too. They are called *excerpts* or *ostinatos*. Although I have already explored riffs in the chapter on improvisation, I would like to revisit it here with some additional thoughts.

Embellishing and changing riffs is a time-tested method for developing improvisational skills. Riffs convey the scale material and the melodic contours of a style. When students approach you with a riff they have learned, you are presented with a teachable moment. You can use riffs for teaching theme and variations, speed, chromatic transposition, octave transposition, music reading, music writing, and improvisation. Take advantage of the natural appeal of riffs.

Exercise: Make a Riff Notebook

Objective: The teacher will make a notebook of written versions of famous riffs to teach students.
Process:

- Make a list of the most famous classic-rock riffs that you are familiar with.
- Purchase sheet music with riffs.
- Make copies of the riffs for your students, keeping in mind that you can copy only 10 percent of a musical work without infringing on the copyright.
- Share the riffs with students, especially those who are struggling with the traditional curriculum.
- Have copies available in your song files that are accessible near the exit of your room.

Reading Exercise: Name That Tune

Objective: Riffs are used as short reading opportunities.
Process:

- Begin by writing the first two or three notes of the riff on the overhead projector.
- Have the students find the notes on their guitar.
- Progressively add notes until the students figure out the riff by reading it.
- Play the riff as a class.

Exercise: Theme-and-Variation Techniques

Objective: Students vary riffs to create improvisations.
Process:

- Teach the students a riff, such as Cream's "Sunshine of Your Love." If applicable, write the notation on the overhead, and add the string and finger numbers.
- Provide a short practice pause, and allow students to get acquainted with the riff.
- Play the riff.
- Demonstrate how new riffs can be created by varying the order and/or the rhythm of the notes.

- Here are some theme-and-variation techniques to explore:
    - same order of notes, new rhythm
    - same rhythm, new order of notes
    - new order of notes, new rhythm
    - same rhythm, completely new notes
- Using the original riff as the theme, have students invent their own variations and share them with the class.

Exercise: The Friday Riff Exchange

Objective: Students share what they already know by demonstrating riffs.
   Process:

- Invite students to review music they have been playing for fun.
- Circulate through the room to see if there are students with interesting music to share.
- Ask students if they would be willing to play their music for the class.
- After the demonstration, suggest that they teach their material to others.

Exercise: The Riff Master Class

Objective: Students share their knowledge with the entire class.
   Process: When you discover that a student knows an interesting popular riff, have them teach it to *you* while the class learns by observing.

- Have students flip their guitars into rest position.
- Invite the student who knows a riff to come to the front of the class to teach the riff to you.
- As the student teaches you the riff, generate questions and comments that will be useful for the entire class.

Exercise: Play a Riff Starting on Different Frets

Objective: Students benefit by transposing the riff they know into other keys.
   Process:

- If necessary, adapt the riff so there are no open strings; this makes it *moveable*.
- Play the riff starting on different frets. For example, start on fret 3, 4, 5, etc.
- Recite the key names as you move up the neck—G, G#, A, etc.
   Advanced Variation: Learn how to play the riff in the same key, but starting on each string. For example, if the first note is A-5/6, start on 12/5, 7/4, 2/3, 10/2, and 5/1.

Exercise: Riffs for Speed Building

Objective: Students will loop a riff, getting faster and faster.
   Process:

- When a student shows you a riff he or she has learned, demonstrate how to loop the riff, getting faster and faster.
- Teach the word *accelerando*.
- Encourage them to play it as fast as possible.

Exercise: Transposing Riffs into Three Regions

Objective: Students learn to play a riff by starting in three different octaves—low, middle, and high.
   Process: In order to use a riff for improvisation, students need to be able to play it in the upper as well as lower registers. Explain that starting in the lower register and moving to the higher ones is one way of building the excitement of a solo.

- Recall our discussion of octave paths in chapter 32. Find the starting note of the riff in the low, middle, and high octaves. For example, if the first note is A, the starting notes are as follows: 5/6, 7/4, 10/2.
- Learn, and then demonstrate, the riff starting on these notes.
- Once students know the riff in three octaves, have them scramble the riff into an improvisation.
- Be sure students work in all three octaves.

VII

THE GUITAR ROOM, GUITARS, AND INDEPENDENT STUDY

36

Setting Up the Guitar Room and Equipment

For better classroom management, teach from the back, as well as the front, of the room.

Your setup may reflect your teaching style and teaching space. I have set up my teaching space so I have easy access to the following (photo 36.1):

- the students
- overhead projector
- microphone
- drum machine
- stereo
- computer with iTunes

MOVEMENT AND SEATING ARRANGEMENT

If possible, set yourself up so that you can circulate through the class as well as teach from the microphone. Circulating allows you to monitor student progress using the five-second-quiz technique or to simply greet everyone and be sure they have the necessary materials on the stand. As a change of pace, teach from the back of the room. This is a proven way to improve student engagement. Here are some suggestions for making your guitar-teaching space efficient and effective.

- *Overhead projector.* An overhead projector enables you to create teaching examples as they are needed. Make several transparencies of large staff paper, guitar grids, etc. It is useful to use your baton or a laser pointer to help students follow the music.
- *Interactive white board.* With an interactive white board you can use teaching examples directly from your computer. With either the touch-sensitive board or a digital pen, both you and your

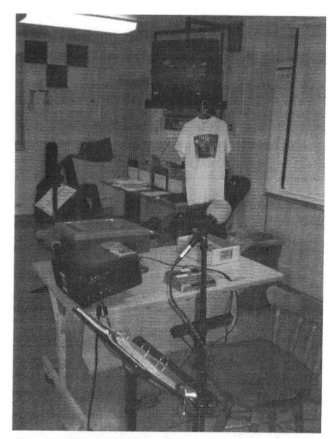

Photo 36.1: The teaching station

students can use the board interactively.
- *Conductor's baton as a pointer.* When circulating the room and working with a student one-on-one, you can use the baton to point to fingers and frets without violating a student's personal space.
- *Utility tables and file boxes.* Have a table near your exit that has open files for every student (photo 36.2). They will put worksheets, songs, and other materials in the file to be used with

Photo 36.2: Student file boxes

Photo 36.3: Coffee house, sound, and light

their song portfolio and practice kit. Inexpensive cardboard file boxes are available at your local office-supply store. In addition to a student files, there should be a file box with extra handouts and songs for students to take and enjoy at home or to add to their portfolio/practice kit. Another utility table for extra books, special handouts, paper, crayons, markers, and other supplies should be available.

- *Storage drawer for accessories.* You will need a drawer or box for guitar strings, picks, capos, tuners, and other items that you may sell to students.

- *String display and storage.* Pound three inches of sturdy wire into the wall from which to mount strings. The wire should be thin enough such that the ball end of the string slides over it. Welder's wire is available at your local hardware store for this purpose. Have a student aide label each string by name and gauge and sort the strings onto different wires.

- *Acoustic foam.* Because of the sheer volume twenty-five guitars can produce, you can reduce the echo in your room by attaching acoustic foam to your ceiling and walls. Use double-sided poster-mounting tape so that you can move the panels if necessary.

- *Broom and cleaning supplies.* Teach students that cleaning up is a necessity to maintaining any comfortable learning space. At the end of the day assign a guitar monitor, or remind the class daily to organize the guitars along the wall. Stack the chairs so you can easily sweep the floor. Have a broom handy for this purpose. Take pride in your work space, and treat it with care.

- *Quick access to worksheets and music paper.* You will benefit from having a variety of music-theory worksheets at your fingertips. Students who forget their guitars or need special reinforcement in a particular area will appreciate the special opportunity to work on something productive. Devise a system that enables you and your students to have quick access to staff papers, tablature papers, grid papers, and the like.

- *Music posters or murals.* If possible, have tasteful, educational, framed music, art, or history prints mounted. For your classroom or performance space, enlist your art department to create large murals of guitar and music themes (photo 36.3). Murals may be painted on particleboard and then mounted to the wall. Make the room a fun place to be by giving the room a fresh coat of paint. We have named our two rooms Guitar Heaven (rehearsals and performances) and Guitar Haven (classroom instruction).

- *Performance space with sound and lighting.* To make your performances more appealing, obtain special lighting, such as black lights, stage lighting, neon lights, or other creative lighting options. Lunch concerts on Fridays provide students added incentive to practice and are a good recruiting tool.

- *Music stands.* To avoid clutter, you can assign two students to a stand. Teach students to monitor and care for the materials. On my stands I have the method book, a song book, an ensemble book, and a folder for reference sheets and special proficiency handouts.

- *Bass guitars.* Playing bass is a natural interest of many students. Have one or two on guitar stands, and invite students to play them. Having a student play bass adds an extra musical dimension to your class sound. If possible, you can model bass playing to generate interest. Start with the simple root bass.

- *Television with video or DVD player or computer with DVD drive.* Videos and DVDs are available that can expand your student's view of the world of music. Before watching a video, pose thought questions and compile a list of things to listen for that could be included in a written summary.

- *Computer or MP3 player attached to your stereo.* Make playlists of songs you want to use to create anticipation for your lessons. Purchase examples from iTunes or other music-download site. Use an adapter or docking station to connect to your stereo system.

- *Practice room or space.* There will be times when the students will benefit from open practice time. Many band rooms have adjacent practice rooms that provide students with the space they need for independent learning. If you don't have practice rooms, check with your administration regarding using the hallway or other adjacent space.

- *Drum machine.* The drum machine serves to keep the class together and adds excitement to the class environment. Place the drum machine within arm's reach of your teaching station. Plug it into your stereo system via your mixer. Develop students' independent rhythm skills so that the drum machine adds a nice sound but does not become a crutch.

- *Audio mixer.* Use an audio mixer to direct signals from your teaching microphone, vocal microphones, drum machine, computer, and other devices into your stereo (photo 36.4).

- *Recorder.* Recording or making podcasts of your class provides a way for students to listen to, and reflect on, their progress. It also

Photo 36.4: Mixer and stereo system

Photo 36.5: White board

motivates students to do their best. The best microphone for recording classrooms is the Crown PZM30.

- *Class set of pencils and crayons.* There are many opportunities in guitar class for creating diagrams. As preparation for the professional world, it may be helpful to create sample textbook pages that explain concepts.

- *Earplugs.* Prolonged exposure to sound can result in ringing in the ears. Visit your local audiologist to be fitted for musician's earplugs. These plugs reduce the volume without changing the tone and are well worth the price.

- *Ergonomic chair and lumbar pillow.* To save energy during the day you may find it helpful to sit on an armless professional office chair or stool. This is a matter of personal preference.

- *Teaching microphone.* A microphone is very useful for saving your voice and managing the class. It is much easier for students to hear you if you use a microphone.

- *White board.* Having a white board mounted to the wall enables you to post the current proficiency requirements and learning goals, as well as important performance dates and other information (photo 36.5).

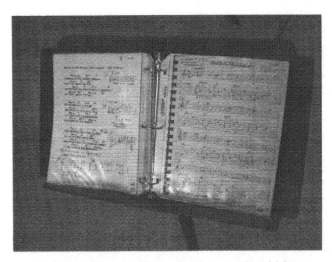

• *Guitar library.* The guitar room should have a guitar library consisting of resources that include methods, songbooks, videos, magazines, and recordings from a variety of time periods and genres. Three-ring binders or folders work well as class songbooks (photo 36.6). I have found that it is best to keep it simple—don't overload your folders. For recreational song performance I use the overhead projector.

SUPPLIERS AND PUBLISHERS

Most of the equipment you need is available through your local music store or through the *Musician's Friend Catalog*, found online at www.musicians friend.com. For guitar methods and accessories, a good source is The Guitar Accessories and Manufacturer's Association website, found at www.discoverguitar.com/.

For classical-guitar materials I recommend Guitar Solo Publications, online at gspguitar.com. For American music, as well as historical methods, supplements, and technique, Mel Bay Publications is a good choice, whose website is found at melbay.com. Nancy Marsters, whom I view as the mother of classroom guitar, has materials available at www.classguitar.com/index2.html. Will Schmid, whom I view as the father of classroom guitar, has publications available through Hal Leonard Publications, whose website is found at www.halleonard.com/. Finally, my materials are available through my website at www.guitarmusicman.com or through Mel Bay Publications.

For music pedagogy, I recommend *Discovering Orff* by Jane Frazee (Schott Publications) and *Teaching Instrumentalists* by Stanley L. Schleuter (Schirmer Books).

37

Guitars and Accessories

Beginners especially need a guitar that is inviting rather than discouraging.

GUITAR SIZE

Students need to have a guitar that matches their size. You wouldn't wear a shoe that pinches or is so large it slips, and similarly you shouldn't struggle to play a guitar that doesn't fit. Young children should use a three-quarter-size guitar or even a ukulele that is tuned like a guitar. They will also benefit from using a utility stool on which to rest both feet. Students should be able to comfortably reach the entire length of the neck with their left hand. If they can't reach the first three frets comfortably, a capo should be attached higher up the neck anywhere between the second and fifth fret. The right arm should be able to reach the strings without straining. Nylon-string guitars are easier to play than steel-string. A strap or a footstool is necessary to hold the guitar in place.

GUITAR SETUP

All guitars require proper setup for ease-of-play. Beginners especially need a guitar that is inviting rather than discouraging. The ease of a guitar's play depends on several factors, especially the distance of the strings from the neck, which is referred to as the *action*. If you purchase a guitar from a reputable shop, they should adjust the action as a service to you. If you buy from an individual, catalog, or other source, there is no guarantee that the action of the instrument is properly set up. If the strings are hard to push, the action is probably too high.

Some factors influencing ease of play follow:

• height of the bridge

• height of the nut
• angle of the neck (truss-rod adjustment)
• thickness (gauge) of the strings
• nylon or steel strings
• thickness of the neck
• width of the neck

PURCHASING A GUITAR

When purchasing a guitar, students should plan to spend several hours of practice time at the music store. Part of the guitar culture includes getting to know the people at the local store. A knowledgeable sales person can help students choose a guitar that matches their size. The three main things I look for when buying a guitar are

1. ease of play, size, and comfort;
2. tone quality, and
3. beauty (part of the appeal of playing the guitar is the sheer beauty of the instrument).

PRICE AND BRAND

The best guitar is not always the most expensive one. You can't always judge a guitar by the brand. Take time to get acquainted with the guitar, and think for yourself. Guitars must feel and sound right, regardless of the price or brand. I personally like Fender, Yamaha, Alvarez, Ovation, and Takamini, but there are many others that are good.

CARE OF GUITARS

• Avoid extremes of cold or hot. Keep them away from radiators. Do not leave them in hot or cold cars. If you must leave the guitar in a car at extreme temperature, do not open the case until the guitar has time to gradually change temperature.

- Always wash you hands before playing the guitar.
- Touching the soundboard with your fingers will leave fingerprints. Instruct children not to touch the front of the guitar except when playing demands it.
- Never lean guitars against the wall, stand them on end, lay them on the floor, or rest them on chairs. These positions are prone to falls or even being stepped on.
- To clean my guitars I use a damp paper towel and a dry cloth. The damp towel is squeezed as dry as possible. After wiping the guitar down, I dry it immediately. If the idea of using a damp towel scares you, a good wood-furniture polish will also work. Commercial guitar polish is also available.

STRINGS

I recommend the nylon-string guitars for beginners because the strings are easier to push than steel strings. If a student has a steel-string guitar, suggest using lightweight strings at first. The lightweight strings are easier to push but have less volume and tone.

TYPES OF GUITARS AND STYLES

- **Nylon string, classical-style guitar** Good for finger-picking, solo guitar, and ease of play for learning
- **Steel-string acoustic** Commonly used for vocal accompaniment, strumming, and song leading
- **Electric guitar** Commonly used for playing rock, blues, and jazz. Electric guitars are not recommended for classroom use because they are too loud and provide a distraction. You may want to offer a Friday show-and-tell for students to bring and demonstrate their electric instruments.

PICKUPS FOR ACOUSTIC GUITARS

Electric pickups are recommended for students who plan on performing publicly. Many acoustic guitars come with built in pickups and tuners. The built-in tuners are especially helpful for beginning students.

TWELVE-STRING GUITARS

Students may ask about twelve-string guitars. Twelve-stringed instruments are much more difficult to play and tune and should not be used for learning. If a twelve-string is the only kind of guitar the student has, suggest stringing it with only six strings and try using a capo.

ACCESSORIES

Guitar strap. I urge all my students to use a guitar strap. The strap enables the guitar to remain steady, even while the player enjoys a variety of sitting or standing positions. Even classical guitars can be fitted with straps. If necessary, have the folks at the music store (don't cringe) drill a hole in the end of the guitar so an endpin and a strap can be attached.

Guitar stand. A guitar stand is useful for a classroom guitar instructor because it provides a safe place for your instrument when you need to attend to other things. It is useful for students to have a guitar stand at home so that the guitar is easy to pick up and practice. I believe that the guitar should be at arm's reach in the home. If it is in the case, it is less likely to be played.

Footstool. Use of a footstool is the traditional way of elevating the guitar to playing position. Footstools are available from your local music store. If you know someone who is handy with woodwork, you can have one made. A wooden box, with the dimensions of 6" x 7" x 8", provides versatility of height. For young children, use a utility stool large enough to support both feet.

Capos. It is nice to have several capos on hand. They can be a lifesaver for students with small fingers or for students with guitars that have impossibly high action.

Guitar tuners. One of the most common reasons people discontinue playing guitar is because they cannot tune them. (The other reason is that they don't have good music to play. That is why we create a song portfolio and practice kit as a final project.) Be sure all your students can tune the guitar before graduating from your class. Electric tuners are relatively inexpensive and are recommended. I use the clip-on type and leave it permanently attached.

Picks. Picks come in a variety of sizes and shapes. Students should experiment to see what they like. My recommendation is to use a standard-size pick in a heavy weight. Heavier picks tend to have a fuller sound and last longer.

Song folios. One of the goals of class instruction is to provide students with the skills they need to purchase and play from the published songbooks of their choice. Having songbooks of popular artists in your guitar library provides an incentive for students to learn how to read music.

Strings. The guitar classroom should be stocked with extra sets of both nylon and steel strings. The lighter-gauge strings are easier to play for beginners. The strings that most commonly break on the steel-string guitars are the trebles, especially the high E. Have lots of high E strings on hand. On the nylon-string guitars the D strings have a tendency to break, so buy extras of these as well.

Song binders or folders. Have binders or folders on the music stands to manage your special handouts.

Home practice space, music stand and chair. Students should set up a comfortable music-practice space at home. The space should be free of distraction and should include a comfortable chair, a music stand, a guitar stand, and any other practice materials. Urge parents to help students set up a comfortable, appealing space.

SETTING UP YOUR CLASSROOM MUSIC STORE

Selling picks, strings, tuners, string winders, and capos provides a service to the students and can help you to raise some petty cash for classroom items. Check with your administration regarding school policies.

HOW TO CHANGE STRINGS

A picture is worth a thousand words in this case, so I recommend you visit your local store, purchase some strings, and ask them to demonstrate changing one string. If you do not have a store nearby, check in your guitar method for instructions. If you do not have a guitar method, carefully study a guitar that already has strings, and use it as a guide. The process is very logical but does take some practice and hands-on experience. String winders are highly recommended to save time.

As a note of caution, many beginners will over-tighten new strings until they break. Always pluck the string as you turn the tuning knob so that you can hear and feel how tight the string is getting. The string should always have plenty of flexibility to it. Change strings when the tone gets dull or you want to experiment with different weights. Included in the appendix to this book are two "Stringing a Guitar" worksheets that may be a good reference for those stringing a guitar for the first time (figures 6.1 and 6.2).

38

Independent Study

Independent study should not be treated lightly and must be approached with a plan.

Independent study may be a way to serve students whose schedules don't allow them to be in your regularly scheduled classes. Success can only be achieved if there is the right balance of structure and creative independence. The student must be of sufficient age, experience, and maturity so the instructor can predict success in advance. Students interested in independent study should have a meeting with the instructor to discuss the requirements, procedures, and grading. Parents should be notified and involved in supporting and encouraging the student. The student will work with the instructor to compile a repertoire list and personal list of written goals.

If the student agrees to the rigorous terms of the course, they will meet with the instructor at the instructor's convenience a minimum of once a week to present a progress report and a written practice journal. They should be encouraged to also present and other written portfolio entries, such as music, repertoire lists, magazine articles, original songs, etc.

The final product consists of a portfolio and an in-class lecture-performance. The structure detailed below gives the independent study legitimacy.

WRITTEN COURSE OF STUDY AND REPERTOIRE PROPOSAL

The instructor will present the student with a written course of study. For example, the table of contents of a method book with highlighted entries would work. I use the table of contents from my own publication *Guitar Essentials*, available through www.guitarmusicman.com. After the student has agreed to the proposed course of study, she must submit a written

repertoire proposal. Once the repertoire proposal is revised and accepted by the student and teacher, the independent study may be approved, but only with the additional following requirements.

Portfolio

The student will compile three copies of an independent-study portfolio: one for the student to keep, one for the instructor, and one for the principal or administrator. The portfolio consists of a three-ring binder with the following items:

- cover sheet, professionally designed, with name, date, place, and artwork
- table of contents
- current repertoire list
- list of future goals
- copy of the written course of study and repertoire list already mentioned
- detailed written daily practice record (figure 38.1), which also includes quantifiable metronome markings, page numbers, and skill listings as provided on the worksheet.
- daily journal entries, written on the back of the practice record, describing and reflecting on the student's practice routine, using complete sentences and legible handwriting
- music sheets
- photos, clippings, graphics
- written summary of the semester of approximately five hundred words
- written outline of lecture-performance

Lecture Performance

The lecture performance will be presented to a guitar class at the mutual convenience of the student and instructor. The presentation will last a minimum of thirty minutes and will consist of the following:

LESSON AND PRACTICE RECORD

Lesson Date:
Name:

Skills:	Mon	Tues	Wed	Thur	Fri	Sat	Sun
Scales and Patterns:							
Intervals:							
Slurs, Strength:							
Chord Progressions:							
Triads:							
Arpeggios:							
Strumming and Accompaniment:							
Reading Music:							
Song:							
Song:							
Improvisation; Play Along							

Figure 38.1: This sheet may be photocopied for class or other groups within purchaser's institution only. This provision does not confer any other rights to the purchaser or his or her institution.

- performances of techniques such as scales, arpeggios, and chord progressions
- discussion of practice methods and progress
- interview with the instructor in front of the class
- engaging the audience with questions and interaction
- performance of solo guitar pieces and/or vocal piece with accompaniment
- discussion with the audience of the elements of the repertoire including melody, harmony, accompaniment, artist background, social/geographical significance, and vocal style

Grading

- **A** Detailed, professional portfolio that meets all requirements; well-organized presentation; a minimum of three proficient solo-guitar pieces
- **B** Well-organized but less-detailed portfolio; good presentation requiring some assistance; two proficient solo pieces
- **C** Sketchy portfolio; presentation requires prompts by the instructor
- **D** Incomplete portfolio; performance of excerpts only

Blank Grid Diagrams

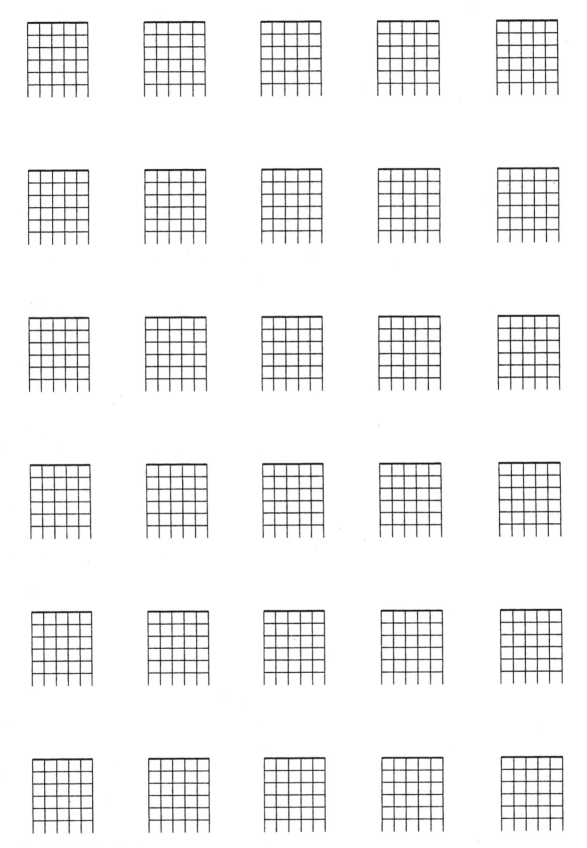

Figure A.1: Small chord grids

Figure A.2: Medium chord grids

Jumbo Grid

Figure A.3: Jumbo chord grids

BLANK SONG SHEET

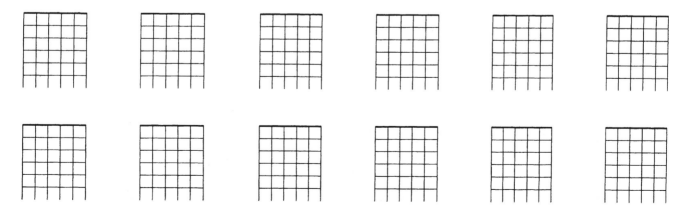

Figure A.4: Lyric Sheet (twelve small grids)

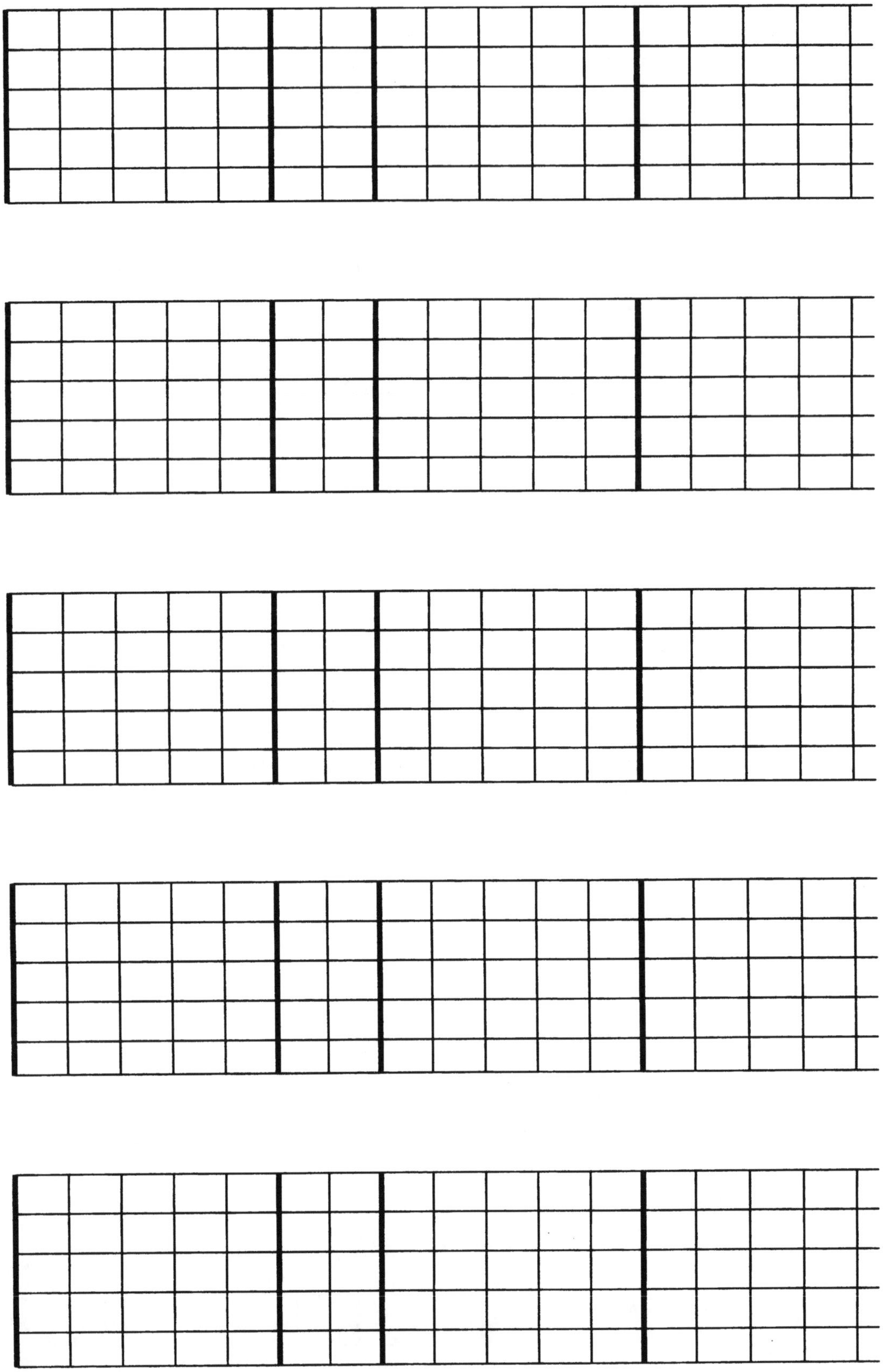

Figure A.5: Fret chord grids

B

Blank Staff

Figure B.1: Staff paper (six staves)

Figure B.2: Staff paper (eight staves)

Figure B.3: Staff paper, jumbo

Figure B.4: Large tablature/staff conversion worksheet

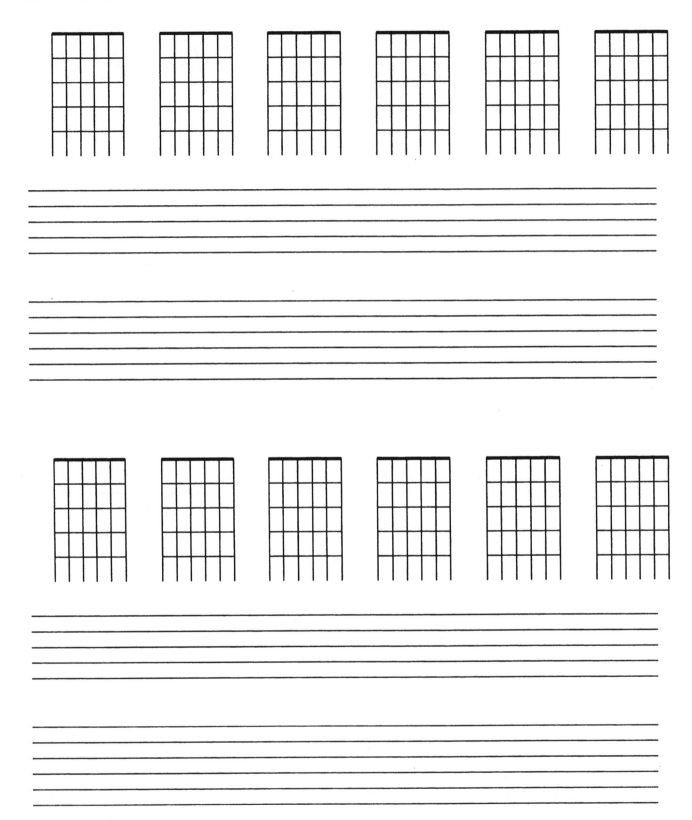

Figure B.5: Grid/staff/tab conversion worksheet

Figure B.6: Grid/staff conversion sheet

Figure B.7: Tablature/staff conversion worksheet

Worksheets

BLUES FORM AND LYRICS

Add Your Own Lyrics in the spaces below the words.

Verse:

Get out-ta that bed, . . . wash your face and hands ....

— — — — —,   —   —   —   —   — ....

Get out-ta that bed, . . . wash your face and hands ....

— — —— —, . . .   —   —   —   —   — ....

You get in that kit-chen . . . and rat-tle those pots and pans ....

— — — — — —, . . . — — — —   — — — ....

Chorus

Shake, rat-tle and roll, . . . shake, rat-tle and roll, ...

—   — — — —, . . . —   —   — ——   — ....

Shake, rat-tle and roll, . . . shake, rat-tle and roll, ...

—   — — — —, . . . —   —   — ——   — ....

Have to do right, to save your dog-gone soul ....

—   — ——,   — —   —   —   —   — ....

Figure C.1: Blues song writing

BLUES PROGRESSION PRACTICE SUMMARY

Variations:

Progressions 1–5 may be played entirely with seventh chords.
Vary the strumming patterns or arpeggios.
Play entirely with barre forms or triads.

	I			IV	I	V	I	
1	C			F	C	G	C	
2	G			C	G	D	G	
3	D			G	D	A	D	
4	A			D	A	E	A	
5	E			A	E	B7	E	
6	Emin			Amin	Emin	B7	Emin	
7	Amin			Dmin	Amin	E7	Amin	
8	Dmin			Gmin	Dmin	A7	Dmin	
9	A7(13)			D7(9)	A7(13)	E7(9)	A7(13)	
10	Amin7			Dmin9	Amin7	E7(♯9)	Amin7	
11	D7(9)			G7(13)	D7(9)	A7(13)	D7(9)	
12	Dmin9			Gmin7	Dmin9	A7(b13)	Dmin9	

Figure C.2:

BLUES PROGRESSION WORKSHEET

	I				IV		I		V		I	
1	C											
2	G											
3	D											
4	A											
5	E											
6	Emin											
7	Amin											
8	Dmin											
9	A7(13)											
10	Amin7											
11	D7(9)											
12	Dmin9											

Figure C.3:

CONCERT INTERVIEW: QUESTIONS TO ENHANCE LISTENING

1. What is the name of the group?

2. What is the origin or meaning of the name?

3. What is the overall message/mission of the group?

4. Who are they trying to appeal to?

5. What is the instrumentation of the group?

6. Who are the members of the group?

7. What is the education/experience of the members?

8. Where is the group based?

9. What record label are they on? What other labels have they been on?

10. In what other groups have the individuals played?

11. Who are they similar to?

12. What are their musical influences?

13. What is the style of music that they play?

14. What is the history of that style? The geographic roots...

15. Compare and contrast them with a similar group and a far different group.

16. Is there a gender factor to their music?

17. What is the symbolism/message of their appearance?

18. Is there a geographic influence to their music?

19. Is the music innovative? How is it innovative? In what way?

20. Is it acoustic or electric based?

21. Are the tunings standard or alternate?

22. What special effects or technology are they using?

23. Comment on the recording quality/production/methodology.

24. How big of a roll do the vocals play?

25. Who would you compare their vocals to?

26. Are their vocal harmonies 2 parts, three parts, triads, or intervals? Which intervals?

27. Is their music simple or complex?

28. Why does it appeal to you?

29. What kind of harmonies do they use? Chords, power chords, seventh chords?

30. What role does improvisation play in their music?

31. What role does virtuosity play in their music?

32. What scales or modes does the lead guitar player use?

33. What kind of guitar, amp, and effects are they using?

34. Does the group have a "signature" rhythm, or sound?

35. Are the members formally trained or self-taught.

36. If you were going to have a lesson with them, what would your top three questions be?

37. Who told you about the group? Where did you hear about them?

38. Could their music be performed "unplugged"?

39. Is their music playable by hobby guitar players?

40. Do they have printed music available?

41. Is their music something you would like to play?

42. Could you learn their music by ear?

43. How long have they been together and what changes have they undergone?

44. Where did you hear them?

45. What were the ticket prices?

46. Was it worth the price? Why?

47. Was their music tailored to live performance or recording?

48. Why is their music entertaining?

49. Was the music uplifting or depressing?

50. How important is volume in conveying the music?

51. Would you recommend this music to your friends, parents, or guitar teacher?

52. From what tradition do they originate?

53. Are there any other observations or analysis that you are able to convey?

54. Who is their audience? What are the demographics?

Figure C.4:

PARENTS INTERVIEW

Student Name:_____

Parents Names:_____

Telephone:_____

Instructions: Interview your parents to learn more about the role music has played in their life. Return the interview for class discussion.

1. What styles of music play a part in your life now? This includes both secular music for entertainment, and/or sacred music for worship:

2. Who are currently your favorite bands and/or performers?

3. What is it that you like about them?

4. When you were a teenager, what styles of music did you listen to? Who were your favorite artists and bands?

5. What styles of music do Grandma and Grandpa like?

6. How did your taste in music change over the years? List your music preferences and also significant historic reflections on the period.

Childhood music:

Historical context:

Teenage music:

Historical context:

College music:

Historical context

Adult working years:

Historical context:

7. Did you every play in an instrument or in a band?

8. Do we have any relatives that are significantly involved in music making?

9. What do you know about the music of our ethnic heritage?

10. State how your musical interests have changed since elementary school.

11. What songs would you like me to learn?

Figure C.5:

DEVELOPING ONGOING, INTERACTIVE, TWO-WAY CONVERSATIONS BETWEEN PARENTS AND TEACHERS

Dear Parent:

I am reaching out and inviting parents to become partners in the learning process of your sons or daughters. It is my goal to develop relationships with parents that are ongoing, interactive, and two-way conversations. Here are some things to consider.

Things you can do to be a partner in the learning process

_____ Be sure your student has a *music stand, comfortable practice space, method book, guitar strap, etc.*

_____ Students are eligible for extra credit if they *produce a written practice-time-log-journal*, which is signed and verified by a parent. This is optional.

_____ Work with your student and collaborate on the *Portfolio Final Project.* Be sure they have a three-ring view binder. Making requests and suggestions to help them collect songs from our songbook. Take photos of your student with their guitar and their friends. The portfolio is an exercise in archiving an exhibit entitled, "My Year in Guitar." Make suggestions of interesting articles and clippings and photos that would be of interest to your student fifty years from now. Suggest songs that would be enjoyed by your grandchildren and great grandchildren.

_____ Student are eligible for extra credit by attending our monthly *Family Night Sing Along Gatherings.* Come and enjoy.

_____ Attend one of my public performances.

_____ Sing or play with your student.

_____ Ask your student to teach you about guitar.

_____ Ask your student about the current proficiency skill, and how it relates to what they have already learned, and where their learning might be headed.

_____ Teach your student the meaning and benefits of the word "proactive." Encourage them to talk with me after class about questions, suggestions, materials, and requests.

_____ Read through the song list provided in the syllabus with your student.

_____ Obtain private instruction as a supplement to class.

_____ email me with ideas, feedback, and questions eckelss@sd5.k12.mt.us

Figure C.6:

PARENT QUESTIONNAIRE

Student Name:_____
Parents Names:_____
Telephone:_____
email:_____

Please answer the following questions for my records.

_____ What materials can I provide (if any) to help create a personalized learning agenda for your son or daughter?

_____ What can you tell me about your student's learning style, challenges, gifts, and strengths that can help me serve him/her better?

_____ Are you involved in a field that is connected to music in some way? Would you consider coming to class to be interviewed about the connection of music to your field? Examples: ministry, athletics, healing arts/medicine/physiology, dance, theater, art/photography/creative arts, guitar building/woodwork, advertising/marketing, anthropology, history. Are you knowledgeable about the music of your cultural/ethnic ancestry? Comments and Ideas:

_____ List any other ideas about the class or your student that can help me improve my effectiveness as a teacher.

_____ Do you, or any of our extended family play an instrument? It is extremely useful to have *family members visit the class* to share their knowledge. Would you consider setting a date to come to class?

_____ May I make a follow-up call to monitor your student's progress and needs?

_____ Is there anything I should know about any special discipline considerations?

Thanks you again for your consideration. I hope your participation is a great experience for you and your son/daughter.

Steve Eckels
eckelss@sd5.k12.mt.us

STUDENT INTERVIEW

Name: Date: Class Period: Phone #_____

Instructions: Help me get to know you as a person. Feel free to write on the back side if you need more space.

1. What is your full name? Do you have any tips to help me remember your name? Were you named after anyone?

2. How old are you? Where and when were you born?

3. What is your favorite class? Why?

4. What is your least favorite class? Why?

5. Tell me about the music and performers you like.

6. What is your favorite song? Why?

7. Are you involved with any youth groups such as church, clubs, etc.?

8. Do you have a job outside of school?

9. What role does music play in your life? What role would you like guitar to play in your life?

10. Name your favorite book and movie and why you like it.

11. What are your hobbies or activities? Sports, theater, music, service, etc.

12. If you do not live with your parents, whom do you live with? Would you share some information on your family background and situation?

13. What is your father's profession? How many years of formal education beyond high school has he taken?

14. What is your mother's profession? How many years of formal education beyond high school has he taken?

15. Name a special adult you admire and who serves as a role model. What do you like about them?

16. List the places you have lived and the approximate dates.

17. Looking back on life from old age, define what success is for you. What would you like to do for an occupation?

18. What about life or the world makes you sad?

19. Tell me about your pets.

20. Finish one of these sentences about guitar class: Guitar class would be better if. . . . Guitar class would be great if. . . .

Figure C.7:

READING PRACTICE WORKSHEET

Name:_____Class Period:_____Date:_____

Instructions: Chose a piece of written music to work on. Use the following procedures to learn the music. Indicate how many minutes you spend on each step. Practice all the steps. Make special notes indicating your thought process. Write comments on the back describing your progress.

Procedure:	Minutes:
1. Review the Natural Note Scale; increase speed; increase ability to play without looking; increase knowledge of note names.	
2. Play small scale-loops for speed and string crossing.	
3. Locate the key-tone throughout the piece.	
4. Play the scale of the piece. For example C-C.	
5. Identify steps, skips, and leaps in the music.	
6. Recite the note names in the music.	
7. Locate the highest and lowest notes in the music.	
8. Play the piece in whole notes.	
9. Loop individual measures until you can play them by memory.	
10. Link one measure to the next.	
11. Identify and work out challenging parts such as leaps and unusual rhythms.	
12. Loop the entire piece for smoothness, expression, tone, and memory.	
13. Locate a good spot to start the next practice session.	
14.	
15.	

Figure C.8:

SING ALONG LIST AND CHORD THEORY

Key of C—C, F, G, Amin

On Top of Old Smoky
Clementine
Kumbaya
Amazing Grace
When the Saints Go Marching In
Where Have All the Flowers Gone?
My Country 'Tis of Thee
Are You Sleeping?
Row, Row, Row Your Boat
I've Been Working on the Railroad
If I Had a Hammer
He's Got the Whole World in His Hands
Rock My Soul

Key of G—G, C, D, Emin

Good Night Irene
Old McDonald
Let it Be
Red River Valley
Country Roads
Down By the Riverside
Puff the Magic Dragon
This Land is Your Land
This Little Light of Mine
Worried Man Blues
King of the Road
Proud Mary
Twist and Shout

Key of D – D, G, A7, Bmin

Rock Around the Clock
Hound Dog
You Are My Sunshine
America the Beautiful (a capella)
Swing Low Sweet Chariot
Home on the Range
Michael Row the Boat Ashore
Oh Susanna
Rock My Soul
She'll Be Commin' Round the Mountain
Tom Dooley

Chord Theory

Scale Steps:

1	2	3	4	5	6	7	8
C	d	e	F	G	a	b	C

The primary chords are:

I	IV	V

Chord Families for Strumming:

I	IV	V	vi
C	F	G	amin
G	C	D	emin
D	G	A(7)	bmin

Figure C.9:

SINGING CHECKLIST

Posture Check

Sit or stand tall; sternum high; ribs expanded

Stretch and relax jaw—open and hold for thirty seconds

Lower larynx and tongue—ka, ga, ya, surprise-breath

Cup the tongue; make space for sound to pass from larynx through throat

Sing words with no pitch/no air; whisper word with air/no pitch. Goal: relaxed face

Breathing Check

Breath in for five seconds, hold for ten (or more), exhale for five (or more) seconds. Regular repetition is important to build muscle strength and control.

Variations:

Pant while holding the breath and use hand motions to reinforce abdominal motion.

Inhale suddenly, then exhale with a long hiss.

Hiss in various rhythm and dynamic patterns including stacatto, legato, articulated legato.

Exhale as long as possible

Inhale, suspend, exhale, recover, and use hand motions to reinforce the movement.

Keep ribs expanded even on exhale; feels like sternum is rising (but it is not).

Vibration Check

Yawn/Sigh: Should not be breathy, but bell like; contented and restful

Variations:

Repeated staccato attacks/onsets.

Ascending and descending/voice flexing.

Vary registration from heavy to light, light to heavy;

Octaves, smaller intervals, and long glissandi and trills.

Add lip trill with pulses; tongue trill.

Carefree mini-scales and arpeggios.

Rattle/Scrape: Pinched glottis into clear tone and back to pinched.

Wedge high tones: begin with falsetto and wedge in heavy registration.

Figure C.10:

Resonance Check

Hum scales and songs loud enough to buzz/ping; teeth apart; throat open

Sing Vowels beginning with N

Ae – Child saying, "nyae, nyae, nyae, nyae," angry.

Vowel circle: EE, A, AH, OH, OO, OH, AH, A, EE

Pronunciation Check

Examine passages of songs for:

Vowel shaping.

Compound consonants.

Preparatory Consonants: Consonant ahead of the beat, and vowel on the beat.

Ta/da; pa/ba; ka/ga; fa/va; la;

Pitches.

Listen   carefully.

Experiment   with varied shapes of mouth and remember what sounds best.

Practice

SONGWRITING CATEGORIES

Assignment: Choose a popular song and rewrite the lyrics using one of the categories listed below. Follow that up by changing the melody and chords to enhance the expression of the new lyrics.

Relationships

Searching for love

Heartbreak

Wedding songs

Romance/hugs and kisses

Engagement and marriage

Nature—earth, sea, sky, farm

Children/play

Philosophical

Political

Places

Ethnic

Historical events

Joy of living

Songs about work

Graduation

Religious

Prayer

Grace

Biblical history

Suffering

Redemption

Dancing

Brotherhood/friendship

Nostalgia

Freedom

Slavery

Peace

Disasters

Fire, flood, wrecks

Party songs

Teenage life

Tribute to a person

Animals

Mythology/legend

Murder

Inspirational

Sadness/blues

Trains, planes, travel

The road, highway

People and personalities

Silly songs

Women/men

Seasons

Lullabies

Funny songs

Patriotic

Fishing

Meaning of life

Change the world

Stars and night

Family, husband, wife

True stories

Time

Dragons

Figure C.11:

PROFICIENCY PLANNING WORKSHEET
SEMESTER:

	Repertoire	Skill	Reading	Assessment Type
1				
2				
3				
4				
5				
6				
7				
8				
9				

Figure C.12:

Glossary

Accessory Success on guitar can be enhanced with the use of several accessories. Here are the most common:

Footstool Used to elevate the left leg, which raises and stabilizes the guitar.

Guitar strap Raises and stabilizes the guitar.

Guitar stand Holds the guitar safely out of the case when not in use. Other advantages are that the guitar is accessible for playing and is an important part of the interior decoration of the home.

Plectrum Formal term for the pick.

Practice portfolio Three-ring binder, which the students use to collect and organize their repertoire pieces and other handouts.

Action The distance of the strings to the neck. Low action is desirable, because the guitar is easier to play. High action indicates the guitar need to be adjusted.

Acture Term coined by Moshe Feldenkrais combining the words *action* and *posture*. Since the body is never motionless, it is only appropriate to study the body positions in the context of movement.

Assessment technique:

Composition exercise Students are given a group of notes and rhythms to work with and are asked to write short phrases within certain parameters.

Constructed-response test (CRT) The student reads an essay related to a specific topic and then answers a set of questions based on the essay. In addition to the content itself, the purpose of the CRT is to give students practice reading and writing.

Exit card Short written work that demonstrates students' knowledge of content for a specific day. Work is collected and filed near the exit of the classroom.

Melodic dictation Students notate the melodic example that the instructor has played. The answers are given immediately, and the class then plays the examples. This is a highly recommended exercise.

Nomenclature exercise The student is provided with a melody and is asked to indicate (1) the appropriate fret, which is the small number to the left and slightly above the note head, and (2) the string number, which is the small number inside a circle and located either above or below the note.

One-on-one Student performs proficiency skills for the instructor. To save time, the instructor may move from student to student asking for short examples, or each student may play an example for the class. After performing the excerpt, each student receives a proficiency slip that provides feedback on hand position and flow.

Performance Given by individuals or small groups playing songs together.

Proficiency slip A small slip of paper that provides feedback, and a written record of a student performance. The proficiency slip may be used for individuals, ensembles or for extra credit.

Self-assessment summary Students give themselves a grade and then justify their grade based on a written summary of their knowledge. This may be in the form of a letter to the instructor.

Small group The instructor sits with a group of approximately four or five students. The advantage of this method is that the instructor does not have to repeat the same explanation to every student.

Spot quiz Each student, directed by the instructor, demonstrates a technique or excerpt in a minimum amount of time.

Written worksheet Especially useful for learning the staff and the fundamentals of music notation. Typically, musical symbols or notation are provided, and the student adds the appropriate identification.

Baton Conducting devise that is indispensable as a pointer regarding finger placement on the fingerboard.

Bel canto Italian term meaning *beautiful singing*, frequently used to describe classical guitar tone.

Bending note To get an authentic blues sound, the guitarist stretches the string, which bends the pitch in a sharp direction. The most common is on the raised fourth degree of a blues scale. To achieve the raised fourth, you bend the fourth until it reaches the desired sound. The raised third, referred to as the neutral third, is also a commonly bent note.

Brace Right-hand technique used in which a finger or fingers are anchored on a string, or on the guitar to provide support for the thumb or other fingers.

Broom According to Montessori education philosophy, having students participate in cleaning the room develops personal attributes. These attributes include gratitude, humility, service, and community. Coincidentally, the broom motion is a type of stroke, and therefore adheres to scientific principles found in guitar playing: preparation, backswing, stroke, contact, and follow-through.

Cantilever motion The reciprocal motion of the pelvis and spine. For example, when the pelvis rocks to the left, the head and spine arch to the right.

Capo A clamp used to raise the pitch of the guitar, to teach barre forms, or to make the guitar easier to play.

Comprehensive lesson The comprehensive lesson consists of the Five S's: (1) strength, (2) scales (or other tonal material), (3) sight reading, (4) skills, such as accompaniment and improvisation, (5) songs and singing.

Concert interview One way to approach the goal of describing music is for the instructor to interview students during class who have been to concerts.

Covey, Stephen An inspirational speaker known for his book, *The Eight Habits of Highly Effective People*. The habits are of value to teachers and students alike. They are: (1) begin with the end in mind, (2) be proactive, (3) put first things first, (4) seek first to understand then to be understood, (5) synergize, (6) think win-win or no deal, (7) sharpen the saw, and (8) find your voice, and help others to find theirs.

Fingering concepts, left hand:

Active and passive fingers Fingers in use are referred to as active. The passive fingers are worthy of equal attention because they are the fingers that are likely to be used next.

Barre As a harmonic instrument, guitar has the unique advantage of being able to transpose chords by sliding the hand from fret to fret. To do this, the first finger emulates a capo by clamping the strings across a fret. A barre may be full or partial. Nomenclature for a barre is *C* followed by a Roman numeral indicating the fret. For example, a barre on the fifth fret would be indicated as CV.

Buddy system For efficient movement, fingers need to remain close to the fingerboard. When the fourth finger is being used, fingers 1, 2, and 3 may rest on the string in a support role. When the third finger is being used, fingers 1 and 2 may rest on the string. Using this principal helps prevent fingers from "popping up," which is inefficient in terms of motion.

Common finger When changing between two chord forms, there may be a finger that is common to both chords. When this is the case, it is useful to use the common finger as a pivot or brace for hand motion.

Glide finger When changing between two chord forms, there may be a finger that can glide on the string into the next form.

Gray tone Muted tone produced by fingering a chord or note but not pressing it. Using gray tones in practice allows the student to focus on finger placement without concern for strength.

Pinch accent Accent created by the alternation of gray tones and clear tones in a strumming pattern.

Position number Roman numeral used to indicate the location of the left hand on the neck. For example, in second position, the first finger would be stationed at the second fret, the position is indicated as II; for fifth position, the first finger would be stationed at the fifth fret and indicated as V. Beginning guitarists are primarily concerned with open position (first position), which includes the open strings and the first four frets.

Proprioception The ability to sense body or finger position by feel rather than by sight. The mastery of scales and scale patterns is one of the best ways to develop proprioception.

Relative shapes When two chord shapes have a similar shape they are described as relative shape. Taking advantage of relative shapes is a useful strategy for making efficient use of motion between chords.

Preparation gesture The practice of prepositioning the fingers of the left hand before they are needed. When changing chords, the preparation gesture is to begin left-hand movement an instant before the required beat. Prepositioning also facilitates string crossing and descending scales.

Tracks/railing Fingers may use strings as references for shifting positions when moving up and down the neck. The strings may be compared to a railing, or railroad track. In violin pedagogy this in known as *riding the rails*.

Fingering concepts, right hand

Alternate picking Right-hand picking technique in which the plectrum (pick) plays a down and up pattern that is synchronized with the down and up beat.

Free stroke Right-hand finger stroke in which the fingers do not touch the adjacent string. Used for accompaniment patterns.

Follow-through Right-hand technique in which the fingers return to home position immediately after the stroke.

P-i-m-a The abbreviations for the fingers of the right hand:

Pulgar thumb
Indice index finger
Medio middle finger
Anular ring finger

Planting The right-hand preparation gesture of placing the fingers on the string before using them.

Rest stroke right-hand picking technique in which a finger comes to rest on an adjacent string after performing a stroke. Used for melody.

String set The numbers of a group of strings needed to perform a specific task. For example, beginning finger-picking patterns usually use the thumb on the root plus string set 1, 2, 3.

Five forms There are five basic major chord forms on which all other chords are based. The forms are C, A, G, E, and D and spell the word *caged.*

Fraction notation Notation shorthand in which the fingering of a pitch is written as a fraction with the fret being placed over the string. For example, 1/2 means the first fret of the second string.

Freight train Practice technique used to develop speed in which a short phrase is looped slowly and gradually speeded up.

Gray tone Muted tone resulting from pushing the string down only half way. Practicing gray tones helps to develop lightness of touch and a graceful hand form, both of which are necessary for speed.

Guitar science The study of how the guitar works. Includes inquiry into the study of motion, practice methodology, the elements of music, and the instrument itself.

Hammer-on Ascending slur. (See *slur.*)

Heuristic Learning by discovery. Referred to also as constructivism. The instructor's role is to guide the student's process of self-discovery. Summarized with the phrase, What students discover independently, they retain.

Home position/neutral position The starting position for an exercise. A useful term for group instruction, "after plucking the note return to home position before plucking the next one."

Home tone The key tone of a piece of music. A useful term for giving verbal cues while reading music.

Imitation teaching techniques:
    Echo The instructor plays or sings a phrase, and the students echo the phrase in response.
    Mirror Students spontaneously imitate the actions of the teacher.
    Overlapping Students imitate the instructor, who then overlaps the students with another pattern.

Inversion Referring to the order in which a chord tone is fingered. In other words, the chord-tone order may be 1-3-5 (root position), 3-5-1 (first inversion), 5-1-3 (second inversion).

Keyboard position Indicates that each finger of the left hand is designated to a separate fret, most commonly the first finger on fret one, second finger on fret two, and so on. Keyboard position is useful for reading music because the guitarist does not need to look at his or her hands. Keyboard position is only one of multiple guitar positions.

Kinetics Branch of mechanics that studies the actions or forces that produce changes in motion. In the case of guitar, it involves primarily the motion of the hands and arms. Guitar students benefit from experiencing the practice and learning process used in other disciplines, especially athletics and dance. (*Kinesiology* is the study of body movement; *kinesthesia* is the sensation of body movement.)

Line reading Music reading is much easier when scale or interval contours are observed, rather than decoding each individual note. Line reading may be encouraged by the rule, Never read one note at a time; always read groups of notes. This is the same way we read language, by word or groups of words, not by letter.

Luxuriant tapestry of sonority A poetic interpretation of the essence of music, coined by composer Paul Hindemith.

Master class Teaching technique, which involves the instructor giving an individual lesson while the class observes.

Milestone The achievement of an important skill that marks a new and higher level of performance ability.

Motivation Teachers are motivators. Motivation of students is cultivated in two ways: Intrinsic motivation stresses internal factors, such as self-expression, worship, the heart and soul, and the human instinct to play and explore. Extrinsic motivation stresses external factors, such as grades, awards, social status, money, gender bonding, etc.

Muslish Term I coined, combining the words *music* and *English,* referring to the practice of reciting the letters of music as words. For example, A-B-C is pronounced as a three-syllable word with the accent on the second syllable: Abc.

Muting:
    Left-hand muting By lying across the strings, the index finger of the left hand can effectively mute them, which prevents unintended strings from resonating. Most frequently used with moveable power chords.
    Right-hand palm mute Muting the strings with the palm of the right hand to create a muffled or percussive tone.
    Thumb mute The thumb of the right hand may be used to mute strings when their resonance is not required.

Nomenclature Set of symbols used in guitar music to indicate neck position, string number, finger number, slides, bends, barre fingerings, and other specific guitar techniques.

Open mind In performance psychology, the mind must be focused and open at the same time—open to expression of the soul, yet focused on the required motions. When the motions are fully mastered, the mind is more able to be open to musical interpretation and expression.

Orff guitar Many of the teaching principles of Carl Orff transfer well to guitar. The prepared-instrument concept translates to guitar by learning pieces on one string and by playing pieces in hand-bell style, where each student is give only one or two notes to play. Another useful Orff concept is the creating of abstract soundscapes. A good example would be creating the mood of the tropical rainforest using freely created textures on an E-minor chord before starting the song "El Condor Pasa." Finally, the concept of a bordun (the interval of a fifth) in Orff practice is the same as the use of a power chord in guitar.

Olympic guitar All aspects of a healthy lifestyle contribute to mental and physical skills necessary to play an instrument. Students should be encouraged to pursue good nutrition, mental health, physical fitness, and the study of any discipline that would enhance physical and mental performance.

Parts of the guitar Knowing the parts of the guitar is essential for both teacher and student as a means for giving and receiving instructions. Most method books contain diagrams showing the following parts:

Bass strings The lower-sounding three strings, usually wound and of thicker diameter.

Bout The curved perimeter of the guitar that separates the front from the back.

Bridge The narrow plastic unit, to the right of the sound hole, over which the strings rest.

Fret Metallic strips dividing the neck into half-steps.

Nut The narrow plastic unit, near the tuning pegs, over which the strings rest.

Rosetta The design around the sound hole

Sound hole The hole in the center of the soundboard.

Soundboard The front of the guitar. The soundboard is important to tone.

Treble strings The higher-sounding three strings of thinner diameter.

Planting A right- or left-hand preparation gesture in which the finger is positioned before it is needed.

Play A human and mammalian instinct that must be preserved and nurtured in order to achieve satisfaction and fulfillment in practice and performance.

Power chord Interval of fifths used in rock music. Also referred to as a *bordun* in Orff music education.

Practice concepts:

Creating silence Silence is one of the elements of music. As such it should be practiced especially at the beginning and end of playing a song.

Gauging Testing or measuring the elements of touch, such as pressure, distance, or location.

Muscle memory The conscious mind cannot work fast enough to guide finger action. Therefore a system is needed to ingrain the preconscious or *muscle memory*. Graduated speed exercises are essential to playing becoming automatic. Examples include (1) using repeated notes and gradually decreasing the repetitions and (2) starting slowly and gradually speeding up.

Open practice Students benefit from free experimentation and heuristic learning. Open practice provides students time to ingrain the proficiency skills or to browse materials. Open practice gives the advanced student a chance to mentor fellow students and the instructor time to monitor student progress.

Practice loop Taking a small excerpt, measure, or phrase and repeating it over and over to allow the muscles to remember the pattern.

Practice point–guided practice Short practice intervals during which students review the preceding material or prepare for the next group activity. Practice points also provide a good opportunity for the instructor to circulate the room and monitor student progress.

Preliminary (prelim) It is desirable to use a song as a vehicle for learning skills. With this in mind, the instructor should demonstrate the performance goal and then guide the students through the necessary preliminary steps, or prelims, to reach the end goal.

Relay exercise Students may be assigned short excerpts of a song to be played as a relay. Excerpts may range from individual notes ("play C whereever it occurs") to individual measures. Relays may be used in ensembles, solo guitar pieces, or single-line melodies. Similar to the procedure used for hand bells.

Rotation of parts When playing ensemble pieces, students benefit from playing all the parts. The rotation may take place at the end of the piece or during a piece.

Running tone, standing tone, and walking tone Students may be encouraged to discover the relationship between notes and chords. Students listen to notes of the chromatic scale played by the instructor that are played simultaneously with a designated chord. By ear, students determine if each note is a standing tone (root or chord tone), walking tone (chord embellishment, such as a ninth), or a running tone (highly dissonant passing tone).

Proprioception Awareness of the position of one's body. In the case of guitarists, this is especially important regarding the position of the hands.

Pull-off Descending slur. (See *slurs*.)

Reference scale The moveable C and G scales performed in the second position are good examples of reference scales. Scale degrees are used as reference numbers to construct chords. For example find degrees 1, 3, 7, and 9 based on the root 6, G scale in second position. Similar interval and chord-building exercises may be accomplished using the C scale in open position.

Rest position Position in which students mute the strings of the guitar with the left and right hand when the instructor is talking. The instructor requests rest position at the end of every song.

Riff Short, repetitive ostinato pattern used in pop music. Famous examples are "Iron Man," "Smoke on the Water," and "Sunshine of Your Love." Riffs can be used to the instructor's advantage for sight reading, fingering technique, and improvisation. Riffs may be thought of as composition kits, because they include available notes for improvising and idiomatic melodic contours and rhythms.

Scaffolding Verbal cues or teacher accompaniment that provide students with help or support; this support is gradually and methodically eliminated as students gain independence. For example, when playing a song, the instructor plays and sings with the students. During the third verse, the instructor only sings. Finally, the instructor only conducts while the students perform independently.

Selective strumming For chords to sound right, their roots must be the lowest strummed notes. Therefore, in order to emphasize the root, the guitarist must learn to strum select groups of strings. For example, if a chord has its root on the fifth string, the guitarist must strum only five strings, beginning with the root. The rule for finding the chord root is that the root is always the lowest *fretted* note, unless the chord is an E, A, or D, in which case the root is an open string.

Simulated guitar/arm guitar It is helpful in guitar education to be able to simulate the neck of a guitar without actually having one in your hand. Place the right forearm across the chest at a diagonal to simulate the angle of the guitar neck. You may then do left-hand exercises and demonstrations on your arm instead of the neck. A computer keyboard (disconnected from the computer) may also be used for useful effect.

Skill builder Short, free-flowing scale pattern played repetitively to develop speed, lightness, and finger memory. For example: 0 1 3 1, 0 1 3 1, etc.

Slice Right-hand stroke in which the index finger plucks the string at a diagonal as the result of a clockwise motion of the forearm. Used for melodic bel canto passages.

Slur Technique of producing a note either by pulling-off or hammering-on instead of plucking with the right hand.

Socratic method The use of guided questions, as employed by Socrates, to assist students in developing problem-solving skills.

Socratic relay Practice technique used for solo guitar or ensembles in which each participant contributes only a small segment of the whole piece.

Strength concepts:

Digital patterns Numerical finger patterns. Common left-hand examples, on one string, include: 1 2 3 4, 4 3 2 1, 1 3 2 4, 4 2 3 1, 1 3 4 2, 4 2 1 3. Digital patterns may also be played while maintaining a barre or by using slurs.

Opposing motion Type of left-hand digital pattern in which the fingers trade or alternate strings and gradually create larger and larger intervals. For example, place fingers 2-1 on strings 4-3: E/G#. Next, have them switch strings: D#/A. Continue switching strings, making the intervals wider, until you reach strings 6-1. As a variation, keep passive fingers fixed or resting on the G string.

Fixed-finger exercises Series of independence exercises in which a group of fingers remains fixed or stationary, while another finger moves in a prescribed pattern. The chord-ingraining exercise out-home, up-home, in-home is a good example.

Isometrics Exercises for the hands that target specific muscle groups and accelerate progress by improving finger independence and strength.

Parallel intervals Strength and finger-independence exercises, which make use of intervals moving in half-steps (by fret). The most famous is chromatic octaves, popularized by Andres Segovia. Also useful are parallel fifths. In class guitar parallel-interval exercises works best using repeated notes and progressively reducing the repetitions. For an advanced variation, play broken intervals and move only one finger at a time.

Tapping Technique in which the notes are sounded by hammering-on with the right hand. When combined with left-hand hammering-on and pulling-off, tapping results in speed patterns.

Transposition Raising or lowering a melody or chord. Transposing E and A chords is a useful concept in relating how barre forms are created.

Triad A three-note chord consisting of scale degrees 1-3-5 presented in varying order. Triads are frequently played on the treble strings and used for accompaniment, harmonizing a melody, or as a reference point for improvisation. Triads are frequently performed in inversions. In other words the chord tone order may be 1-3-5 (root position), 3-5-1 (first inversion), or 5-1-3 (second inversion).

Tuning terms:

Beats When two strings approach a unison one can hear a pulsing sound referred to as *beats*. When the strings are in perfect unison, no beats are heard. Therefore, learning to hear beats is a valuable step in learning to tune the guitar.

Directed tuning Students are instructed as a group to play one tuning note as conducted. Students determine if they are high or low in reference to the group and make the necessary adjustments to the tuning knob. In addition to tuning, this drill provides practice in group precision.

Ear tuning/interval tuning Learning the sound of the intervals of fourths and thirds, and using them to tune the guitar. The most common reference song used for this purpose is "Amazing Grace."

Electronic tuner Inexpensive device that indicates correct pitch for each string. Highly recommended.

Spot tuning The instructor plays a reference pitch and then points to each individual student, who in turn plays the respective note individually and receives comments. Allow approximately three to five seconds per student.

Staccato tuning The instructor plays the reference pitch. Students then play their respective string quietly and muted. This enables everyone a better chance to listen and hear the reference pitch.

Tuning arpeggio Picking pattern in which the guitarist tunes each string relative to the preceding string group. Ascending, the string order is 6, 6 5, 6 5 4, 6 5 4 3, 6 5 4 3 2, 6 5 4 3 2 1; descending, the order is 1, 1 2, 1 2 3, 1 2 3 4, 1 2 3 4 5, 1 2 3 4 5 6.

Unison tuning The most common form of individual tuning. A reference pitch is provided on the sixth string, fifth fret (5/6). The sixth string functions as the reference string, and the fifth string functions as the variable string, which must be adjusted until it forms a perfect unison with the reference note. This pattern is continued on all string sets except between strings three and two. In this case the reference fret is on the fourth fret.

Two-for-one exercise There are frequent opportunities to do exercises that provide two or more benefits to the student. For example, by practicing the roots of a song, the student learns (1) the root of the chord and (2) the location and name of the pitch.

Waggle Golf term for adjusting posture, balance, and distances by moving back and forth until a balance point is discovered. Waggling is useful in guitar for students discovering their optimal hand position.

About the Author

One of the strengths of this book is that **Steve Eckels** is both a virtuoso guitarist and a master classroom teacher. Since his father was a master potter, and his mother the chair of a college education department, Eckels's background as an artist and teacher is part of his family tradition and heredity. Eckels is a skilled potter in his own right. Before writing this book, he wrote over twenty guitar books for Mel Bay Publications and Alfred Publications. His experience as an author includes arranging and recording guitar music of diverse styles, including Western, folk, blues, gospel, Latin, world music, that of Stephen Foster, Native American, Gregorian chant, mariachi, and others. His published classroom guitar supplements include *A Modern Method for Fingerstyle Guitar*, *Blues for the Young Beginner*, *Fingerstyle Classics Made Easy*, *Latin American Music Made Easy*, *World Music Made Easy*, and *Guitar Techniques and Ensembles*. His catalog of recordings includes classical masterpieces, original compositions, and arrangements of American traditional music. His articles on guitar instruction have been featured in *Teaching Music*, *Fingerstyle Guitar Magazine*, *Cadenza Magazine*, *Teaching Guitar*, and *Guitar Sessions Webzine*.

Eckels began developing the guitar program at Flathead High School in Kalispell, Montana, in 2000. His program, which consists of four semesters of guitar, now employs additional instructors who are specialists in band, orchestra, and choir. He has carefully listened to the concerns and needs of these teachers in developing this book. Other inspiration for this book comes from participants in his summer workshop for teachers, Teaching Classroom Guitar, which he codirects annually in Kalispell, Montana, with his wife, Barbara.

Eckels has taught at the collegiate level at Berklee College of Music, New Mexico State University at Las Cruces, The University of Wisconsin at Superior, and Northland College in Ashland, Wisconsin. He was one of the first students to graduate with a bachelor's degree in applied guitar from Berklee College of Music (1978), where he studied with William Leavitt. He received his master's degree in guitar from New England Conservatory (1981) and his music-education certification in band, choir, and general music from Northland College in Ashland, Wisconsin (1984). His interest in improving classroom guitar instruction has included independent study in the areas of Orff education, Montessori education, Waldorf education, Feldenkrais: Awareness Through Movement, and violin technique and pedagogy. He has studied classical guitar with Christopher Parkening and classroom-guitar pedagogy with both Will Schmid and Nancy Marsters. Elements of this book were also inspired by his work toward national certification by the National Board of Professional Teaching Standards.

For information on workshops, books, and recordings visit www.guitarmusicman.com.

Made in the USA
Lexington, KY
11 August 2015